Statism in Plymouth Colony

KENNIKAT PRESS

NATIONAL UNIVERSITY PUBLICATIONS

SERIES IN AMERICAN STUDIES

Under the General Editorial Supervision of

JAMES P. SHENTON

Professor of History, Columbia University

HARRY M. WARD

Statism in Plymouth Colony

National University Publications
KENNIKAT PRESS
Port Washington, N. Y. • London

Library of Congress Catalog Card No.: 72-91177
ISBN: 0-8046-9036-7

Manufactured in the United States of America

Published by
Kennikat Press, Inc.
Port Washington, N.Y./London

PREFACE

The study of individual freedom has been a neglected aspect of American history. We take for granted the freedoms of the Bill of Rights, and most investigation on the subject concerns itself with the legacy of English constitutional development and the constitution-making of the colonists. Although there has been important work on the colonial legal systems and the internal structure of democracy and society, little attention has been paid to the confrontation of the individual with the state. A measure gauging the actual liberty possessed by free men is to determine the reach and demands of the corporate whole upon the individual citizen, and by the same token to determine the capacity of the individual to assert himself in the pursuit of his own public or private happiness.

Statism—like most "isms"—defies any precise definition; but it may be said to be the placing of extensive controls in the state at the expense of rights of the *individual,* and, it may also be added, the exercise of power by the state for the sake of power. The very nature of the state is to follow a course of self-preservation and to protect itself from its constituency. It becomes an end unto itself. It tends to seek tools of control above responding to the needs of the people; and when there is a response it is to accommodate interest groups rather than the people at large.

It was America's fortune that institutions sprang up in the fresh air of frontier conditions, in which freedom was expansive and tyranny could be checked by a safety valve—if not geographical at least through the open-endedness of society. But these conditions of early America are no longer externally available for Americans today. Americans must now decide upon the value of freedom and adjust it internally. Yet, if we are to understand the nature of liberty in America, we must start with the past. It is this concern that has led the author to probe individual liberty vis-à-vis the state in the formative period of American history.

Plymouth Colony is an ideal subject. The half century of the colony's history and the relative smallness of the colony provide a perfect microcosm. The Pilgrims started from a state of nature. They had no particular axes to grind, except to live in peace and security unmolested and to maintain a minimum of a religious commonwealth. The settlers of the colony were a simple folk, and—if it is true of any people—they were less imbued with greed and certainly with less mercantile or quantitative ambitions than settlers elsewhere. The growth of the colony was rapid, and hence one can trace the rise and need for the state. They faced the problems of preserving their organic community intact. Finally, public policy stands as a contrast of moderation compared to the more zealous Puritan neighbors.

Topics for this study are selective; though reflecting the germinal aspects of the colony's history, they are also relevant to the questions of statism that could be raised in any given society. It is assumed the reader has a general familiarity with the Pilgrim story and the history of the Puritan colonies of New England.

In quotations, original spellings are left as they are, except in most instances to extend shorthand abbreviations and to change such quirks of alphabetical usage as "j" when intended for "i" or "v" for "u". The ten days needed to bring dates under the Gregorian calendar have not been added, but January 1 rather than March 25 has been taken as the first day and month of the year.

The resources of many libraries have been used in the preparation of this study. I am grateful for the fine services of the Virginia State Library, and particularly to Milton C. Russel and his excellent staff. Especially I wish to thank Plimoth Plantation, Inc. for a research grant that made this study possible. Arthur G. Pyle, Education Projects Director for the Plantation, has offered encouragement from time to time.

CONTENTS

Statism in Plymouth Colony

Chapter One

COMMUNITY

Before disembarking upon the wintry shores of the promised land, the Leyden Pilgrims combined themselves into a civil body politic. As much as they would have preferred to live by the invisible church, they were realists enough to know that men make government. The Pilgrims thus became the first Englishmen in America to establish government by a rudimentary convention form, unconnected with any powers conferred by a public or private authority abroad.[1]

Although the Mayflower Compact was intended to serve as a temporary expedient to establish law and order until charter privileges could be received, the Pilgrims considered their act to be the foundation of a permanent civil society. They were not troubled that their combining together to form a government could only be a legal fiction under English law.

It may well be argued that the Pilgrims had no clear understanding of political incorporation and that they sought merely to establish a primitive, communitarian society, bound together by like-minded persons and a long-standing intimate friendship.[2] *Mourt's Relation* calls the Mayflower Compact "an association and agreement," and Bradford simply refers to a "combination made by them before they came a shore." It did not become a "compact" until 1793.[3]

But the Pilgrims were aware that they were creating a community. They would probably have concurred with a seventeenth century definition that a community "is a perfect coming together of free men, associated for the sake of enjoying the advantages of law and for the common utility." [4] And they must have been mindful that the community gives rise to a sovereign authority—the state—an entity in itself, comprised of a legal value of interests and an ethical power residing in law and spiritual authority.[5]

Whether viewed as a "plantation covenant"[6] or as an extended church covenant, the Mayflower Compact was a departure from the church covenant idea.[7] Among the last words of advice from Pastor John Robinson to the Pilgrims before they left on their perilous voyage was the necessity of broadening the church covenant to include "using amongst your selves civill governments." Yet the new community in the New World should be recognized to be under divine auspices. Robinson cautioned that a distinction should be made between the holy authority of the governors and the governed:

> let your wisdome and godlines appeare. not only in chusing shuch persons as doe entirely love and will promote the commone good, but also in yeelding unto them all due honour and obedience in their lawfull administrations . . . .[8]

Since the Mayflower Compact mentions a "covenant" framed "solemnly and mutualy in the presence of God", the Pilgrims imply that magistrates to be chosen to administer the laws and ordinances are invested with a holy authority. The will of God transcends both particular and majority interests. What the Pilgrims were yet to learn was that the claim of divine authority by the magistrates would afford a convenient subterfuge for the state to protect itself from its constituency.

From the point of view of their Separatist principles, the Pilgrims were putting into effect a corollary of the federal theology. They had lived under the covenants of grace and church, but now was their first opportunity to establish a civil covenant. It would fall to the more sophisticated Puritans—like John Winthrop, John Cotton, Thomas Hooker, John Eliot, and

Thomas Shepard—to give full expression to the meaning of this covenant, and official sanction could be found in the acceptance by the Puritan colonies, including Plymouth, of the Cambridge Platform of 1648. The founders of Plymouth Colony would not have agreed with the idea of social stratification in the civil covenant, which John Winthrop expounded while he, similarly to the Pilgrims of a decade before, was on the ocean-crossing of the *Arabella*. But the Pilgrims believed in Winthrop's assertion, as the whole history of the colony attests, that the consummation of the civil covenant depended upon their fulfillment of mission. If they fail, in their witness to the world, in the planting of a holy commonwealth, and seek after the golden calf rather than God's laws and ordinances, then God will cast them out. As Winthrop was to put it quite succinctly:

> Thus stands the cause betweene God and us, wee are entered into Covenant with him for this worke, wee have taken out a Commission, the Lord hath given us leave to drawe our owne Articles wee have professed to enterprise these Actions upon these and these ends, wee have herupon besought him of favour and blessing: Now if the Lord shall please to heare us, and bring us in peace to the place we desire, then hath hee ratified this Covenant and sealed our Commission, [and] will expect a strickt performance of the Articles contained in it, but if wee shall neglect the observation of these Articles which are the ends wee have propounded, and dissembling with our God, shall fall to embrace this present world and prosecute our carnall intentions, seekeing great things for our selves and our posterity, the Lord will surely breake out in wrathe against us be revenged of such a perjured people and make us knowe the price of the breache of such a Covenant.[9]

In the civil covenant (or, to borrow the phraseology of Perry Miller, the "national" or "communal" covenant),[10] the Pilgrims contracted for an external relationship with God, whereby they would be judged as a people and a society rather than merely as individuals or church members. To secure the blessings of God, the community must conform to His will. He had sifted a whole nation that He might send choice seed into the New World; if His people neglect their calling, the covenant will be voided, and God will discontinue His favor. It was imperative that the community recognize the sovereignty of God, only under whom there could be perfect freedom. No man or man-made law or institutions should be placed above the divine will. By holy covenant, as with Abraham and his descendants, a chosen people must bear the continuing responsibility of meeting their end of the covenant. This meant that the governing of a community rested with the people as a whole and by their free consent. It also meant that the common good must always be kept in sight, both because of the responsibility that the people bore and because of the vision of a holy commonwealth that God had given them.

An experiment in planting the Heavenly City on earth required a small compact community. Any spreading out of the population or conflict between the interests of the church and the government would undermine the cohesion necessary for the social control of the utopia.[11] The saints must keep in mind that they are a people apart. "The main ends for which the Lord gathereth and preserveth his church upon earth," wrote John Robinson, "are that he might have a peculiar people, separated unto himself from all other peoples, to call upon his name in faith and to glorify him their heavenly Father in their holy conversation, whom he also might glorify in the end of their faith, the salvation of their souls."[12] The Lord provided room for his chosen people in order that they might live in a community untainted by the corruption of the world. "He hath placed thee in *Rehoboth,* in a peaceable place," John Cotton was to tell John Winthrop and company upon their departure for America. "This we must discerne, or els we are but intruders upon God . . . if a man doe remove, he must see that God hath espied out such a Countrey for him."[13]

The holy community entailed a closed society. The prevention of subversion to the established order should be the constant concern of everyone. As early as 1617, the Pilgrim leaders found, in submitting a self-evaluation to the Virginia Company, that

> We are knite togeather as a body in a most stricte and sacred bond and covenante of the Lord, of the violation we make great conscience, and by vertue wherof we doe hould our selves straitly tied to all care of each others good, and of the whole by every one and so mutually.[14]

No man can live apart from the community. The Pilgrims

not only accepted this truism, but, by virtue of their common religious purpose, considered their community a private association, which added to the sense of social cohesion. As long as church and town were closely related and coterminous in jurisdictions, harmony could be maintained. The full, weight of the community must be used to prevent disruption.

For a people who had deemed their liberties repressed in England, it may seem ironical that the Pilgrims in the new–found–land would place such a priority on unity. In spite of the many tribulations over the years and that they themselves were dissenters, the refugees from Scrooby had acquired little respect for a positive protection of the right to dissent. If they had to leave their homeland in order to form their kind of community, they were entitled by that sacrifice to keep that community free from subversive influences. William Hubbard, looking back on the founding of Plymouth, undoubtedly caught the rationalization of the Pilgrims in establishing a social order based upon unity.

> That which our Savior once affirmed concerning a kingdom, is as true of the smallest colony, or puny state or least society of mankind, that if it be divided against itself it cannot stand; and how can divisions be avoided where all sorts of people are to be at their liberty, whether in things civil or sacred, to do all that doth, and nothing but what doth, seem good in their own eyes?[15]

By birthright, the Pilgrims were Englishmen, and the best of Englishmen they would strive to be in the New World. Their long exile in the Netherlands, where they had felt the sting of discrimination and had been unwilling to surrender their cultural identity, had imbued in them an affection for country unmatched by other early New England settlers. Except for the Cromwellian period, one does not find the Plymouth fathers expunging references to the king in their laws and oaths as did the Puritans at Massachusetts. The Pilgrims thought they retained the good will of the king; and "who can doubt or call in question the lawfulness of inhabiting or dwelling there, but that it may be as lawful for such as are not tied upon some special occasion here, to live there as well as here." But "as the enterprise is weighty and difficult, so the honor is more worthy, to plant a rude wilderness, to enlarge the honor and fame of our dread sovereign."[16] In the New World the Pilgrims considered them-

selves entitled to all the liberties enjoyed by Englishmen in the
realm. When they sat down to codify their laws in 1636 they
made this point clear.

> Wee the associates of New-Plymouth Coming hither as freeborn
> subjects of the State of England endowed with all and singular the
> privileges belonging to such being assembled; doe ordaine Constitute
> and enact that noe act imposition law or ordinance be made or im-
> posed upon us at present, or to come but such as shall be imposed
> by Consent of the body of the associates or their representatives
> legally assembled; which is according to the free liberties of the
> State of England.[17]

But knowledge of the subtle complexities of English law was
meager at best, since the Pilgrims had long been refugees from
the home country and none were lawyers. Thus they would have
to follow common sense in setting up a community in accord
with the English constitutional system and to improvise in order
to meet the conditions of a primitive society. Obviously there
would be some divergence between a community made from a
state of nature and the English municipality or parish; and, as
time would wear on, without direction from abroad, the disparity
would widen. In general intent, however, the Pilgrims wanted to
conform to English principles of government as they understood
them. They were much "on the same ground," as Hubbard
states, "that Pacuvius sometimes advised his neighbors of Capua,
not to cashier their old magistrates till they could agree upon
better to place in their room. So did these choose to abide by the
Laws of England, till they could be provided of better."[18]

Upon the return of the *Mayflower* to England, friends of the
Pilgrims learned that the colonists wanted to secure a patent
from the newly formed Council of New England. A patent issued
by the Virginia Company earlier to John Wincob, who had
expected to accompany the Pilgrims to America, of course had
no validity for a settlement outside of the Company's jurisdiction.
It is probable that the Pilgrims before leaving England had already
arranged for a patent with Ferdinando Gorges and associates,
who were re-organizing the New England Company into the
*"Councill established at Plymouth, in the County of Devon, for
the planting, ruling, and governing of* New-England, *in America."*
The charter of the Council passed the seals in November 1620.[19]

In a pure sense, the Council of New England was not a corporate body of stockholders, as the Virginia Company, but merely a council of forty persons to grant lands and fishing privileges.[20] Too poor to establish a general government for New England, the Council considered its settlements as subordinate plantations, which would allow a settlement to exercise local political power and proprietorship.[21] Later, when New England would be "raised unto so much eminence," the Council would seek to put the government of the New England colonies into its own hands, through the appointment of a hierarchy of officials.[22]

The patents (1621 and 1622) obtained through the Council of New England, provided for powers of local government within the larger corporation. Legally, however, the constitutional base of Plymouth Colony was nothing more than that of a sub-proprietary. The patent of June 1, 1621 granted to John Peirce, acting for the adventurers (stockholders) of the Plymouth enterprise, conferred one hundred acres of land to each New England settler, on condition of a quit-rent of two shillings an acre after seven years, and gave hunting and trading privileges. During the seven year period, Peirce and associates could request a formal incorporation of the settlement by the Council, and "in the meane tyme untill such graunt [be] made, it shalbe lawfull for the said John Peirce his Associate undertakers and Planters their heires and assignes by consent of the greater part of them to establish such Lawes and ordynaunces as are for their better government, and the same by such Officer or Officers as they shall by most voyces elect and choose to put in execution."[23] Actually the granting of government powers had no validity since the Plymouth settlers were not agents of the Council and the Council had no authority to act in this capacity.[24]

Although taken out in the name of the adventurers, a second patent issued to John Peirce in April 20, 1622 sought to convert Peirce's status from trustee to a single proprietorship. This patent was in the form of a deed poll[25] rather than an indenture and required only one person (Peirce) to act in matters concerning the deed. The significance of the change was not lost on William Bradford, who perceived that Peirce could act as a lord of a manor with seignorial powers over the Plymouth settlement. He "mente to keep it to him selfe and alow them what he pleased, to hold of him as tenants, and sue to his courts as cheefe Lord."

But "the Lord marvelously crost him." Having set out twice in a vessel heavy laden with cargo and passengers, Peirce had to return both times to port in England because of unruly seas. Already burdened by great expense, Peirce decided to reassign this patent back to the full body of adventurers. Complaints by the Pilgrims to the Council of New England because they had not been consulted also influenced the decision.[26] Action taken by the Council on March 25, 1623 reinstated the patent of 1621 and ordered "undertakers and Servants now settled or to bee settled in Plymouth aforesaid should remaine and continue Tennants unto the Councell established for the managing of the foresaid affaires of New England."[27]

Because of this experience in the Council's granting away their rights and the dwindling financial support from the adventurers, the Pilgrims were ready to get out of both arrangements.[28] As a result of Isaac Allerton's negotiations in 1626, an agreement was reached for the London adventurers to assign their shares to each adult man then resident in Plymouth (these would be called "Old Comers" or "Purchasers"), with Bradford and eleven associates, in return for a monopoly of the Indian trade, to assume the financial obligation. The "Purchasers" would share in the future division of assets. With this dissolution of the partnership with the London capitalists, the Plymouth colonists now secured a patent directly from the Council of New England. The Warwick (or Bradford) patent of January 13, 1630 granted to the Plymouth residents powers of legislation—thus recognizing the form of government that the colony had already taken. Of course, laws enacted in the colony must conform to the laws of England, and the Council reserved the right to impose limitations on government in the future.[29] The colony and the company were now one and the same. Although again the Council's conferring governmental rights had questionable constitutional validity, assurances came from an order of the Privy Council in 1632 that "if things were carried as was pretended when the patents were granted . . . his Majestie would not only maintaine the liberties and privileges heretofore granted, but supply any thing further that might tend to the good governmente, prosperitie, and comforte of his people ther of that place, etc."[30] The colony, however, was still legally a fief of the Council of New England, and after 1635 of the king; yet, the self-governing corporation of the settlers resident at Plymouth was acknowledged *de facto*.

On April 25, 1635 the Council of New England surrendered its charter. Individual proprietary interests, however, would be maintained by certain members, principally by Ferdinando Gorges and his heirs, and meetings would continue until 1638.[31] Gorges himself would receive an ill-fated appointment as Governor-General of New England. But the Plymouth colonists were now free to go their own way, unfettered from the meddling of a private company abroad. With most of the original debts to the adventurers discharged, the Plymouth General Court agreed to a final division of assets of £300 to each of the "Purchasers" or "Old Comers." Bradford and associates resigned their trusteeship for the patent; and in March 1641 the patent was surrendered to the whole body of freemen.[32] Thus the rights of the patent and full ownership devolved upon the Plymouth self-made corporation.

Looking at the first years of Plymouth Colony one can find truth in J. F. Jameson's remark that "political democracy came to the United States as a result of economic democracy." Under a typical joint-stock company arrangement, whereby settlers pool their profits in a common stock, Plymouth of the early 1620's was a communality. The Pilgrims had agreed that, for a period of time, wealth was to be held in common and the houses and residential plots were to be considered as belonging to the common stock. This arrangement was to cause some irritation to the Pilgrims, who were soon to adjudge that in building a settlement they were enlarging their individual shares as against the shares of the English stockholders.

Early Plymouth, however, cannot be considered a communist society. It was a capitalistic enterprise. Each settler, sixteen years old and above, received a share valued at ten pounds in money; an additional share was given for each domestic servant accompanying a settler, and two shares could also be received for bringing over a person over sixteen years of age. As full partners in the stock company, the Pilgrims had incentive—even if the important motive for immediate private gain was circumscribed— to improve the investment. After seven years, they would share in the division of capital and profits according to their own stake in the enterprise.[33]

In the New World, as John Smith put it:

> The most of them live together as one family or houshold, yet every man followeth his trade and profession both by sea and land, and all for a generall stocke, out of which they have all their maintenance, untill there be a divident betwist the Planters and the Adventurers . . . . all the masters of families are partners in land or whatsoever, setting their labours against the stocke, till certaine yeers be expired for the division.[34]

Out of working side by side for the common good, the Pilgrims could expect to plant the roots of an ideal community. Even though they disparaged the idea of communism, toiling together in the secular vineyard would produce the cohesion necessary to make their settling in a strange land a success. Cooperation and disinterestedness in one's individual gain in deference to the good of the whole was a theme constantly reiterated by the Pilgrim leaders. The first sermon preached at Plymouth suitably took as its text: "Let no man seek his own, but every man another's wealth" (1 *Cor.* x, 24). Robert Cushman asked that the Pilgrims keep in mind the motives that brought them to the New World "in memory for ourselves and those that shall come after, to be a remedy against self-love, the bane of all societies; and that we also testify to our Christian countrymen, who judge diversely of us, that though we be in a heathen country, yet the grace of Christ is not quenched in us. . . ." Everyone should work as hard as he could and share his fare with less fortunate neighbors. No one should be forced to beg or lose his "majesty," the image of God. "And as you are a body together, so hang not together by skings and gimocks, but labour to be joynted together by flesh and sinewes." [35] Edward Winslow warned the early settlers at Plymouth that "three things are the overthrow and bane . . . of plantations." Besides ambition of would-be leaders and "carelessness" in sending over supplies, foremost to be feared was "the vain expectation of present profit, which too commonly taketh a principal seat in the heart and affection. . . ." No man should expect "fruit before the tree be grown" or become "seekers of themselves, but the common good of all for whom they are employed." [36] Troubled by complaints coming from Plymouth against the idea of a collective community, James Sherley, the treasurer for the London adventurers, exorcised those who wished to "withdraw themselves, tempting God and despising their neighbours." Persons so inclined cannot have their cake and eat it too; they "must look for no share or part in any of these things; but as they will be a commonwealth alone, so alone they must work, and alone must eat, and alone they must be sick and die. . . ." [37] But for a utopia pinioned on the capitalist motive, it was inevitable that the settlers would soon insist upon their individual preferment.

It is not surprising that the first breach in the collective order came from the sheer desire to stay alive. Writes William Bradford in 1623: "All this whille no supply was heard of, neither knew they when they might expecte any. So they begane to thinke how they might raise as much corne as they could, and obtaine a beter crope then they had done, that they might not still languish in miserie." Thus it was decided "that they should set corne every man for his owne perticuler, and in that regard trust to them selves; in all other things to goe on in the generall way as before." Assigning each family land for its own use proved an instant success: "it made all hands very industrious, so as much more corne was planted then other waise would have bene by any means the Governor or any other could use. . . ." Bradford soon concluded that a "common course and condition" might satisfy the "vanitie of that conceite of Platos and other ancients," but men are not wiser than God and in Plymouth the trial with communism bred "much confusion and discontent" and retarded "much imployment." [38] The arrival in 1623 of "Particulars," men who were not bound by the joint stock company agreement, served to drive a further wedge in the village communism. Such malcontents as John Oldham, resenting exclusion from landholding, the fur trade, and government, stirred up a round of dissension in both the colony and the company that would hasten the division of property in 1627. [39]

The mixture of realism and idealism in the Pilgrim idea of community approached utopia perhaps even more than the early settlers themselves realized. They had all the ingredients for the perfect commonwealth, insofar as it rests in the machinations of man: a social compact literally entered into in a state of nature; a pervasive myth commanding the ultimate allegiance of the governors and the governed and distraining the passions of man; and a sense of common weal tempered with the belief that each individual is entitled to better himself as he sees fit. In looking ahead at the total perspective of the colony, one wonders if the Plymouth settlers, had they been left alone from outside interference and had they possessed greater resources, would have held to the dream of a perfect commonwealth as long as they did. Utopia, so it seems, can only exist in a condition of poverty, and then but for a moment. A taste of Eden brings about a longing for a past that almost was. As time passed, the Pilgrim founders became aware that during the deprivation of the early years they had come close to a perfect society. Thus there would be the temptation to make their state reactionary; but the seeds of democracy sown during the first years made possible accommodation to change.

NOTES

1. The Virginia Company in February 1620 had granted the Pilgrims "liberty till a form of Government be here settled for them, of associating unto them divers of the gravest and discreetest of their companies to make orders and ordinances for the better orderinge and directing of their servants and business." Quoted in Arthur Lord, "The Mayflower Compact," *AASP*, XXX (1920), 289. Technically, however, the Pilgrims landing at Cape Cod were outside the jurisdiction of the Virginia Company.

2. For the idea of intimacy as a factor in the Pilgrims seeking a democratic but closed social order, see Charles E. Park, "Friendship as a Factor in the Settlement of Massachusetts," *AASP*, XXVIII (1918), 60-62.

3. *Mourt's Relation* (London, 1622), ed. Dwight B. Heath, The American Experience Series (New York, 1963), 17; William Bradford, *History of Plymouth Plantation,* ed. Worthington C. Ford *et al.,* 2 vols. (Boston, 1912), I, 189, hereafter cited as *Bradford Hist.;* Lord, "Mayflower Compact," *AASP,* XXX (1920), 279.

4. Quoted from Hugo Grotius, *De jure belli ac pacis,* in H. Krabbe, *The Modern Idea of the State* (New York, 1927), 19.

5. *Ibid.,* 95-96.

6. To A. C. McLaughlin, the Mayflower Compact was one of several things: a "transmutation of a church covenant into the practical foundation of a self-governing community . . . . first of a series of plantation covenants, used by the founders of little towns and communities in New England," and merely an old "sea law," by which passengers governed themselves during a voyage. Andrew C. McLaughlin, *The Foundations of American Constitutionalism* (New York, 1932), 19-21. Similarly, the settlers at Nethunsek (Salem) "by common consent of the old Planters . . . . combined together into one Body Politicke." Francis Higginson, *New-Englands Plantation, Or, a Short and True Description of the Commodities and Discommodities of that Countrey* (London, 1630), reprint (New York, 1943).

7. Champlin Burrage, *The Church Covenant Idea: Its Origins and Development* (Philadelphia, 1904), 86.

8. John Robinson to John Carver [July] 1620, *Bradford Hist.* (1912), I, 134.

9. John Winthrop, "A Modell of Christian Charity," *Winthrop Papers,* 5 vols. (Boston, 1929-47), II (1931), 294-95.

10. For discussion on the theological ramifications of the civil covenant, see Herbert W. Schneider, *The Puritan Mind* (Ann Arbor, reprint 1966), chapter 1; Perry Miller, *The New England Mind: The Seventeenth Century* (Boston, reprint 1961), 398-431, 464-78; Perry Miller, *The New England Mind: From Colony to Province* (Boston, reprint 1966), 21-28, 68-78.

11. A. Mervin Davies, *Foundation of American Freedom* (New York, 1955), 62-63.

12. John Robinson, "A Justification of Separation from the Church of England: Against Mr. Richard Bernard his Invective," (1610), Robert Ashton, ed., *The Works of John Robinson,* 3 vols. (London, 1851), II, 119.

13. John Cotton, "God's Promise to His Plantations" (1636), *Old South Leaflets,* III, No. 53, 7-8.

14. John Robinson and William Brewster to Edwin Sandys, Dec. 15, 1617, *Bradford Hist.* (1912), I, 76.

15. William Hubbard, *A General History of New England from the Discovery to 1680* (1682), *MHSC,* 2d Ser., V (1848), 61.

16. *Mourt's Relation,* 93.

17. Plymouth Colony Laws (1636-71), Nov. 15, 1636, MS., p. 6, Boston Public Library. This is a slightly different wording from the

printed laws, which omit such phrases as "privileges belonging to such being assembled" and "doe ordaine Constitute and enact." (*PCR,* XI, 6.)

18. Hubbard, *General History, MHSC,* 2d Ser., V (1848), 62.

19. For the charter, see William Brigham, ed., *The Compact, with the Charter and Laws of the Colony of New Plymouth* (Boston, 1836), 11-18. Possibly the Pilgrims had an understanding with Sir Ferdinando Gorges before leaving England. Richard A. Preston, Colonial Schemes of Sir Ferdinando Gorges, (unpubl. Ph. D. diss., Yale University, 1936), 153.

20. Joseph S. Davis, *Essays in the Earlier History of American Corporations* (*Harvard Economic Studies,* XVI [Cambridge, 1917]), 34.

21. L. D. Scisco, "The Plantation Type of Colony," *AHR,* VIII (1903), 269-70.

22. Sir Ferdinando Gorges' Observations on New England, May 12, 1634, Bancroft transcripts, I, 121, NYPL. Officers to be appointed included: Lord Governor or Lord Lieutenant; Lord Bishop; Chancellor; Admiral; Master of Ordinance; Secretary of State, and other assistants, with power to erect courts of justice, decide boundaries, settle subordinate officers, etc.

23. For the patent, see *Bradford Hist.* (1912), I, 246-51; printed also in "The First Plymouth Patent," *MHSC,* 4th Ser., II (1854), 158-63.

24. Preston, Gorges (Ph. D. diss.), 154-55.

25. A deed poll is "a deed testifying that only one of the parties to the agreement had put his seal to the same, where such party is the principle or only person, whose consent or act is necessary to the deed. And it is therefore a plain deed, without indenting and is used when the vendor only seals and there is no need of the vendee's sealing a counterpart, because the nature of the contract is such, as it requires no covenant from the vendee." Quoted from Jacob's *Law Dictionary* in C. M. Andrews, *The Colonial Period of American History* (New Haven, 1934), I, 282n.

26. *Bradford Hist.* (1912), I, 306-9; William Bradford, *Of Plymouth Plantation,* ed. Samuel E. Morison (New York, 1967), 124n.; J. G. Bartlett, "John Peirce of London and the Merchant Adventurers," *NEHGR,* LXVII (1913), 147-53.

27. Charles Deane, ed., *Records of the Council of New England, 1622-38, AASP,* V (1867), Minor Publications #4, 92.

28. See Bradford to Cushman, June 9, 1625, *Governor Bradford's Letter Book, MHSC,* 1st Ser., III (1794), 36.

29. Printed in Brigham, ed., *The Compact . . . Laws,* 21-26.

30. Order of Privy Council, Jan. 19, 1633, *Bradford Hist.* (1912), II, 144-45. This was among the first reports of the Committee on the New England Plantations (twelve members appointed by the Privy Council), headed by Archbishop Laud. For the functions of the Committee see C. M. Andrews, "British Committees, Commissions, and Councils of Trade and Plantations, 1622-75," *Johns Hopkins U. Studies in Hist. and Pol. Science,* Ser. XXVI, Nos. 1-3 (Baltimore, 1908), 15-17. Surprisingly the Separatism of Plymouth Colony did not bother the Committee.

31. Preston, Gorges (Ph. D. diss.), 282-84.

32. Bradford, *Of Plymouth Plantation,* ed. Morison, 428-30 and 429n.

33. *Bradford Hist.* (1912), I, 104-6. For a discussion of the fiction of the "half profits" system and dual control, see William Scott, *The Constitution and Finances of English, Scottish and Irish Joint-Stock Companies to 1720,* 3 vols. (Cambridge, Eng., 1910-12), II, 306-8.

34. John Smith, *The Generall Historie of Virginia, New-England, and the Summer Isles . . .* (1624), facsimile ed. (Cleveland, 1966), 247.

35. Robert Cushman, "The Sin and Danger of Self-Love," (preached Dec. 1621—pub. in London, 1622), in Alexander Young, ed., *Chronicles of the Pilgrim Fathers of the Colony of Plymouth, 1602-25* (Boston, 1844), 255-62.

36. Edward Winslow, *Good Newes from New England* (1624), abridgement, *MHSC,* 2d Ser., IX (1832), 76.

37. James Sherley *et al.* to William Bradford *et al.,* Dec. 18, 1624, *Bradford Letter Book, MHSC,* 1st Ser., IV (1794), 31.

38. *Bradford Hist.* (1912), I, 298-303.

39. See Ruth A. McIntyre, *Debts Hopeful and Desperate: Financing the Plymouth Colony* (Plymouth, Mass., 1963), 30-32.

Chapter Two

DEMOCRACY

As the Pilgrims came to America to avoid "the heirarchy, the cross in baptisme, the holy dayes, the book of Common Prayer, etc.," [1] so did they seek a democracy in government. They were aware that a group tightly joined together for a common purpose could best keep their mission intact by giving to each member an equal voice in the affairs of government. The joint-stock company arrangement also furthered unity and a sense of equal responsibility.

The Pilgrims would soon discover, however, that an inclusive majoritarianism in their government could have a character of its own outside the collection of individual wills. The majority will could be equated with the original holy sanction of their first coming together. A society founded on the principle that the majority rules creates a justification for the state to exist as an entity separate from the people on the presupposition that the state, legally constituted, is always the majority. Thus the state is the body politic: it determines its membership and the reach of its own authority. The minority must accommodate itself to

18

the interests of the majoritarian state. In Plymouth there would be no room for political parties or checks and balances, other than shifting public opinion. The majoritarian state encourages apathy. Assuming the constant mandate of the people, it is prone to act for rather than by the people. As population expanded and became more diffuse, power gravitated all the more into the hands of the established leaders in Plymouth.

Certain criteria can be used to measure, structurally, democracy in Plymouth Colony: the extent of the franchise; actual representation; the fluidity of office-holding; and the degree of responsibility borne by the citizen.

Early government in Plymouth appears to have been conducted by informal meeting of all the free male adults. Since the colonists were in intimate daily acquaintance with each other, what "laws and orders" needed to be passed or officials to be elected was done in the spirit of a confirmation procedure rather than as legislative business. Until the introduction of a representative system, provided for in 1636 and implemented in 1638, all matters were transacted by the company of freemen as a whole.[2] Newcomers, who were not stockholders, probably were not allowed to participate in the government; but with the termination of the stock company in 1627 they were apparently freely admitted into the political corporation in order to broaden the base of support in paying off the colony's debts.[3] During the early years, therefore, Plymouth was relatively a pure democracy.

When the colony in 1636 institutionalized the practice of electing officials "onely by the freemen according to the former custome," it also provided for an oath, which was to become one of several requirements for the freemanship. The oath of freemen was essentially a loyalty oath or, as it was later extended to the inhabitants of the towns, an "oath of fidelity." The 1636 oath reads:

> You shall be truly loyall to our Sov. Lord king Charles his heires and successors. You shall not speake or doe, devise or advise any thing or things act or acts directly or indirectly by land or water, that doth shall or may tend to the destruction or overthrow of this present plantations Colonies or Corporation of New Plymouth, Neither shall you suffer the same to be spoken or done but shall hinder oppose and discover the same to the Governor and Assistants

of the said Colony for the time being or some one of them. You shall
faithfully submit unto such good and wholsome laws and ordnances
as either are or shall be made for the ordering and government of
the same, and shall endeavor to advance the growth and good of
the severall plantations within the limits of this Corporation by all
due meanes and courses. All which you promise and sweare by the
name of the great God of heaven and earth simply truly and faithfully to perform as you hope for help from God who is the God of
truth and punisher of falsehood.[4]

During the civil war in England the words "our Sovereign Lord
king Charles his heirs and successors" were eliminated, and "the
State and Government of England as it now stands" was substi-
tuted; in 1658 the latter clause was replaced by "our Sovereign
Lord the Kinge his heires and Successors."[5] Such an oath to
uphold the state indirectly supported the church. By making an
oath of fidelity universal, an individual was bound to the will
of the majority in policy affecting religion. Technically it did
not matter whether the person taking the oath was regenerate
or unregenerate since he was merely pledging to preserve the
security of the state.[6]

The oath of fidelity for freemen was soon extended to the
admittance of inhabitants into the towns. In 1643 the General
Court ordered that "all those persons in every Towneship within
this Government that have not taken the Oath of fidellyty etc.
and do refuse to take it depart the Government."[7] As early as
1636, it was the practice that no person could be admitted as an
inhabitant of the colony without "the leave and likeing" of the
Governor and two assistants.[8] Such legislation was aimed at
denying subversive religious elements the franchise, while at the
same time in effect making the colony magistrates the sole
judges of voter qualifications on the local level. Since some of
the towns were remiss in requiring an oath of fidelity for admission as an inhabitant and non-freemen could customarily vote
for deputies and other business in the town-meetings, the General
Court in 1669 ordered that no person could vote in the town-
meetings without taking an oath of fidelity.[9] Petitioners for the
incorporation of a new town were also required to take an oath
of fidelity "for the state of England and this present government
of New Plymouth."[10]

To compound the matter, town residents refusing to take the oath of fidelity were to be fined £5 annually.[11] When this law was first passed in 1658, however, thirteen persons of Sandwich each were fined £10; in the two following years twelve persons were fined annually £5 each for not taking the oath of fidelity.[12] When the two itinerant Quaker interlopers, Humphrey Norton and John Rouse, refused to pay the fines, they were whipped and imprisoned.[13]

Largely through negative restrictions added over the years rather than through a definite electoral code, Plymouth Colony narrowed the voter franchise. To be admitted a freeman one had to petition the General Court, and this could be done only after a year's residence in the colony.[14] A candidate for the freemanship had to have the approbation of the freemen of his own town, and his petition had to be presented to the General Court by the deputies of his town.[15] Thus it is presumed that if a person were not on good terms with the town's elite, he would have no chance to become a freeman. The General Court in 1669 also stipulated that voters in town-meetings have a "twenty pound ratable estate" and be "of good conversation." [16] Later it was required that non-freemen and non-freeholders had to have a £30 ratable estate to vote for deputies, and in order to apply for freemanship one had to be twenty-one years old and to have his religious orthodoxy certified by his neighbors. In 1685, the £20 ratable estate requirement could be lifted if a person be "generally known and approved by the Court." [17]

Actually the qualifications for freemanship and the franchise were not severe. But the colony and town governments were closed corporations to those who digressed from the general conformity. Although the colony did not require test oaths for the franchise, several laws were passed excluding persons of different religious views than that of the majority from the right to vote. In 1650 the General Court ordered

> That forasmuch as there are Risen up amongst us many scandalus practises which are likely to prove destructive to our churches and Common peace; That whosoever shall heerafter set up any churches or publicke meetings diverse from those allreddy set up and approved without the concent and approbation of the Government or shall continew any otherwise set up without concent as aforesaid

shalbe suspended from haveing any voyce in towne meetings and presented to the next generall court to Receve such punishment as the court shall think meet to Inflict.[18]

In 1659 Quakers "or such as shall contemptuously speake of the lawes thereof" were singled out along with "such as are judged by the Court grosly scandalouse, as lyers, drunkards, swearers, &c" to be disfranchised.[19] The colony records contain a number of examples of persons being disfranchised for Quakerism as well as for drunken or lewd conduct. It is important to emphasize, as did the Plymouth authorities to the royal commissioners in 1665, that the concern was the maintenance of civil order rather than the forced conformity of religious belief.[20] Nevertheless, that the state saw a threat to its security in allowing radical religionists the enjoyment of civil liberties speaks for itself. In the 1680's Quakers were beginning to have their local suffrage rights restored by the colony.[21]

Before 1636 almost all freeholders were freeman.[22] Undoubtedly some male adults living in an extended family without property of their own were disqualified. As new towns were founded the ratio between the number of male adults and those admitted to freemanship widened. Most settlers of new towns were very young[23] and thus did not meet the usual age requirements of twenty-one or twenty-four[24] or the one year residency. It can be assumed also that most settlers only had a secondary concern for the responsibilities of freemanship, and waited until they had established themselves in a community before they applied for admission into the colony corporation. Usual estimates of those constituting the freemanship at any given time, as supported by the recent study of George Langdon, are between twenty-five and thirty per cent.[25] For example, in 1643 there were 227 freemen among 560 men capable of bearing arms,[26] and in 1670, out of an estimated adult male population of 1000, 359 freemen were listed.[27] In addition to the restrictions of property, Quakerism, servitude, age, and residency, general apathy held down the number of freemen.[28] In spite of the apparent narrow franchise, most adult males could become freemen if they cared to, and a majority (slightly over fifty per cent) sometime in their lives did.[29]

As the colony expanded and government grew more complex,

interest on the part of the people waned. Plymouth would become less a plebiscatory democracy and more an elitist representative government. Power gravitated into the hands of the few. The creation of a representative system in March 1639 had the effect of increasing the powers of the magistracy. Previously they had represented a single constituency of the people in both legislative and executive functions. Now, with the provision for town deputies or "committees" (two from each town and four from Plymouth) "to joyne with the Bench to enact and make all such lawes and ordinances" for the good of the whole colony, much of the legislative burden would be taken off the magistrates, who, still elected directly by the freemen at large, could give more attention to the enforcement of the laws and policy-making. The deputies would sit in several short legislative sessions, where their votes combined with the votes of the magistrates in the same chamber could determine the laws, but the magistrates would have continual tenure throughout the year. The freemen at the annual court of election had the power of a referendum to rescind any legislative measure,[30] but there is no indication that they ever exerted this veto. Nevertheless, this was a built in check-and-balance against any intractability of the deputies, who did not have to be freemen and who could possibly be misdirected from the interests of the whole by virtue of their particular representation.

When the representative principle was put into effect in 1639, the assistants (including the governor) had one-third of the votes in the unicameral legislature: eight assistants[31] and sixteen deputies from the seven incorporated towns.[32] With new towns added, the proportion of deputies to the assistants increased: for example, 1642—eighteen deputies; 1652—twenty-two; and 1685—forty-two.[33] Towns did not always send a complete committee of deputies. In 1667, Sandwich, because "of theire scarcitie of men fitt for publicke imployment," was allowed by the General Court to send one deputy.[34] It appears to have been the practice to permit the newer towns to send only one deputy if they wished. Bridgewater, founded in 1656, never elected a second deputy until 1689.[35] Despite the fact that a town not choosing deputies faced a fine of 40s. and each deputy elected but not appearing at the General Court was to be fined 20s.,[36] delinquencies went relatively unpunished.

The office of deputy was monopolized by a few public spirited men, who, in the early years after the town planting, were invariably original proprietors of the town lands. After the General Court required the towns to appoint boards of selectmen in 1662,[37] most deputies were also selectmen.[38] Plural office-holding on the town and colony level enhanced the oligarchic control of those with the greater stake in society.

All town affairs were under the authorization or overview of the General Court, including the naming of local officials, the bounds of authority for the town-meetings, and local ordinances and policy. This will be borne out more fully in subsequent chapters. Fines were levied by the General Court for anyone appointed but refusing a local office, such as constable or marshal.[39] The towns placed their own fines upon "listed townesmen" for each absence from a town-meeting.[40] In order to promulgate orders of the General Court or to compel consideration of any business, deputies could convene town-meetings.[41]

If representative democracy in Plymouth was top-heavy, local inhabitants seemed content because in theory at least all power derived from the whole body of freemen at the annual court of election. But inevitably, as in any republic, there would be differences over the fundamental right to be taxed fairly with one's consent. Occasionally contention arose between town and colony concerning the rate fixing powers of the General Court in taxation for the general use. Each town was annually assessed for taxes according to the estimated value of livestock and improved landed property in the township; inhabitants, through town levies, then paid their share in such commodities as wheat, corn, butter, pork, or peas. The General Court required towns to appoint raters, and if this were not done or if raters neglected their duties a town was fined £5. Failure to make assessments within a time limit by raters also would lead to a fine on the town.[42] Since raters were taxpayers themselves, they had the tendency to report conservatively the property assets of their townships. But the General Court set the final apportionment of taxes, and sometimes a town would consider its share of the colony's taxes disproportionate in comparison to other towns. Indeed, it seems that Scituate, with a much higher rate than any of the other towns, bore an undue share.[43]

The General Court could order a town to follow greater equity in the rating for taxes, as in the case of Bridgewater where persons with "dorment lands" were being taxed more heavily than those "that live mostly upon the spoyle of youer commons."[44] Quaker protest over exclusion from serving as raters eventually led the General Court in 1681 to permit Quakers to serve in this capacity "soe long as they carry civilly and not abuse theire libertie."[45] The inhabitants of Rehoboth in 1669 petitioned the General Court that they were being taxed more than their just proportion.[46] Fortunately for the colony leaders, the tax burden was not high, and protests were scattered and infrequent.

But in 1685 the huge rise in taxes caused by the war debt and price inflation stirred wide discontent among the subsistence farmers of Plymouth—the full opprobrium, however, would fall upon the councilors of the Dominion of New England. The policies of the Dominion government of high rating of livestock, on which Plymouth residents were especially dependent, rating of houses, and taxing all persons over sixteen years old on the basis of owning £20 in taxable property whether they did or not, were among grievances of Plymouth colonists in a petition to the crown. The new rating was held "neither just or legal," and the king was reminded that the Plymouth settlers had sacrificed their lives and had suffered many "dangers"—"at our own proper charge and costs"—in order to make the colony a success.[47] They had won the right to tax themselves, and the Dominion government should at least respect the rating policy of Plymouth colony that had been in effect for a half century. Essentially, the Plymouth colonists were claiming the right of the colony to internal taxation.

Legislative business in the General Court was hardly more than a rubber-stamping of pre-arranged decisions. There appears to have been little deliberation. Debates and roll calls went unrecorded. With the deputies constantly below full representation, no attempt was made to establish a quorum or house rules. Standing committees were unknown, and special committees were only used for periodic revision of the laws or as boards of arbitration in local disputes, such as laying out boundaries. From the course of events, it can be assumed that the only divisive issues were the Quaker problem, the support of the ministry, and the nature of offensive and defensive war in connection with the Dutch and Indian wars.

Laws made outside of code revision were probably agreed to informally before presentation to the General Court, much like the practice of modern town councils or county courts. The governor presided over the legislative sessions and thereby guided the course of legislation. A curious feature of the colony records is the omission of references to bills before the General Court; only the enactments, in the form of orders, laws, or ordinances are mentioned. The Plymouth fathers shared the Puritan penchant for clear and uncontested authority in government.

In the authoritarian democracy of Plymouth, the magistrates (the governor, assistants, treasurer) held full sway. Their election came from the popular sovereignty manifested in the annual court of election by the freemen, but their right to rule came from God. In essence, the will of the people and of God were one— each buttressed the other. The freemen would bestow the office, but from the time of election, a magistrate would be responsible only to God. If he veered from the straight path, he could be ousted at the next election by the freemen, who were inclined to follow the dictates of the other magistrates in wishing to cast out one of their own. As did the children of other Zions in seventeenth century New England, the Plymouth settlers believed that a mystical power pervaded the act of governing. Thus respect for the combined popular and divine authority in government accounts much for the paternalism in Plymouth Colony and, for that matter, much of the apathy of the inhabitants.

In spite of the rather exclusive character of the freemanship, it is surprising how little was expected of freemen. Theoretically, having the power to review all enactments and to compel the governor to hold a special session for that purpose,[48] in practice they confined their functions to electing the magistrates in the annual court of election (held originally in March and then in June). The introduction of vote by proxy in the annual court of election (first accorded to Rehoboth in 1646 and general- ized in 1652) did not promote a sense of corporate authority among the freemen since the simple act of a proxy vote was an isolated balloting in the election of the magistrates. What per- centage of freemen continued to attend in person the courts of election can only be speculative. For non-attendance they had to register their intent and reasons with the deputies at the town meetings.[49]

Any freeman could vote for whom he pleased for governor, assistant, or treasurer, but presumably he designated the office for his nominees. For assistants, seven persons receiving the most votes were elected; if one or more of these did not assume the office of assistant for whatever reason, persons with the next most votes would be declared elected. Refusal to serve as governor if elected entailed a £20 fine; £10 for declining the office of assistant.[50] Thomas Prence and Miles Standish were absent at the first session of the General Court in 1637 and therefore were not sworn in.[51] In 1638 Edward Winslow and John Jenney were absent at the first General Court and Timothy Hatherly outright refused to serve. John Browne, who stood next in the order of votes, replaced Hatherly, who was cited as liable for fine at the future discretion of the Court.[52] After 1647, the number of assistants was reduced to six.[53] James Brown refused to serve in 1683, but apparently was not fined.[54]

Once a person became a magistrate, Plymouth freemen were reluctant to turn him out. Similar to other New England governments, the Plymouth magistracy had a self-perpetuating quality. Unlike Massachusetts, the office of commissioner of the United Colonies was passed around solely among the magistrates. Plymouth did not have a country party in the deputies, as did Massachusetts, and hence the magistrates could secure the office of commissioner of the United Colonies without opposition. For the seventy-one years after Carver's death in 1621, the colony had only five governors. After a single term each of Hinckley and Cudworth as deputy governors in 1680 and 1681 respectively (the office was instituted in 1680 because of Governor Winslow's ill-health), William Bradford Jr. was the sole deputy governor from 1682-92. The colony had only seven treasurers and four secretaries (not considered a magistrate)— both offices began in 1637. Only twenty-nine assistants held office during the whole life of the colony, which is remarkable since this was an elective office and during most of the period there were six or seven assistants at a given time.[55]

Service in the magistracy called for a high sense of public duty —hence a primary factor for the monopolization by a few men. Emoluments certainly did not exceed the measure of responsibility. Assistants performed judicial duty in the court of assistants and acted as legislators in the General Court. Extra-curricular chores were also time consuming, such as the administration of estates of persons dying intestate.[56] By 1670, however, all colony

officials were salaried, including military officers, marshals, constables, etc. Customarily, around £100 was allocated for the
total salaries of the governor and assistants, £30 for the treasurer, £12 for "necessaries to accomodate the magestrates table,"
and £80 to "entertain the commissioners [of the United Colo-
nies]."[57] Such operational expenses in this later period made up
most of the £275–£300 annual budget. The Plymouth governor
received usually £10 in silver money as an annual salary but
from time to time was allowed "extraordinary charges." Shortly
after Governor Josiah Winslow died, £40 was voted to his
estate.[58] By 1690 salaries had become stabilized: governor, £28;
deputy governor, £12; each assistant, £10; deputy, 6d. per day,
paid by the towns; chief marshal, £8, etc.[59]

The all-embracing authority of the magistrates was somewhat
curtailed with the establishment of counties in 1685. Freemen
of each county now elected associates (Plymouth, 3; Barnstable,
2; and Bristol, 2), who were empowered to hold county courts.[60]

For a people imbued with unity in religion and community,
attentiveness to the education of the citizenry would be expected.
Other than to promote the general usefulness of each citizen,
justification for public education rests upon two major premises,
both relevant to the Plymouth experience. In order to have a
free and responsible society, the young must be educated in its
virtues; especially in Plymouth, with the sense of mission, it was
incumbent upon the older generation to impart the meaning and
objectives of the holy commonwealth to the young. Secondly, a
state naturally seeks its own self-preservation, and education is
the best means of indoctrination. Despite their humble origins,
the Pilgrims harbored no anti-intellectualism *per se;* but as poor
husbandmen and fishermen they could hardly appreciate the
benefit of education beyond its rudiments.

It was resolved in 1624 to establish a common school in
Plymouth, but the matter was put off until a "fit person" could
be found. Parents had the full responsibility of teaching and
catechizing their children.[61] A scheme in 1640 for an academy
at Jones' River, to be under the tutelage of Charles Chauncey,
did not materialize. Several towns boasted schoolmasters before
the passage of a law in 1662 charging each town to have a school-
master, which was made compulsory in 1677 for municipalities
of fifty families. An act of 1671 required parents and masters to

teach their children and servants reading, religion, the laws, and some calling so that they not "prove pests instead of blessings to the country." Negligence by parents or masters merited a 10*s*. fine, and, if continued, 20*s*. after three months. The children could subsequently be taken away after an additional three months. Selectmen of the towns were to keep "a vigilant eye" over the enforcement of this law.

In 1670 the General Court offered all the annual profits from fishing with nets or seines at Cape Cod for mackerel, bass, or herring for "a free schoole in some towne of this jurisdiction, for the training up of youth in literature for the good and benefit of posteritie." The school in Plymouth, originally supported by rents from the common lands, received this subsidy in 1673. Thomas Hinckley, representing the governor and assistants, was appointed to manage the Plymouth school, which thus became the first totally free public school in America—but from 1677-1704 it was on a tuition basis. In 1677, £5 from the fishery was offered to any town setting up a Latin grammar school, and every township of fifty families was to provide £12 in taxes plus voluntary contributions for a free school. Each of the new county seats in 1685 was ordered to establish a Latin school, where each pupil was to pay 3*d*. a week for English instruction and upon entering Latin grammar, 6*d*. a week, with students from other towns admitted free.[62] The colony government, therefore, promoted education and prescribed guidelines, but left a school system entirely up to the towns. The Plymouth authorities had at least taken cognizance of education as a cohesive force in restoring the ancient dedication to a Bible community. They had harkened to the exhortation in the election sermon of 1669: "Let not the Kids of the Flock be forgotten. . . . If you would enjoy your Church Priviledges, and your Civil Peace, labour for *Unity*." [63]

Puritanism crept into the Separatist principles of government held by the Plymouth settlers. They would still subscribe to the idea of John Robinson that in the church "every one is made a king, a priest, a prophet, not only to himself but to the whole body," [64] but in civil polity they put into practice a more aristocratic philosophy. They could agree with Henry Ainsworth, teacher of the "Ancient Brethren" Separatists in Amsterdam. Ainsworth, who had moved away from a democratic position while Robinson had progressed towards it, saw that there must be a clear distinction between the rulers and the ruled, which anticipated John Cotton's famous statement of a later time that democracy was never ordained by God "a fitt government either for church or common wealth. If the people be governors, who shall be governed." As Ainsworth had put it: "So then for *popular government* . . . we hold it not, we approve it not, for if the multitude govern, then who shal be governed? Christian liberty (which all have) is one thing, the raynes of government (which some have) is another thing." [65]

The Pilgrims believed that the people lacked will if left to themselves; the very nature of man required consummate leadership. They could agree with William Hubbard when he said:

> The body of a people are not much unlike the body of waters, which are not apt to move of themselves, if let alone in their own receptacle, but as they receive an impression from a forreign Element, or a power that is above them: and things that are soft and flexible are susceptible of divers, yea contrary impressions.[66]

The good magistrate never acts precipitately on an impulse of the people, who are fickle and can be misled by false notions of self-interest; rather he seeks to follow the will of God. If the transcendence of the divine will into duly constituted authority conflicted with the democratic base of society, it nevertheless lifted the popular mandate to the lofty plane of fundamental law. "Christians should be men of public Spirits" and "especially publick persons" must "not be of private Spirits," spoke the Reverend Samuel Arnold to the freemen assembled in 1674.

> Every Generation hath a common work and something proper, some special service to do for God.
>
> • • •
>
> Publick persons are under a *special Obligation* and *Bond* of Service, the Latine word *officium,* signifies both office and duty, and they have more Service from their Generation then others, and therefore owe more Service to their Generation . . . .
> . . . the best Generation is ordinarily a divided Generation, a mixed Generation, like those in the confused Assembly at *Ephesus* . . . some cry one thing and some another, some are for God, and some

are for *Baal,* whence it is impossible to serve our Generation according to their will, it is more possible to please God then to please our Generation.

. . .

The highest place among men is a service, those in highest place are but Servants to others, such as have the greatest Dignity have the greatest Duty.[67]

Democracy in Plymouth was prefaced by the fact that God governs in the affairs of men. It had the Calvinist connotation that the people must be led in governing themselves. Hence we have the largely negative attitude toward citizen responsibility; threats of fines, loyalty oaths, and the like forced the people out of depraved disinterestedness to exert their civil liberty. Some were called to govern the whole body; others to preside over the parts, while still others were left to serve more humbly. But all were bound as one in holy commonwealth.

NOTES

1. Edward Winslow, *New-England Salamander Discovered by an Irreligious and Scornful Pamphlet* . . . (1647), *MHSC,* 3d Ser., II (1830), 138.

2. *Mourt's Relation,* 59; *Bradford Hist.* (1912), I, 385; *PCR,* XI, 6.

3. George D. Langdon, Jr., "The Franchise and Political Democracy in Plymouth Colony," *WMQ,* 3d Ser., XX (1963), 516.

4. *PCR,* XI, 8, 80.

5. *Ibid.,* 156. Although not entirely accurate, see Charles Evans, "Oaths of Allegiance in Colonial New England," *AASP,* XXXI (1921), 383-85.

6. For John Cotton's justification of the oath of fidelity in Massachusetts, similar to the position of the Plymouth magistrates, see John Cotton, *A Reply to Mr. Williams his Examination; And Answer of the Letters sent to him by John Cotton* (1647), *Pubs. of the Narragansett Club,* 1st Ser., II (Providence, 1867), 90.

7. *PCR,* XI, 43, 118 (1658).

8. *Ibid.,* 109, 191.

9. *Ibid.,* 223 (1669), 248 (1678).

10. *Ibid.,* III, 44-45 (1654).

11. *Ibid.,* XI, 109 (1658), 129 (1661).

12. *Ibid.,* III, 93, 96, 98.

13. *Ibid.,* 139-40 (1658).

14. *Ibid.,* XI, 155 (1658).

15. *Ibid.,* 65 (1656).

16. *Ibid.,* 223.

17. George D. Langdon, Jr., *Pilgrim Colony: A History of New Plymouth, 1620-91* (New Haven, 1966), 88-89n.; Mary E. Hatheway, "The Early Hatheways of Taunton," *Old Colony Hist. Soc. Colls.,* No. 6 (Taunton, 1899), 79.

18. *PCR,* XI, 57.

19. *Ibid.,* III, 167.

20. *Ibid.,* IV, 85-86. An early case of disfranchisement for drunkenness was that of John Combe in 1639. *Ibid.,* I, 132.

21. E.g., Quakers in Sandwich being allowed in 1681 to vote on the disposal of lands and the choice of raters or assessors. *Ibid.,* VI, 71.

22. In 1633 there were 89 ratable persons in the colony and 91 freemen. *Ibid.,* I, 3-4, 9-11.

23. E.g., in early Bristol (1689). John Demos, "Families in Colonial Bristol, Rhode Island: An Exercise in Historical Demography," *WMQ,* 3d Ser., XXV (1968), 49.

24. Langdon, "Franchise and Political Democracy . . . ," *WMQ,* 3d Ser., XX (1963), 519.

25. *Ibid.* The low proportion of freemen in new towns is witnessed in early Yarmouth: in 1643 (after four years of settlement) there were 52 persons capable of bearing arms out of an approximate population of 250, and only sixteen freemen. Charles F. Swift, *History of Old Yarmouth* (Yarmouthport, 1884), 34-35.

26. The 560 is Langdon's estimate. The colony records list 401 (Plymouth, 148; Duxbury, 43; Sandwich, 70; Barnstable, 61; Yarmouth, 52; Taunton, 27), while freemen only are listed from Marshfield (62) and Rehoboth-Seaconck (5). There were no returns from Scituate. All names come to 468. It is reasonable to assume that, including Scituate and other omissions on an individual basis, the number of men capable of bearing arms between ages 16-60 was 500. The list of freemen for 1643 is broken down as follows: Plymouth, 70;

Duxbury, 34; Scituate, 33; Sandwich, 12; Cohannet (Taunton), 15; Yarmouth, 16; Barnstable, 22; Marshfield, 11; Rehoboth, 4; and Nauset, 10. *PCR,* VIII, 187-96.

27. *Ibid.,* V, 274-79. With cancelled names included, there were 363 freemen from 12 towns. See also Albert E. McKinley, *The Suffrage Franchise in the Thirteen English Colonies in America, Pubs. of the U. of Pennsylvania Series in Hist.,* No. 2 (Philadelphia, 1905), 349. An estimate derived from the report of a royal commissioner is found in John G. Palfrey, *History of New England,* 5 vols. (Boston, 1890), III, 36n.

28. For further discussion, see Langdon, "Franchise and Political Democracy . . . ," *WMQ,* 3d Ser., XX (1963), 517-24.

29. *Ibid.,* 519.

30. *PCR,* I, 121; XI, 31. In October 1636 it was proposed that "committees for the whole, be added to the Governor and Assistants, to rectifie and prepare such as should be thought most convenient . . . ." *Ibid.,* I, 43. In 1646 freemen at a court of election could "make or repeale" laws and ordinances. *Ibid.,* XI, 54.

31. Upon the death of Carver in 1621, one assistant was elected (Isaac Allerton); from 1624-37 there were four or five assistants, with the governor during this period having a double vote. See John A. Goodwin, *The Pilgrim Republic* (Boston, 1888), 159. Elected with Governor Bradford in 1639 were seven assistants: Thomas Prence, Miles Standish, John Alden, John Browne, William Collier, Timothy Hatherly, and John Jenney. *PCR,* I, 116.

32. *PCR,* I, 126. In repealing laws and on matters of adjournment, assistants and deputies also decided as one body. *Ibid.,* XI, 56-57.

33. *Ibid.,* II, 40; III, 18; Ebenezer W. Peirce, *Civil, Military and Professional Lists of Plymouth and Rhode Island Colonies . . .* (Baltimore, reprint 1968), *passim.*

34. *PCR,* IV, 159 (1667).

35. *Peirce, Civil Lists,* 40-41.

36. *PCR,* XI, 54 (1646).

37. *Ibid.,* 143. The practice of approving selectmen began in 1666. *Ibid.,* IV, 124. The idea of giving governing authority to a board of townsmen was first tried in Plymouth in 1650. *Records of the Town of Plymouth,* 3 vols. (Plymouth, 1889-1903), I, 29-30.

38. See lists of town and colony office-holding in Peirce, *Civil Lists, passim* and for the towns of Barnstable County, Frederick Freeman, *The History of Cape Cod: The Annals of Barnstable County and*

of its Several Towns, 2 vols. (Yarmouth Port, Mass., reprint 1965), II, 168-69, 239-40, 343-44, 413-14.

39. E.g., Job Bourne fined £4 for refusing to serve as constable at Sandwich in 1672. *PCR,* V, 100.

40. E.g., *Sandwich and Bourne Town Records,* No. 104 of *Library of Cape Cod History and Genealogy* (Yarmouthport, Mass., 1910), 30 (1676); *Ply. Town Records,* I, 32 (1652).

41. *PCR,* XI, 36 (1640).

42. *Ibid.,* 42 (1644).

43. *Ibid.,* VIII, 123 (1667), 137 (1672), 141 (1674), 146 (1676). It was the duty of the chief marshal to collect taxes, to be assisted by anyone he saw fit. *Ibid.,* III, 11-12. After 1685 the responsibility fell on the county sheriffs. The annual colony levy reached an all time high in 1685, £346 10s., because of debts accrued from King Philip's War. *Ibid.,* VIII, 167.

44. *Ibid.,* V, 4 (1668).

45. *Ibid.,* VI, 71.

46. Winslow Papers, MHS, 37. For territory owned by one jurisdiction but lying within another (e.g., Rehoboth and Swansea), the General Court fixed the rates of the local taxation. *PCR,* V, 84 (1672).

47. Thomas Hinckley to William Blathwayt, June 28, 1687, *HP,* 154-59; "The Humble Address of your Majesty's most loyal and grateful Subjects . . . of New Plymouth, Oct. 1687, *ibid.,* 173-80.

48. *PCR,* XI, 80.

49. *Ibid.,* 84.

50. *Ibid.,* I, 5 (1633).

51. *Ibid.,* 53.

52. *Ibid.,* 86.

53. *Ibid.,* II, 115, *passim.*

54. *Ibid.,* VI, 106.

55. See Peirce, *Civil Lists,* 3-5; Samuel Dana *et al.,* "Account of Plymouth Colony Records," *MHSC,* 3d Ser., II (1830), 266-67; cf. Cotton Mather, *Magnalia Christi Americana: or the Ecclesiastical History of New-England . . . 1620 . . . 1698* (1702), 2 vols. (Hartford, reprint 1820), I, 108.

56. In this instance, Cudworth and Hatherly. *PCR,* VI, 15 (1679).

57. *Ibid.,* VIII, 134 (1671), 138-9 (1672). Mass. magistrates did much better: in 1645 the Mass. governor earned £60, and in 1646 and afterwards, £100. *MCR,* II, 84, 113, 124, 246.

58. *PCR,* VI, 44, 63, 253.

59. *Ibid.,* 245-46.

60. *Ibid.,* 247.

61. *Bradford Hist.* (1912), I, 363.

62. *PCR,* V, 107; XI, 233, 237; Goodwin, *Pilgrim Republic,* 494-96; "History of Free Schools in Plymouth Colony, and in the Town of Plymouth with Incidental Notes," *MHSC,* 2d Ser., IV (1816, reprint 1846), 84; Marcus W. Jernegan, *Laboring and Dependent Classes in Colonial America, 1607-1783* (New York, reprint 1960), 98-102.

63. Thomas Walley, *Balm in Gilead to heal Sions Wounds . . .* (1669), Evans #146, 16, 19.

64. Quoted in G. P. Gooch, *The History of English Democratic Ideas in the Seventeenth Century* (Cambridge, Eng., 1898), 76.

65. Quotes from Henry M. Dexter, *The Congregationalism of the Last Three Hundred Years as Seen in its Literature* (New York, 1880), 353.

66. William Hubbard, *The Happiness of a people in the wisdome of their Rulers directing and in the obedience of their brethren . . .* (1676), Evans #214, 15.

67. Samuel Arnold, *David serving his generation . . .* (1674), Evans #185, 2-6.

Chapter Three

MERCANTILISM

"Lay not up for yourselves treasures upon earth," said Jesus, "for where your treasure is, there will your heart be also." The Pilgrims, however, could also find ample justification in the Old and New Testaments for laying up earthly goods. Indeed "one spetiall motive" of their coming to America was the "holding of house and lands."[1]

The Pilgrims believed that all members of society should have equal opportunity in economic self-improvement. Each person should be able to work toward bettering himself and to rise in worldly possessions. The constant striving strengthens moral character and subordinates immediate pleasure to the preparation for tomorrow. God expected his children to be self-reliant and steadfast, and through the perfection of the moral will they could control nature and make their holy experiment a witness to the world. Like the Puritans, the Plymouth settlers fitted their economic life into their overall conception of retributive justice, that persons reap their own just rewards whether on this earth or in the hereafter.[2]

36

Acquisition of worldly goods, however, should not be an end in itself, for if one follows only his self-preference he will lose sight of the Heavenly City. Robert Cushman's sermon, preached during the early days of the settlement, set the tone for the Pilgrim view of economic individualism. Taking his text from the first epistle to the Corinthians, Cushman entreated his fellow emigrés not to become "covetors," who "seek their own by seeking riches, wealth, money." There is a "difference between a covetous worldling and an honest, thrifty Christian—it is lawful sometimes for men to gather wealth, and grow rich even as there was a time for Joseph to store up corn; but a godly and sincere Christian will see when this time is, and will not hoard up when he seeth others of his brethren and associates to want." Each person should attend to his own "labor" or calling, but he should also be concerned with the greater good of society. Production was the virtue—not the making of wealth.[3] It would fall to the colony government to insure that the individual's quest for improvement and wealth conformed to the general welfare. In order to accomplish this, a degree of mercantilism was necessary.

Mercantilism can be employed in the small as well as in the large state. Basically, mercantilism may be defined as a form of statism, "the doctrine that government should concern itself with stimulating, guiding, and regulating various aspects of the people's lives."[4] Its primary emphasis is the economic sector. Assuming the interdependence of economic activity, government, through various means, stimulates as well as regulates private enterprise in order to promote the general welfare, which is usually equated with the wealth and power of the state.

Adoption of mercantilist policies indicates the insecurity of a state. In a healthful and well-balanced economy and when capitalist enterprise is profitable enough to stand on its own, mercantilist regulation gives way to a *laissez faire* economy. Plymouth Colony, as a new and poor settlement, struggled for existence. Besides the internal problems of subsistence, it faced severe competition from more affluent English and foreign neighbors. Hence it was necessity as much as their Christian mission that led the Pilgrim fathers to provide for governmental interference in the economy. Commerce, agriculture, and industry were promoted and regulated in the public interest.

Before ending the common stock arrangement of the adventurers in 1627, the Pilgrims had little incentive to produce
commodities other than those needed for their immediate sus-
tenance. The adventurers were disheartened by the Pilgrims'
dilatoriness in getting a fishing or fur industry under way; and
the Pilgrims blamed the company for neglect in sending over
supplies. The order of priorities to the Pilgrims was best summed
up in Bradford's quote from an epistle of Seneca: "That a great
parte of libertie is a well governed belly, and to be patiente in
all wants." [5]

Although the Peirce Patent of 1621 had provided for a division
of land in 1624, it did not permit a factory system in furs to be
owned other than by the whole company of adventurers. The
realization by the settlers that all profits would be used to pay the
investors undoubtedly stifled incentive. Misfortune also dampened
the spirit of the Pilgrims in developing a trading enterprise. The
return of the *Fortune* in late 1621, with a few furs and clap-
boards, resulted in its capture by a French privateer and its
cargo confiscated. The crew of the *Little James,* sent over in
1623, refused to fish; and when the ship undertook trade with the
Indians along the southern New England coast, the Dutch had
already taken furs from the Indians and the ship returned empty.
Later, the ship was captured by Barbary pirates. Other trading
expeditions sponsored by the adventurers had little success. It is
not surprising that several colonists—Standish in 1625 and Allerton in 1626—borrowed money on their own for the purpose of
setting up trading posts. Thus by 1627 the Pilgrims were prepared
to breach their contract, which influenced the decision of the
adventurers to dissolve the stock company.

To pay off the indebtedness of £1800 to the adventurers in
return for "all and every the stocks, shares, lands, marchandise,
and chatles, what soever," [6] would require efforts of the colony
to stimulate the production of marketable goods. Furs, always in
high demand in Europe, offered the easiest way for quick profits.

In 1627, the colony granted a monopoly in the "trade for
beaver and other furrs and comodities" to eight "undertakers"
in the colony—William Bradford, Miles Standish, Isaac Allerton,
Edward Winslow, William Brewster, John Howland, John Alden,
and Thomas Prence—and their London "associates"—James
Sherley, John Beauchamp, Richard Andrews, and Timothy

Hatherly. The undertakers agreed to pay the debts of the colony over a period of six years, and after the expiration of this agreement "the whole trade shall returne to the use and benefite" of the colony. The undertakers received possession of the whole stock of furs, beads, corn, hatchets, knives and the like, a fishing shallop, and a new trading sloop. To help subsidize the trade, each "Purchaser" ("Old Comer") was to pay to the governor, on behalf of the undertakers, three bushels of corn (or six pounds of tobacco) annually.[7] Apparently there was no coercion to compel this support since there was sufficient incentive in a contributor being credited with a pound of beaver skins for each bushel of corn.[8]

In 1627 the settlers now had plentiful food and had finally learned how to catch fish,[9] and, therefore, could afford to turn their attention to the fur trade. For nearly a decade their efforts were enormously successful. Although there are no total figures for 1628-30, Bradford reported that, for the period of 1631-36, over 12,000 pounds of beaver and over 1000 of otter skins were sent to England. With a beaver pelt bringing 20s.-24s. and an otter skin 14s.-16s., Bradford calculated that the total debts of the colony of £4770 (which at the time included the remaining undertakers' debt of £1000 and the cost of supplies sent over in the *White Angell* and *Friendship* in 1631) should have been entirely covered by the sale of the furs and skins. But the confused accounts of Sherley and his associates left the Pilgrims still in arrears, and an adequate explanation for the shortage of profits was never given to the Pilgrims.[10]

Because of this failure to pay off the debt, caused by Sherley's ineptitude and probable dishonesty (the other associates and Allerton also came in for blame), the monopoly of the undertakers was unofficially renewed after the original six year period. Not until 1643 did it end when Sherley accepted £400 from the colony for payment of the debt in full. Four of the undertakers had to reach into their own pockets to reimburse the colony for this sum: Prence and Winslow sold their homes, Bradford a farm, and Standish three hundred acres of land.[11]

In spite of the competition from various English traders,[12] the Pilgrims had their most success off the coast of Maine at the Penobscot and Kennebec Rivers. At the Kennebec, the Pilgrims secured a patent from the Council of New England for a strip of land fifteen miles wide on each side of the river, where they built a trucking house for trade with the Abenaki Indians. In 1630, further north, they set up a trading post on the Penobscot, which was beset with all sorts of difficulties, including the arrest and deportation of one of the factors at the trading post for violating a proclamation of the king against trading "powder and shot" with the Indians. Allerton soon deserted the Penobscot venture, and set himself up to the north in competition with the undertakers. In 1635 the trading post at Penobscot was taken by the French from Acadia; a ludicrous attempt to recover it failed when Standish and the captain of a hired ship wrangled with each other, and the Pilgrim force ran out of powder.[13]

The trading post at the Kennebec, where Winslow in one year had obtained twenty hogsheads of beaver, was also the scene of misfortune. In 1634, John Hocking, an English trader from the trucking post on the Piscataqua, tried to encroach on the Plymouth rights at Penobscot; unheeding a warning, he killed a Plymouth trader, and himself was shot dead. The Massachusetts authorities got a one-sided version of the incident and arrested John Alden, who allegedly was a witness to the shooting. It was soon decided, however, that Hocking had been the instigator. A meeting to solve the differences over trading jurisdiction proved abortive when commissioners from the Piscataqua settlement failed to negotiate with commissioners from Massachusetts and Plymouth.[14]

By 1640 the Kennebec trade had sharply declined in profits,[15] and the colony subsequently released the trade to private individuals for terms of seven years. The lessees in the 1650's were Thomas Prence, William Bradford, and Captain Thomas Willett, who had "full and free liberty to improve and imploy the said trade to the best advantage they can for themselves and the countrey." For this privilege they paid the colony £35 per annum. No more than five hundred skins could be taken each year, and the value for one half of the skins was set at 8s. a skin and the remainder at 4s.[16] In 1659 Thomas Prence, Alice Bradford, Captain Willett, and Major Josiah Winslow rented the trade, now all but defunct because of Indian hostilities and the extinction of beaver, for £10 a year.[17] In several years the Kennebec trade was totally abandoned.

Shortly after the Pilgrims established a fur trading post at

Matianuck (Windsor) on the Connecticut River in 1633, they ran into competition from the Dutch at Fort Good Hope (Hartford) and transplanted parishioners from John Warham's church in Dorchester, who claimed territorial rights where the Plymouth post was located. Although most of the Dorchester settlers returned to Massachusetts in 1636, the whole town of Newtown (Cambridge), under Thomas Hooker, resettled the site, and forced the Pilgrims to accept only one-sixteenth of their claims— two small lots and the trucking house. Moreover, Bradford and Winslow were unsuccessful in a trip to Boston to secure a joint front against the Dutch intrusion on the Connecticut. Smallpox among the Indians and the Dutch, winning the Indians over with tools and other equipment instead of corn, which the Plymouth traders had to offer, also contributed to the swift elimination of Plymouth traders from the Connecticut. Further settlement on the Connecticut River and at Narragansett Bay shielded Plymouth from trade advantages on Long Island Sound.[18] Manomet, twenty miles south of Plymouth town, would remain the colony's only trucking house in southern New England; when trade for furs there dried up in the mid 1630's, it continued to serve as a depot in exchange of goods with the Dutch.

With the founding of the Massachusetts Bay Colony, Plymouth was deprived of its earlier arteries of trade in the Boston Bay region, which had been so zealously defended by Standish and company at Wessaqusset (1623) and Merry-Mount (1628).[19]

As the fur trade decreased, Plymouth commercial policy became isolationist. In 1645, the colony declined to join in the formation of an intercolonial stock company to monopolize and control the fur trade, under the auspices of the New England Confederation, because of the fear that the other colonies, with greater capital resources, would place Plymouth at a disadvantage.[20] During the tariff war between Massachusetts and Connecticut of 1645-50, Plymouth took a neutral position, even though affected by the impost duties at Boston and Saybrook.[21]

Regulation of the Indian trade reflected not only a desire to protect monopoly trade privileges bestowed by the colony but also to bolster military security. Trade "directly or indirectly" between a single individual and the Indians was prohibited.[22] Exception was made, however, for a person dealing in "small things" for his own use, such as bargaining for a beaver skin.

This kind of trade on a permanent basis, however, did require the approval of the governor and assistants "or els the Governor to undertake the same, with such partners as he shall like of for the manageing of it, in such wise for the summer season as he shall thinke best for the space of one year." [23] At various times, certain items were forbidden in the Indian trade: powder and shot,[24] boats and rigging,[25] horses,[26] and gold or silver money (penalty twentyfold the amount).[27] Sale of liquor and arms to the Indians was definitely forbidden, although, when Indian relations were stable, licenses for the arms trade could be obtained upon approval of two magistrates or one magistrate and two deputies from one's town.[28] During King Philip's War, trade in guns or ammunition to the Indians was a capital crime.[29] Again, in time of Indian unrest, fines for illegal trade of liquor to Indians were more stiff; hence in 1646, during relative quiet, a fine for each default was 10s., but in 1671 it was £1 10s. In 1670 Jonathan Hatch was fined £3.[30]

Because of the problem of foreigners "lyeing with theire vessells in our harbours trading with the Indians" in liquors, guns, and ammunition, it was enacted in 1677 that no ship from outside the colony could hover off the Plymouth coast "under any pretense whatsoever," upon pain of confiscation of cargo and ship.[31] In the first Dutch war, an embargo was placed upon the export of provisions to the Dutch or French "or other strangers," unless exempted by the governor and two assistants.[32]

Measures were taken from time to time to prevent commodities needed in the colony from being sold at higher prices elsewhere. Sheep had to be brought to Plymouth town for sale at a fixed price, and those not purchased could then be sold out of the colony.[33] By an order in 1672, "Plankes, Boards, Bolts, or Bark" could not be exported.[34] Such articles needed in the Indian trade as corn, beans, or peas could not be conveyed out of the colony "without leave and license of the governour and councell." [35]

Fishing held high prospect for the Pilgrims. They anticipated great profits, which "will give content to all." [36] But the first years were frustrating. The Pilgrims had hoped to secure a monopoly of fishing in New England, but the Council of New England could not grant what it could not receive itself.[37] The early backwardness in learning how to fish, the lack of hooks and nets, the want of an able saltmaker, the death of their ship's carpenter, and the insufficient manpower and resources to make the fishing station at Cape Ann a success proved discouraging. Bradford complained in 1624 that some of the "best men" were wasting too much time trying to fish—"a thing fatall to this plantation." [38]

By the mid-1620's the Pilgrims had gained experience and had the necessary equipment for fishing in the shallows. The waters off Cape Cod abounded with an infinite variety of fish, including mackerel, bass, alewives, sturgeon, halibut, shad, cod, and "our bay is full of lobsters all the summer . . . in September we can take a hogshead of eels in a night, with small labor, and can dig them out of their beds all the winter. We have mussels and others at our doors." [39] Here was a valuable commodity for export and home consumption, not to mention the use of fish for fertilizer and in the Indian trade. The immense profits to be had in the fishing industry are indicated by the fact that in 1639 a hogshead of mackerel brought £3 12*s.*, and a boat could catch twelve hogsheads a week. Unfortunately, Plymouth did not have the resources of its more powerful neighbor to the north. In 1642 Massachusetts exported 300,000 dried fish and had many ships at sea, including five vessels over one hundred tons. Plymouth in the same year could boast only one boat of forty to fifty tons, owned by thirteen persons.[40] It is not surprising, therefore, that Plymouth enacted measures to stimulate and protect its infant industry.

In 1633 the town of Plymouth was given a monopoly in fishing for herring, shad, and alewives, whereas residents outside of the town could only use these fish for bait, unless special permission was granted by the governor.[41] To encourage fishing, the town allotted small parcels of land to individuals for fishing stations.[42] The colony leased commercial fishing rights for annual fees or simply placed an excise on fish taken: for example, 6*d.* per barrel of mackerel (1*s.* 6*d.* for every barrel taken "by any foraigners").[43] The lease of bass fishing rights for a seven year period brought a £30 per annum revenue.[44] For the improvement in nets, seines, and the like, part of the rent for fishing rights could be remitted.[45] Citizens of the colony desiring fishing privileges, by a 1677 order, had to petition the General Court in person.[46]

Since Massachusetts fishermen could not be kept out of Plymouth's waters, certain accommodations were made. Persons who moved out of the colony lost their special privileges,[47] but could be re-admitted under regulations governing non-residents. Few persons in Plymouth cared to fish by seine at the Cape, and therefore the water bailiff was given discretionary power to license non-residents, as long as they were "orderly" and paid the fees.[48] Eventually, it was allowed that one half of the fishermen could come from Massachusetts.[49] An act aimed at Massachusetts fishermen levied a 40s. fine for leaving rotting fish on the beach.[50] Because of the rapid "destruction" of mackerel with nets and seines off Cape Cod, the Plymouth General Court, with approval from the Massachusetts authorities, passed a stringent conservation measure in 1684: no mackerel could be taken "by setting or shooling any nett or sayne," upon penalty of forfeit of all nets and seines used, the fish caught, and vessels so employed.[51]

The need for better supervision of fishing off Cape Cod was undoubtedly given some consideration by the colony in establishing an admiralty court in 1684, consisting of the governor, "with three or foure of the Assistants, and such other substantial persons as the Governor for the time being shall commissionate under the seals of this collonie. . . ." [52]

Protection of monopoly interests in Plymouth was premised upon the distinction between purely private property and that which was affected by public use. In matter of fact, any state is "under necessity of making a choice between the preservation of one class of property and that of the other wherever both existed in dangerous proximity." [53] Because of the scarcity of capital and underdevelopment of industry in Plymouth, however, it had to be reckoned that all industry was essential and involved a preponderant public concern—and hence there was virtually no conflict between individual and public liberty.

In several domestic industries, the General Court left protective authority largely to the towns. The "clearest example of the strong tendency to socialize private capital," writes Clive Day, "appears in the public position given the gristmill." [54] A town gristmill was established as either a public corporation or a private monopoly. In 1633, Stephen Deane received permission to construct a water-powered mill at Plymouth to "beat" all the corn in the colony on condition of paying one pottle for every bushel of meal produced.[55] The General Court the following year ordered that Deane would have to "surrender up his worke and that right and claime . . . whenever a grinding mill shall be sett up at the order and appointment of the Governour and Councell of Assistants." Deane died in 1634 before the mill could be built. Although four freemen were ordered to make preparations for the mill's construction in 1635, nothing came of this plan.[56] In 1637 John Jenney was authorized to build a mill in Plymouth, but no monopoly grant is mentioned, probably because Scituate now had a mill.[57] No encouragement was given by the colony for the erection of sawmills, and as late as 1665 there was only one in the whole colony.[58] Such local industry was left to the municipalities to promote, through the establishment of stockholding corporations with grants of subsidies and monopoly privileges.[59] Thus the colony could concern itself solely with more general matters affecting industry, such as the regulation of trade and standards.

The only iron works in the colony, at Taunton, benefited from oblique legislation: for example, the exemption of laborers on the job from military duty and allowing the foundry to use timber from the public lands.[60] Shipbuilding never got off the ground until after annexation by Massachusetts,[61] and the records are void, except for laws conserving timber on public lands, of any efforts to stimulate what could have been a profitable industry.

It is not difficult to explain why in the period after 1640 the colony left the encouragement of industry to the towns to supply their own particular needs. Certainly there was the dominant belief that government should best preside over fairness and equality of condition, and individual initiative and thrift would be rewarded on their own. Being a poor and thinly populated people, the Plymouth settlers always complained of high taxes; if revenues were to be applied to subsidization of industry, this could be done best on the local level, where one would directly benefit from his tax payment. The overpowering economy of Massachusetts and the dearth of fluid capital were also factors. Priority was given to a self-sustaining economy,[62] and long-term colony monopolies—like the practice of Massachusetts in vital industry such as iron, lead, or salt—were viewed as favoring one locality as against another.

Thus much of the colony economic policy was an inverse protectionism, designed to serve home needs rather than exportation. Timber, iron, and oysters were but several marketable items discouraged from trade by the levy of export duties or by outright prohibition on exports. Plymouth, of course, was hardly in the position to levy impost duties. Nevertheless, the lack of positive inducement to industry was characteristic of the narrowness and defeatism of so much of the public policy..

As befitting the Calvinist penchant for medieval economic theory, the whole area of prices, wages, and labor was intricately regulated. Retail licensing [63] and uniformity of weights and measures—according to common standards in England and Massachusetts [64]—were the chief means for stabilizing prices. A mixed board of the magistrates and others specially chosen determined price values.[65] Agricultural commodities were kept at a fixed price index from 1640 until after King Philip's War, when the colony revised prices upward [66] to conform with inflation in Massachusetts, which aroused bitterness among the money-poor farmers in Plymouth.

Very few prosecutions occurred for profiteering. Although many regulations set wage scales, only one instance is recorded of a colony prosecution for wage oppression.[67] Probably most persons availed themselves of the opportunity to make restitution before being brought to court.

For particular projects or emergencies, persons could be forced to contribute their labor for the good of the colony. Besides military conscription,[68] towns could impress men to work on highways (upon three days warning and a fine of 3s. per day for each default of duty),[69] and the magistrates could impress tradesmen to repair prisons, stocks, whipping posts, or "other Instruments of Justice" [70] and compel any person to serve as a "messenger in the Countreyes busines."[71] All craftsmen were enjoined to apply their "science or trades" within the colony and for residents of the colony, unless permitted otherwise by the magistrates.[72]

The colony regulated all phases of contract labor. Assignments of servants and terms of the indenture had to meet standards set forth by the colony. Freedom dues (originally five acres of land per servant) and proper maintenance and training of youth were among specifications. Indictments occasionally were returned against masters for "barbarous and inhumane" conduct; while the General Court gave its sanction to extra service, fines, or whipping for runaways.[73] The Articles of Confederation of the United Colonies (1643) established comity in extradition of runaway servants, which was also written into the Treaty of Hartford with the Dutch: namely, upon proof to a magistrate of a colony the servant was to be returned.

A workhouse program was introduced in 1642 by the enactment that every township "shall make competent provision for the maintenance of their poor according as they shall find most convenient and suitable for themselves by an order and Generall agreement in a publicke towne meeting."[74] In 1658, the General Court, somewhat exasperated by the increase of "Idle persons or rebelliouse children or servants" wandering about "without any lawfull calling," ordered the construction of a "worke house or house of Correction," to be superintended by an appointee of the Court. The workhouse opened its doors in Plymouth the following year.[75] According to English poor law practice common to all the colonies, Plymouth let the localities bind out poor children and orphans; specifically this was a duty of the town selectmen. Much of the social and sumptuary legislation may be regarded as basically economic in intent. This will be treated in social context in later chapters.

Economic regulation in Plymouth paralleled development in the other Puritan colonies. It differed, after 1640, in that there was less centralization in the promotion of industry and trade. For the implementation of standards and fair practices, Plymouth, like other colonies, relied chiefly upon local government. Much of the economic statism, as did not derive from English and Puritan influences, originated simply from the need to establish routine order that all governments must have and to adjust to New World conditions.

NOTES

1. *Bradford Hist.* (1912), I, 127-28.

2. For the Puritan theory of "worldly prudence" see Ralph B. Perry, *Puritanism and Democracy* (New York, reprint 1964), chapter 12.

3. Cushman, "The Sin and Danger of Self-Love," in Young, ed., *Chronicles,* 255-62.

4. Eugene O. Golob, *The "ISMS:" A History and Evaluation* (New York, 1954), 65.

5. *Bradford Hist.* (1912), I, 372.

6. The agreement between the adventurers and Isaac Allerton, on behalf of Plymouth Colony, is printed in *ibid.,* II, 4-6.

7. *Ibid.,* II, 29-30, 29n. and 31n.; *Gov. Bradford's Letter Book, MHSC,* 1st Ser., III (1794), 60.

8. Letter of Isaack de Rasieres to Samuel Blommaert (1628?), J. Franklin Jameson, ed., *Narratives of New Netherland, 1609-64* (New York, 1909), 113.

9. *Ibid.,* 111, 113.

10. *Bradford Hist.* (1912), II, 129-31, 229-31.

11. See correspondence between the undertakers and James Sherley, 1642-43, *ibid.,* 331-41; Andrews, *Colonial Period,* I, 290.

12. Two English merchants at Pemaquid; Oldham and Richard Vines at the mouth of the Saco River; the Laconia Company of F. Gorges and J. Mason; Walter Bagnall, and later John Winter at Richmond Island off Cape Elizabeth. Nathaniel C. Hale, *Pelts and Palisades: The Story of Fur and the Rivalry for Pelts in Early America* (Richmond, Va., 1959), 104-5.

13. *Ibid.,* 97-98, 102-3; *PCR,* I, 60; *MCR,* I, 192; *Bradford Hist.* (1912), II, 62-5, 134-5; Bradford, *Of Plymouth Plantation,* ed. Morison, 232-33n. Before the capture of the Penobscot post, the French robbed it several times. Winslow was sent to Mass. to secure military aid against the French, but the Plymouth request was refused. The king appointed Francis West Admiral of New England to enforce the royal proclamation against trading without a license, but freebooting continued virtually unchecked.

14. *Bradford Hist.* (1912), II, 175, 187-88; John Winthrop, *The History of New England from 1630-49,* ed. James Savage, 2 vols. (Boston, 1853), I, 155, hereafter cited as *Winthrop Hist.*

15. Roland G. Usher, *The Pilgrims and Their History* (New York, 1920), 234.

16. *PCR,* III, 95 (1656); *Winthrop Papers, Letters to, MHSC,* 5th Ser., I (1871), 396n. Thomas Willett had commanded at the Kennebec post since 1639.

17. *PCR,* III, 170-71. Finally, about 1662, Plymouth sold all rights to Kennebec trading to Edward Tyng, Josiah Winslow, and others for £400. William B. Weeden, *Economic and Social History of New England, 1620-1789,* 2 vols. (Boston, 1891), I, 162.

18. *Bradford Hist.* (1912), II, 216-18, 226-27; *Winthrop Hist.,* I, 125, 134, 165, 182; Goodwin, *Pilgrim Republic,* 392-96.

19. For the subversive and military aspects of these incidents, see Chapters 7 and 8. For the threats to Plymouth trade in the Boston Bay region, see William Roberts, *The Fur Trade of New England in the Seventeenth Century* (unpubl. Ph. D. diss., University of Pennsylvania, 1958), 56ff.

20. *PCR,* II, 82; Weeden, *Economic and Social Hist.,* I, 147.

21. *MCR,* III, 152 (1649), 191 (1650); William Pynchon to John Winthrop, Mar. 9, 1647, *Winthrop Papers,* V (1947), 136.

22. *PCR,* XI, 33 (1640).

23. *Ibid.,* II, 4 (1640); repealed 1669, *ibid.,* XI, 184.

24. *Ibid.,* XI, 33 (1639); repealed 1665, *ibid.,* 215; revived 1667 and repealed 1669, *ibid.,* 219, 225, 237.

25. *Ibid.,* 184 (1656).

26. Sale of horses authorized, providing tax of 10s. paid. *Ibid.,* 221 (1668), 229 (1670).

27. *Ibid.,* 33 (1639); penalty reduced to five times value of money given Indians, *ibid.,* 244; repealed 1677.

28. *Ibid.,* IX, 65-66 (1646).

29. *Ibid.,* XI, 243 (1676).

30. *Ibid.,* V, 39 (1670); VIII, 135 (1671); XI, 54 (1646). Ordinaries selling liquor to Indians were fined for each default 20s. *Ibid.,* XI, 218 (1667).

31. *Ibid.,* XI, 246 (1677).

32. *Ibid.,* III, 24.

33. *Ibid.,* II, 17-18 (1641).

34. *Ibid.,* V, 106.

35. *Ibid.,* XI, 4 (1626).

36. *Mourt's Relation,* 85; Robert Cushman to Fuller, Winslow, Bradford, and Allerton, June 10, 1620, *Bradford Hist.* (1912), I, 114.

37. Bradford, *Of Plymouth Plantation,* ed. Morison, 40n.

38. *Bradford Hist.* (1912), I, 353-54, 377-79.

39. *Mourt's Relation,* 84.

40. Palfrey, *Hist. of New England,* III, 55-56.

41. *PCR,* I, 8.

42. E.g., *Ply. Town Records,* I, 106-7.

43. *PCR,* VI, 56 (1681).

44. *Ibid.,* 139 (1684).

45. E.g., *ibid.,* 19 (1679).

46. *Ibid.,* V, 243.

47. John Prince and Nathaniel Bosworth's Petition to the Government of Plymouth, June 8, 1671, *MHSC,* 1st Ser., VI (1800), 127.

48. *PCR,* V, 104 (1672).

49. *Ibid.,* 245 (1677).

50. *Ibid.,* XI, 220 (1668), 228-29 (1670), 131, 206 (1661).

51. *Ibid.,* VI, 140 (1684).

52. *Ibid.,* 139; that is, if Plymouth were to benefit from the Admiralty Court. Of course, the main purpose of this court was to secure Plymouth's aid in curtailing privateering, piracy, and violations of the Navigation Acts.

53. Quote from Justice Stone, *Miller* v. *Schoene* (1928), in Robert L. Hale, "Force and the State: A Comparison of 'Political' and 'Economic' Compulsion," *Columbia Law Review,* XXXV (1935), 200.

54. Clive Day, "Capitalism and Socialistic Tendencies in the Puritan Colonies," *Annual Report of the Amer. Hist. Assoc. for . . . 1920* (Washington, 1925), 234.

55. *PCR,* I, 8. Without citing authority, S. E. Morison says Deane's mill was actually established in 1633. Bradford, *Of Plymouth Plantation,* ed. Morison, 145n.

56. *PCR,* I, 22, 35.

57. *Ibid.,* XI, 26, 30.

58. George Carr to [Sec. Lord Arlington?], Dec. 14, 1665, *CSP,* (1661-68), #1103.

59. E.g., in 1654, a mill built by twenty-two stockholders, with a subsidy of £20 from the town. Freeman, *History of Cape Cod,* II, 53.

60. *PCR,* III, 89 (1655); IV, 46 (1663).

61. See Samuel E. Morison, "New Light Wanted on the Old Colony," *WMQ,* 3d Ser., XV (1958), 363.

62. High prices for English commodities was a major factor in the 1640's for Plymouth turning to new production: e.g., wool, leather, and

iron. Darrett B. Rutman, *Husbandmen of Plymouth: Farms and Villages in the Old Colony, 1620-92* (Boston, 1968), 19.

63. See Chapter 6 for licensing inspection of a sumptuary nature.

64. *PCR,* XI, 13, 198 (1636), 38 (1641), 115 (1652), 113 (1658).

65. *Ibid.,* I, 36 (1635), 54 (1637).

66. See Dana, "Account of Ply. Col. Recs.," *MHSC,* 3d Ser., II (1830), 268-69 for the price pattern; also Alanson Borden, *Our County and its Peoples . . . Bristol County* (Boston, 1899), 19. In 1679 prices dipped slightly before spiraling. Although the General Court occasionally made pronouncements on common agricultural problems, such matters were usually left to the towns, e.g., ringing of hogs (*PCR,* I, *passim* and for a typical violation, see Simeon L. Deyo, *History of Barnstable County, Massachusetts* [New York, 1890], 266) and bounties for pests (e.g., the town of Plymouth's requirement to bring in heads of blackbirds and crows, with 12*d.* fine for neglect. *Ply. Town Records,* I, 164 [1680]).

67. See Richard B. Morris, *Government and Labor in Early America* (New York, 1946), 78 and footnotes for documentation.

68. See Chapter 8.

69. *PCR,* XI, 194 (1646). Authority for building highways was vested in juries empaneled from the towns concerned. *Ibid.,* I, 58 (1637); III, 15, 61 (1652); I-VI *passim.* After the establishment of counties, justices of the peace handled cases of neglect to appear to work on highways. Taunton Town Records, Nov. 4, 1701, 151.

70. *PCR,* XI, 88, 164 (1658), 258 (1682).

71. *Ibid.,* 121, 206 (1658).

72. *Ibid.,* 4 (1626).

73. For further discussion, see Morris, *Government and Labor,* 12, 345, 403-5, 440, 475. Concerning authorization of whipping of a runaway servant in the presence of the governor and magistrates, a successful suit by a servant for not being taught a trade, and extension of servitude for an Indian, see *PCR,* I, 7 (1633); III, 51 (1654); VI, 152 (1685), resp.

74. *PCR,* XI, 111-12.

75. *Ibid.,* 120 (1658), 126 (1660).

Chapter Four

THE RELIGIOUS CORPORATION

The Pilgrims believed in the coterminal responsibility of church and state in promoting moral and social discipline. Church and state were rigidly separate in polity but complemented the work of each other. The two covenants—civil and church—derived from the same body of people. The interaction of church and state constituted an establishment for religion—in a sense, they were a "dual corporation." [1] Although having been dissenters against the hierarchal control of the Church of England, the Pilgrims held no brief against church establishment *per se,* only that it reflect the majority will of congregational authority.

In America, the Pilgrims had the task of re-creating their religious community and a civil body politic as well, both bound by the ties of kinship and neighborhood they had known in England. But the challenge to build any society they wanted to out of the wilderness void fortified their feeling of Providential sanction and their utopian vision of "the triumphant and glorious Church." The Pilgrim search for a "lost community," [2] therefore, provided impetus to the mutual succor of church and state.

Although the Pilgrims had a broader view of toleration and liberty of conscience at the outset than did their Puritan neighbors and they would be amenable to the forces of religious and social pluralism, the two corporations of church and state labored strenuously to preserve an exclusive holy commonwealth. The General Court and the magistracy held sway in religion primarily by three means: oversight of church policy; requirement of localities to maintain and support a ministry acceptable to the general good; and enforcement of the first four of the ten commandments.[3] The churches as a corporation exercised authority in the community by setting membership standards and keeping moral discipline. Since church members were usually admitted inhabitants of the political corporation and vice versa, ostracism by the church carried great weight.

As good Calvinists, the Pilgrims made a distinction between the civil and ecclesiastical authority of Moses and Aaron. They did, however, allow that certain areas of religious authority affecting behavior directly concerned the state. Before their emigration to America, the Scrooby band in Holland had to face squarely the issue of magisterial power in compelling the performance of religious duty. In contemplating a move to the New World, they could not afford to deny the religious authority of a king, from whom they sought permission to settle on his foreign lands. The seven articles drawn up by the Leyden Church and "sent to the Councell of England" acknowledged the king as the "Supreme Governor," to whom "obedience is dewe . . . either active, if the thing commanded be not agaynst God's word, or passive if itt bee, except pardon can bee obtayned. . . . Wee believe that no sinod, classes, convocation or assembly of Ecclesiasticall Officers hath any power or authoryty att all but as the same by the Majestrate given unto them."[4] The Pilgrims, therefore, did not object so much to legitimate state authority as they did to the establishment of ecclesiastical authority over the churches. Pastor John Robinson noted that when the civil authority acts in accordance with the true principles of religion, it has the sanction of God. Thus the magistrate

may alter, devise, or establish nothing in religion otherwise than Christ hath appointed, but [he may] use his lawful power lawfully for the furtherance of Christ's kingdom and laws.

It is true they have no power against the laws, doctrines, and religion of Christ: but for the same, if their power be of God, they may use it lawfully, and against the contrary. And so it was in special foretold by John, that "the kings of the earth should make the whore desolate, and naked, and eat her flesh, and burn her with fire." [*Rev.* xvii, 16][5]

Once settled in the New World, the Pilgrims were more insistent on limiting the authority of the state in religion, but still held firm to Robinson's idea that the magistrate is bound by the sacred nature of authority itself to do the will of God. The mature statement of the Pilgrims for state concern in matters of religion is given in the introduction to the revised law code of 1658:

And although wee hold and doe afeirme that both Courts of Justice and majestrates whoe are the minnesters of the lawe are esensially Civill; Notwithstanding wee conceive that as the majestrate hath his power from God soe undoubtedly hee is to Improve it for the honer of God and that in the upholding of his Worship and service and against the contrary with due respect alsoe to bee had unto those that are really consiencyous though differing and decenting in som smaller matters; but if any really or in pretence of consience shall professe that which eminently tendeth to the Inundation of Civell State and violation of Naturall bonds or the overthrow of the churches of God or his worship that heer prudence is to bee Improved in the enacting and execution of lawes . . . .[6]

Although separation between church and civil officeholding was strictly maintained,[7] the colony government in effect held a veto over the selection of ministers of the churches. At first, the Pilgrims were dubious of having a settled ministry—as Separatists, they believed in the non-proselyting nature of the church—and elder Brewster could attend to the needs of the flock.[8] The first ministerial prospect, John Lyford, received censure, and community pressure mobilized by Governor Bradford was used to prevent his assuming the pastorate because of his factiousness and intention to bring the Pilgrim church into the Anglican fold.

As new congregations were formed,[9] the Plymouth magistrates usually offered no objections to the election of a minister, whose status as a clergyman continued only while he was a member of a particular church.[10] The governor and assistants heard petitions from church factions contesting an election of a pastor, but followed the practice, as long as the elected minister was deemed orthodox, of accepting the majority decision of the church.[11] On one occasion the General Court directed the constable at Yarmouth to arrest Joseph Hull, an "excommunicant," and to present him to answer "his doings" to the General Court if he attempted to exercise the ministry.[12] In order to prevent a schism in a church from turning into secession, the magistrates could use persuasion and "such other means" to keep a minister in line with his congregation, especially when there was evidence of "plaine Obstinacye against an Ordinance of God." [13] Persons responsible for setting up "any Churches or publicke meetings diverse from those allreddy set up and approved" without the consent of the colony government were to be "suspended from haveing any voyce in towne meetings and presented to the next generall court to Receve such punishment as the court shall think meet to Inflict." [14]

Beginning in 1657 each township was required to give financial aid to a minister approved by the colony government. Four men were to be chosen by each town

> or Incase of theire Neglect Chosen by any three or more of the Majestrates to make an equall and just proportion upon the estates of the Inhabitants according to theire abillities to make up such a Convenient maintainance for his Comfortable attendance on his worke as shalbee agreed upon by the Church in each township where any is with the Concurrance of the Rest of the Inhabitants if it may be had or by the Majestrates aforsaid incase of theire apparent Neglect and that . . . Incase there bee any other way wherby any township doe or shall Agree that may effect the end aforsaid this law not to bee binding to them.[15]

Thus the towns could provide maintenance through means of their own choosing. For example, Eastham paid part of its minister's salary of £50 per annum by taking a hogshead "out of every whale that shall be cast up in this town;" [16] while Bridgewater provided its pastor an annual salary of £20-£30 and "his Diet" out of a direct levy on real estate.[17] Eventually the General Court appointed two collectors of the minister's revenue in each town.[18] For towns new and sparsely populated, the colony government subsidized the minister's salary.[19]

Occasionally persons were haled before the court of assistants for refusal to pay taxes for the ministerial support, and, if still obdurate, they were fined double the amount.[20] What the colony could do when a town refused to support a minister never reached a final test. Dartmouth, under repeated court orders to provide for an orthodox minister in the 1660's-70's, never did comply; it is small wonder that many persons considered the destruction of Dartmouth in King Philip's War as an act of God's vengeance.[21] The royal commissioners in 1664-65 forced a reluctant concession from Plymouth that rival churches could maintain their own ministers and be exempt from supporting those of the established Puritan faith.[22] But the colony never fully endorsed this view. Efforts to compel support, however, during the Andros regime were thwarted by action of the council of the Dominion of New England.[23] After incorporation with Massachusetts in 1692, ministerial support was enforced, and if a town refused to maintain a ministry, the court of quarter sessions, upon complaint, could fine the selectmen or other assessors.[24]

It may be noted briefly that marriages in Plymouth came wholly under civil authority, contrary to English canon law. Governor William Bradford performed the first marriage, that of widower Edward Winslow in 1621. Thereafter, it was customary for the General Court to designate a person in each town to perform marriages.[25] A magistrate could void parents' refusal to consent to a marriage or, in the case of servants, that of a master, who acted from a "senistery or Covetuous desire." [26]

Missionary work among the Indians fell under the authority of the state, or more particularly, under the auspices of the commissioners of the United Colonies, as it did for all the Puritan colonies. The commissioners applied the funds and equipment received from the Society for the Propagation of the Gospel in New England.[27] Three Plymouth preachers worked in this vineyard. William Leverich, who gave up his Sandwich pastorate because "divers of his people" had "cast off all the Ordinances of God" and "at last came to be seduced by every idle spirit," experienced some success among the Nausets; but he failed to learn their language, and moved to Long Island in 1653.[28] Richard Bourne, who followed Leverich, had the Indian church covenanted in 1670—witnessed by six magistrates. John Cotton (Jr.), Plymouth's pastor from 1669 to 1697, also preached to the Indians and revised Eliot's Indian Bible. In 1674, it was reported that there were eight Indian churches in the colony, containing 497 persons. Unfortunately, the governor and assistants were not very successful in preventing encroachment upon the tribal lands of these praying Indians.[29]

The Pilgrim churches pursued a more separatist way than their brethren of the Bay Colony, and hence they had little use for ecclesiastical authority beyond local churches. Although John Robinson had approved of synods and thought that "no man can endure to be withdrawn from, nor easily dissented from, by another, in his way of religion,"[30] the Pilgrims preferred to let individual churches decide upon doctrine and church polity. However, as time went on, the Plymouth churches found they were faced with the same problems of heresy and subversion as Massachusetts, and the colony came close to the pattern of Massachusetts in maintaining uniformity in religion, under the encouragement, if not the sanction, of the magistracy.

When Plymouth had only one church, Bradford and other leaders kept a check upon any tendencies threatening to corrupt their reformed church. Although a hands off policy was followed by the government and the mother church towards new churches, the divergent ideas that soon developed proved startling. Charles Chauncey, first as teacher at Plymouth in 1640 and shortly afterwards pastor at Scituate, turned out to be too rigid a Separatist—differing on baptism, communion, and church membership. Censure for his views was obtained, however, not from the government but from churches of Massachusetts and Connecticut.[31]

Challenged directly by the Gortonists and a Presbyterian element headed by William Vassall,[32] the Plymouth authorities became receptive in the mid-1640's to the idea of positive action to maintain uniformity in religion. To counter complaints by religious malcontents and because of the possibility that the English government would compel all its subjects to accept a Presbyterian creed, Edward Winslow, as agent for both Massachusetts and Plymouth, was dispatched to England. Fortunately for New England Puritanism, the Presbyterian ascendancy in England was short-lived. It was during this period of uncertainty, however, that the second synod at Cambridge was held, with Plymouth represented by at least one delegate—Ralph Partridge of Duxbury. Partridge was a member of the three man committee that wrote the famous Cambridge Platform. The synod had been convened by the Massachusetts General Court, thus acknowledging John Cotton's earlier advice that the best way to curtail religious subversion was through a "Synod with consent of civil Magistrates." Cotton had also warned: "Sheepe set at libertie from the fear of Wolves, will straggle further from their Shepheard, then when they resent danger."[33] The Plymouth magistrates took no action concerning the synod, but some of the clergy were skeptical that synods were as capable of as much "evil" as the English government or "discontented persons."[34]

But it is significant that, after the acceptance of the Cambridge Platform[35] by the Massachusetts General Court in 1648, the Plymouth Government showed a deference to follow its broad outline as far as it related to civil authority—witness the government support of the clergy and the increased state intervention to promote obedience to the Mosaic code.

Although there would always be a basic difference on church polity between the Plymouth and Massachusetts churches—the Plymouth churches allowing less pastoral authority—the churches of both colonies developed a visible degree of mutual reliance. As early as 1640, the Reverend John Wilson was brought from the Bay Colony to attempt to settle a dispute between the pastor and church at Green's Harbor (Marshfield).[36] It became customary to have general approval from sister churches and "civil government" in the selection of pastors and other church policy, regardless of boundaries between the colonies. In this respect, the Massachusetts Puritans felt a paternalistic responsibility towards the Plymouth churches:

> yet are the Mattachusets far from deserting them, esteeming them highly, so long as their Governments maintain the same purity in Religion with themselves, for indeed this is that they have spent their whole travel for, and therefore if Plimoth, or any of the other shall draw back herein, the chiefest end of their confederation would be lost . . . .[37]

Early testimony to the intercolony, coordinate church and state repression of disfavored religious views is given by one of the Baptists:

immediately the adversary cast out a flood against us, and stirred up the spirits of men to present my self and two more to *Plymouth* Court, where we met with 4 Petitions against our whole company to take some speedy course to suppress us, one from our own Plantation with 35 hands to it, one from the Church (as they call it) at *Tanton* [Taunton], one from all the Ministers in our Colony, except two, if I mistake not, and one from the Court at *Boston* in the Mathatusets under their Secretaries hand; whereupon the Court straitly chargeth us to desist, and neither to ordain Officers, nor to Baptize, nor to break bread together, nor yet to meet upon the first day of the week . . . .[38]

But even on this question there was a breach in the "confederacy by faith, by neighbourhood, by fellowship," evoking a reprimand from the Massachusetts General Court, because Plymouth allowed "some unsettled brethren to goe into the bottome of the Bay of Cape Cod."[39]

The relation of Plymouth churches to churches outside the colony, however, remained only on an informal basis. No messengers from the churches of Plymouth attended the Ministerial Convention of 1657 or the Synods of 1662 and 1679.[40] But during the 1670-80's, the General Court promoted councils of church elders within the colony to decide upon the limits of toleration and form of worship.[41]

Church membership did more than signify the elect; it conferred a status and responsibility in the safeguarding of the purity of the community. The church itself was a covenant of persons who had a special calling from God. John Robinson had defined the true church as "a company of faithful and holy people, with their seed, called by the Word of God into public covenant with Christ and amongst themselves, for mutual fellowship in the use of all the means of God's glory and their salvation."[42] No one became a member except through his volition and strong desire to share in the perfecting of the community.[43]

The church—Separatist[44] and soon also the New England Puritan—consisted of persons having undergone a religious experience and who repudiated "such former pollutions wherein we have been defiled and inthralled."[45] As Ralph Barton Perry has noted, a church covenanted among the elect leads to a dual orthodoxy: "the inner faith of the regenerate and the outward conformity of the unregenerate. No greater uniformity than this can be expected on the assumption that many are called but few are chosen."[46]

Although the Plymouth General Court passed laws against persons practicing religion contrary to the will of the majority,[47] it did not attempt to dictate to the churches their policies of admitting members. However, the Plymouth commissioners joined in a resolution of the United Colonies of New England:

> That a due watch be kept and continued at the doors of Gods house, that none be admitted as members of the body of Christ, but such as hold forth effectuall callinge and thereby union with Christ the head, and that those whome Christ hath receaved, and enter by an expresse covenant to attend and observe the lawes and dutyes of that spirituall Corporation, that Babtisme, the seale of the Covenant be administered onely to such members and their imediate seed, that Anabaptisme, familisme, Antinomianisme and generally all errors of like nature which oppose, undermine and slight either the scriptures, the Sabboth or other ordinances of God, and bring in and cry up unwarrantable Revelations, inventions of men, or any carnall liberty, under a deceitfull colloure of liberty of conscience, may be reasonably and duly supprest . . . .[48]

In selection of membership, the churches exercised review of the orthodoxy of applicants. A change in residence necessitated not only application for admission in the new church but also dismission from one's former church. If a person was under discipline, dismission was not granted.[49] In forming a new church, dismission from the original church also had to be secured.[50] Membership required oral confession. Although the Old Colony did not adopt the Half-Way Covenant, the churches, nevertheless, fell in line; and persons who were shy could be heard in private by the elders.[51]

The colony did not try to institute an inter-covenanting of the churches until the outbreak of King Philip's War caused a soul-searching. Hitherto, although each church had entered into its own local covenant, the Plymouth churches were regarded as an extension of the Leyden church. Upon a resolution of the General Court, at an appointed time in July 1676, the Plymouth churches covenanted with God, and "after confession of the prevailing evils of the times, they entered into strict engagements (through the assistance of divine grace) for personal and family reformation."[52]

Church members were subject to disciplinary action of the church, which served to supplement and fill the void in the legal system of the colony. Distinction was made between two types of public offenses: private offenses and those committed before two or more witnesses. In disciplinary cases, the church in an open meeting acted as a court, with judicial safeguards afforded the accused. The object of a church trial was to secure acknowledgement for sin, and if repentance was deemed sincere, the church member might be restored to full communion. If not, however, or if a person evaded a summons, he suffered the extreme penalty of excommunication—which, in effect, meant, besides the denial of church privileges, social ostracism by the church community.[53]

During the first years at Plymouth all offenses came under the political authority, and the first offenses dealt with by the church did not occur until after the arrival of the first ordained minister, John Lyford, who himself was the first miscreant.[54]

Although about every offense conceivable came before the church—sometimes preceded by a court conviction—aggravated crimes against the person appear in the church records only rarely.[55] Excommunication or the lighter sentence of censure was meted out frequently by Plymouth churches for violation of the sexual mores. Other cases involved business ethics and sundry categories, such as "given to Idleness . . . slacked in the duty of prayer," "Scandalous Carriage . . .," perjury, and suspicion of theft. Absenteeism or infractions during the worship service, such as refusing to take communion, were causes for church trial.[56] Women were censured or excommunicated for abusing their husbands, and, in 1689, Mrs. Dorothy Clarke was briefly excommunicated for pulling Josiah Cotton, son of the Plymouth pastor, bleeding from a tree.[57] It is interesting to note that matters of slander and reproach between individuals were usually left to litigation in the courts.

The elders of the church would meet after a church service to compare notes on their observations of the conduct of their church brethren.[58] In the Plymouth church

the Ruling Elders with the Pastor made it their first spetiall worke together to passe through the whole towne from family to family to

enquire into the state of soules and according as they found the
frames either of the children of the church or others, soe they
applyed counsells, admonitions, exhortations and incouragements,
which service was attended with a blessing, for in divers with whom
God had begun his work, it prevailed to stirre them up to lay hold
of the covenant . . . .[59]

Thus, whenever possible, the elders tried persuasion to get a
backslider to reform, but if the bad behavior was persistent, then
a case was made to the church. A finding of bad conduct in a
meeting of the elders was tantamount to a bill of presentment.

After mid-century, the decline of church authority was every-
where evident. The second and third generation Pilgrims seemed
to be forsaking "their errand into the wilderness," and "some
woful villages" on the outskirts of the colony began "to live
without the means of grace."[60] Plymouth pastors, no less than
their colleagues elsewhere, issued jeremiads on the doleful
condition of the people in neglecting their religious mission.
Thomas Walley, in an election sermon to the General Court in
1669, contended "the Country is a sickly Country." If the people
wished to save their destiny they had the means. "We have
Gileads Balm, and Gileads Physicians," exhorted Walley; "we
have the Means of Healing. . . . God is yet our Sion, we have
healing Ordinances, the Preaching of the Gospel, the Seals of
the Covenant of Grace, Magistrates that would heal the Sicknesses of Sion, and Ministers that mourn for the hurt of the
daughter of Sion."[61]

Governor Danforth of Massachusetts wrote Governor Prence
in 1665 that New England was growing "too wanton, against all
order in church and common weale, and stood in need of a
whip, to reduce them to their old primitive resolution. . . ."[62]
The Plymouth churches could also heed the platform of the Synod
of 1679-80, drawn up by messengers of the Massachusetts
churches: "God hath a Controversy with his New-England People
is undeniable," and, therefore, "in order to Reformation, it is
necessary that the Discipline of Christ in the power of it should
be upheld in the Churches;" it was also "incumbent on the
Magistrate" to give encouragement to the ministry.[63]

The loss of spiritual leaven in Plymouth society can be attributed to a variety of sources. An assessment would include the

unsettled political conditions, the effects of the Indian war, social mobility, the toleration (under royal pressure) of Quakers and Baptists,[64] or, as recent scholarship avers, the "pluralistic" nature of New England Puritanism.[65] Or perhaps it was because Puritanism commanded too dedicated allegiance and excellence. It did not offer the relief and comfort men need in religion. As Page Smith has pointed out, the Puritans in the late seventeenth century were undergoing an anxiety crisis; the breakdown of a sense of involvement between God and man, which was never too strong among a people who at best could only doubt their state of grace, was turning them to despair.[66] As the power of the church over men's lives declined, the state became more the policeman of one's moral conscience. The rapid expansion in the law and prosecution of sumptuary crimes in the late period of Plymouth's history and the efforts to define church establishment, especially after the union with Massachusetts in 1692, attest to the weakening of the church and the encroachment of political authority. Had the purity and unity of the primitive society envisioned by the Plymouth founders been attainable, church and state would be separate.

NOTES

1. This is a phrase of Judge Lemuel Shaw, and its implication in later Massachusetts history is the subject of John D. Cushing's provocative article, "Notes on Disestablishment in Massachusetts, 1780-1833," *WMQ*, 3d Ser., XXVI (1969), 169-90.

2. The search of the Separatists for a "lost community" is discussed from the view of their antagonists in David B. Quinn, "The First Pilgrims," *WMQ*, 3d Ser., XXIII (1966), 387-88 and their English roots in Timothy L. Smith, "Congregation, State, and Denomination: The Forming of the American Religious Structure," *ibid.*, XXV (1968), 158-60.

3. See Chapter 6.

4. S/ William Brewster and John Robinson, quoted in Ashbel Steele, *Chief of the Pilgrims: The Life and Time of William Brewster* (Philadelphia, 1857), 316.

5. "Of Religious Communion, Private and Public" (1614), Ashton, ed., *Works of John Robinson,* III, 277. Robinson held that ministers could only have "a true and lawful *calling"* from "particular congregations"—and hence there was no need of "prelates." John Robinson, "A Manumission to a Manuduction or Answer to a Letter . . ." (1615), *MHSC,* 4th Ser., I (1852), 194.

6. *PCR,* XI, 73. For slightly different wording—e.g., "Churches of Christ"—see Laws of Plymouth Colony, 1636-71, MS., p. 11, Boston Public Library.

7. E.g., John Done, named a deacon in the church, was "freed from the office of Assistant in the Common weale." *PCR,* I, 23 (1634). Although this action was taken at the request of Done and the church, it appears that normally no one holding a church office was considered for a colony post.

8. For capsule biographies of prominent ministers of the colony, see Mather, *Magnalia Christi Americana* (1820 ed.), 212-14; Daniel Neal, *The History of the Puritans . . .* (1732-33), 3 vols. (London, 1837), I, 617ff. For the problem of retaining a minister in Plymouth, in addition to Bradford's *Hist.,* see John Cotton, "An Account of the Church of Christ in Plymouth . . ." (1760), *MHSC,* 1st Ser., IV (1795), 108-9. New churches were encouraged to elect pastors as speedily as possible. Hence, as early as 1643 eleven towns each had pastors. Hubbard, *General History, MHSC,* 2d Ser., VI (1848), 663. On Roger Williams versus the non-apostolic mission of Separatist ministers, see Edmund S. Morgan, *Roger Williams: The Church and the State* (New York, 1967), 40-45.

9. For the formation of the first church and township outside of Plymouth town, see John Lothrop, Diary (copied from the original in 1769 by Ezra Stiles), Yale University Library; Harvey Pratt, *The Early Planters of Scituate* (Scituate, 1929), 26-27; Joseph B. Felt, *The Ecclesiastical History of New England,* 2 vols. (Boston, 1855-62), I, 217-18.

10. For Puritan Massachusetts in this respect, see Horace Ware, "Was the Government of the Massachusetts Bay Colony a Theocracy?" *PCSM,* X (1907), 163.

11. E.g., Yarmouth Church (1667). Swift, *Old Yarmouth,* 89-90. In a dispute over who should be preacher at "Secunke," the General

Court intervened and decided in favor of a Mr. Sims over a Mr. Miles. Thomas Prence on behalf of the Court of New Plymouth (abstract), July 4, 1666, *CSP,* (1661-68), #1230.

12. *PCR,* II, 53 (1643). Hull had been excommunicated at Barnstable for "breaking communion with us." Amos Otis, ed., "Scituate and Barnstable Church Records," *NEHGR,* X (1856), 38, 41. See Donald G. Trayser, *Barnstable: Three Centuries of a Cape Cod Town* (Hyannis, Mass., 1939), 16 for comment on Hull's activities.

13. *PCR,* XI, 64 (1655).

14. *Ibid.,* 57 (1650).

15. *Ibid.,* 67 (1657).

16. An Eastham ordinance of 1665, quoted in Alice A. Lowe, *Nauset on Cape Cod: A History of Eastham* (Falmouth, Mass., 1968), 74. Such a policy was recommended by the General Court. *PCR,* XI, 135 (1662).

17. "Extract from the Records of the Town of Bridgewater," Feb. 22, 1660, *MHSP,* XIII (1875), 68.

18. *PCR,* V, 37 (1670), 172 (1675).

19. *Ibid.,* XI, 247 (1677). Thomas Hinckley, as an assistant of the colony, used his influence to secure a pastor from Mass. for Barnstable. Records of the West Parish of Barnstable, Mass., 1668-1807, June 10, 1678 and Sept. 19, 1683, photostat, MHS.

20. E.g., *PCR,* V, 31 (1670), 38 (1670), 40 (1670). George Langdon points out that the main problem was forcing persons who had pledged voluntary support to pay up rather than taxing nonchurch members. Langdon, *Pilgrim Colony,* 121.

21. Borden, *Bristol County,* 24.

22. *PCR,* IV, 86 (1665); George Carr to [Sec. Lord Arlington?], Dec. 14, 1665 (abstract), *CSP* (1661-68), #1103.

23. At a Council . . . Boston, June 1, 1687, MA, Ecclesiastical, 40; Minutes of the Council, Mar. 2, 1687, Robert N. Toppan, ed., *Andros Records, AASP,* XIII (1901), 257; Borden, *Bristol County,* 25.

24. I.e., 40*s.* for the first offense; £4 for the second; and £4 for each additional default. Susan M. Reed, *Church and State in Massachusetts, 1691-1740* (Urbana, Ill., 1914), 26-28.

25. *PCR,* III, 155 (1650); Bradford Smith, *Bradford of Plymouth* (Philadelphia, 1951), 154.

26. *PCR,* XI, 190 (1638) and 191 (1636).

27. See Alden T. Vaughan, *New England Frontier, 1620-75*

(Boston, 1965), 255-302; Harry M. Ward, *The United Colonies of New England, 1643-90* (New York, 1961), chapter 11.

28. Henry Whitfield (pub.), "Strength out of Weaknesse; Or a Glorious Manifestation of the further Progresse of the Gospel among the Indians . . ." (1652), *MHSC,* 3d Ser., IV (1834), 180; Vaughan, *New England Frontier,* 299.

29. Daniel Gookin, "Historical Collections of the Indians in New England," *MHSC,* 1st Ser., I (1792), 196-98; "The Mather Papers . . . ," *ibid.,* 4th Ser., VIII (1868), 226n; Vaughan, *New England Frontier,* 299-300. Red tape and infrequent meetings of the commissioners of the United Colonies accounted for arrears in compensation for the Indians. Thomas Hinckley, as governor and commissioner of the United Colonies, had the Indians of Plymouth "under my inspection," including their religious life. At sixteen locations, he reported in 1685, there was an Indian population of 1439 of persons over age 12. Hinckley noted the Indians often desired his help in their courts. Indian judges frequently appealed to him for a decision. The Indians getting liquor from England, as Hinckley saw it, was the major problem. Thomas Hinckley to William Stoughton and Joseph Dudley, April 2, 1685, *HP,* 133-34.

30. John Robinson, "New Essays; or Observations Divine and Moral" (1628), Ashton, ed., *Works of John Robinson,* I, 70; Felt, *Eccles. Hist.,* II, 24.

31. *Winthrop Hist.,* I, 398, Mar. 21, 1640; Edward Winslow to John Winthrop, Sr., Oct. 10, 1640, *The Winthrop Papers, Letters to, MHSC,* 4th Ser., VI (1863), 169-70.

32. The Gorton and Vassall affairs, as protests against the civil establishment, will be treated in Chapter 7.

33. John Cotton, "The Way of Congregational Churches Cleared" (1648), in Charles F. Adams, ed., *Antinomianism in the Colony of Massachusetts Bay, 1636-38, Pubs. of the Prince Society,* XXI (Boston, 1894), 389; Williston Walker, *The Creeds and Platforms of Congregationalism* (Boston, reprint 1960), 179; Williston Walker, *A History of the Congregational Church in the U. S., The American Church History Series,* III (New York, 1897), 158-60.

34. Lothrop, Diary, Apr. 22, 1647, 347, Yale U. Lib. Nathaniel Morton's obituary of John Wilson in 1667 indicates acceptance in Plymouth of the idea of synods with platforms enforced by the magistracy. Nathaniel Morton, *The New-England's Memorial* (1669), (Ply., Mass., 1826), 139.

35. Printed in Walker, *Creeds and Platforms,* 194-237.

36. Thomas Lechford, "Plaine dealing: or Newes from New-England" (1642), *MHSC,* 3d Ser., III (1833), 106-7; John Eliot, "Ecclesiastical History of Massachusetts," *MHSC,* 2d Ser., I (reprint 1838), 200.

37. Edward Johnson, "Wonder Working Providence of Sions Saviour in New-England" (1654), *MHSC,* 2d Ser., VIII (reprint 1826), 15-16.

38. John Clarke, "Ill Newes from New-England or A Narrative of New-Englands Persecution" (1652), *MHSC,* 4th Ser., II, 46.

39. Mass. Gen. Ct. to Ply. Gen. Ct.,—1649, MA, Ecclesiastical, X, 213; Edward Winslow to John Winthrop, Sr., Mar. 28, 1645, *Winthrop Papers, Letters to, MHSC,* 4th Ser., VI (1863), 177.

40. Walker, *Congregational Church,* 175-80.

41. *PCR,* V, 233 (1677); John Myles to Gov. Prence, Mar. 7, 1670, Winslow Papers, MHS, 2; John Cotton to Cotton Mather, Mar. 11, 1684, "Mather Papers," *MHSC,* 4th Ser., VIII (1868), 252.

42. John Robinson's Appendix to William Perkins' "Six Principles of Christian Religion," in Wilberforce Eames, "Early New England Catechisms," *AASP,* XII (1899), 85.

43. Perry Miller, *Errand into the Wilderness* (Cambridge, 1956), 147.

44. The Pilgrims considered their church one of a number of reformed churches—all of which were "true churches" in that they "deal faithfully and bear witness against their [Anglican and Catholic] corruptions." William Bradford, *A Dialogue or the Sum of a Conference between Some Young Men Born in New England and Sundry Ancient Men . . .* (1648), *Old South Leaflets,* II, #49, 22. It is probable that many of the Pilgrims joined the English Reformed Church in Holland (still distinct from the Dutch Reformed Church today), while regarding themselves an independent congregation. Daniel Plooj, *The Pilgrim Fathers From a Dutch Point of View* (New York, 1932), 101.

45. Burrage, *Church Covenant Idea,* 41. The quote is John Cotton's in 1643, by which time he and other Puritan leaders had become more adaptable to the principles of Separatism. "A Letter of Mr. John Cottons . . . to Mr. Williams . . . , *Pubs. of the Narragansett Club,* 1st Ser., I, 16. Cotton's letter to Samuel Skelton, June 13, 1631 had recognized the Separatism in the Salem church without designating the source of the influence. See David D. Hall, ed., "John Cot-

ton's Letter to Samuel Skelton," *WMQ,* 3d Ser., XXII (1965), 478-85. For critics of Perry Miller's view that New England Congregationalism stems from the nonconformist thought of the Mass. Puritans, see Larzar Ziff, *The Career of John Cotton: Puritanism and the American Experience* (Princeton, 1962), 75-78 and Morison, "New Light . . . ," *WMQ,* 3d Ser., XV (1958), 364.

46.   Perry, *Puritanism and Democracy,* 114.

47.   See Chapter 7.

48.   *PCR,* IX, 81 (1646). Ironically, "Paedobaptists," founding a church at Swansea, endorsed the power of the magistracy to repress "damnable heresies." Isaac Backus, *A History of New England with Particular Reference to the Denomination of Christians Called Baptists,* 2 vols. (Newton, Mass., 1871), I, 285.

49.   Emil Oberholzer, Jr., *Delinquent Saints: Disciplinary Action in the Early Congregational Churches of Mass.* (New York, 1956), 25.

50.   E.g., Lothrop, Diary, 323, Yale U. Lib. Dismission from the Plymouth Church granted, Nov. 23, 1634; new covenant formed, Jan. 8, 1635. After the incorporation with Mass., the right to worship privately in one's own family for those living at a great distance from a church instead of attending church required a petition from a town to the Mass. government. E.g., in 1695, petition from the town of Plymouth, Aug. 10, 1695, MA, XI, Ecclesiastical, 98.

51.   Cotton, "An Account . . ." (1760), *MHSC,* 1st Ser., IV (1795), 123. Even with the more relaxed policy towards admission, religious decline in the later period was evident. In Plymouth:

1669–27 admitted to full communion (with oral confession)
1682– 9 admitted to full membership; 24 children baptized
1684– 2 admitted to full membership; 16 children baptized
1687– 5 admitted to full membership; 23 children baptized
1690– 2 admitted to full membership; 19 children baptized
—*Plymouth Church Records, 2 vols.* (New York, 1920-23), I, 144-45, 158-59, 162, 165.

52.   Cotton, "An Account . . ." (1760), *MHSC,* 1st Ser., IV (1795), 124-25; Burrage, *Church Covenant Idea,* 86. The covenant was similarly renewed in April 1692.

53.   Emil Oberholzer, "The Church in New England Society," in J. M. Smith, ed., *Seventeenth-Century America; Essays in Colonial History* (Chapel Hill, 1959), 146-49; Clifford K. Shipton, "The Locus of Authority in Colonial Mass.," in G. A. Billias, ed., *Selected Essays*

on Law and Authority in Colonial America (Barre, Mass., 1965), 144-45.

54. Harry W. Johnson, *Moral Discipline in Early New England Churches* (unpubl. Bachelor of Divinity Thesis, University of Chicago, 1915), 3-5.

55. Oberholzer, "Church in New England Society," in Smith, ed., *Seventeenth-Century America,* 151-53.

56. Lothrop, Diary, *passim,* Yale U. Lib.; Records of the West Parish of Barnstable, Mass., photostat, *passim,* MHS; Otis, ed., "Scituate and Barnstable Church Records," *NEHGR,* X (1856), 38ff.

57. Oberholzer, *Delinquent Saints,* 122, 166-67. For tables of number of cases and the offenses brought before Mass. churches, including the Plymouth and Barnstable churches, 1640-1809, see *ibid.,* 251.

58. Cotton, "An Account . . ." (1760), *MHSC,* 1st Ser., IV (1795), 125.

59. *Plymouth Church Records,* 1669, I, 144.

60. Mather, *Magnalia Christi Americana,* I (1820), 59.

61. Walley, *Balm in Gilead* (1669), Evans #146.

62. Gov. Thomas Danforth to Gov. Prence, Jan. 12, 1665, Winslow Papers, 16, MHS.

63. Quoted in Walker, *Creeds and Platforms,* 433-44.

64. See Chapter 7.

65. Michael McGiffert, "American Puritan Studies in the 1960's," *WMQ,* 3d Ser., XXVII (1970), 36-45.

66. Page Smith, "Anxiety and Despair in American History," *WMQ,* 3d Ser., XXVI (1969), 417-18.

Chapter Five

THE LEGAL SYSTEM

The organization of power in a small community is more likely to be visibly statist, if not materially, than in a government over a large territory and population. The smaller the community the more centralized the power structure: the mitigating forces of federal distribution of power, separation of powers among the agencies of government, and checks and balances are at a minimum. In Plymouth Colony, all power was derived from the center. This is perhaps best evidenced by the legal system, which, in the formulation and administration of law, was thoroughly statistic. Yet, what is intriguing, is that we also find the ennoblement of the individual. Such a contradictory development could only be possible in a little colony, compact and poor but whose citizens were imbued with the ideals of individual dignity and equality.

Statism is best measured by the status of individual freedom, which is bound to be encompassed by enlightened authoritarianism in a small as well as in the large state. The types of law and courts, the procedural and substantive guarantees of the individual when confronted by the authority of the state, and

70

the kinds of crimes and punishment reveal the latitude of individual freedom.

In Plymouth, frontier adaptability and improvisation shaped notions of law and justice derived from biblicalism and the English heritage. It is not within the purview of this study to analyze the legal system, to discern its origins, or to gauge the influence of Plymouth upon the other American colonies. These areas still require thorough investigation, and the question of the legacy of Plymouth in all institutional aspects will undoubtedly continue to divide historians.

For the small band of refugees in the early years, there was little need for a formalized legal system. The first law entered in the records of December 17, 1623 sufficed to set up a working model for justice: the General Court "held that all Criminal facts, and also all [matters] of trespasses and debts between man and man should [be tried] by the verdict of twelve Honest men to be Impanelled by Authority in forme of a Jury upon their oaths."[1] Before the codification of 1636, legal enactments consisted of ordinances governing franchises and other economic concerns, which the Pilgrims patterned from their knowledge of English local law. The only major criminal case was the murder trial of John Billington in 1630. Bradford states that all "due means" were used at the trial, and Winthrop, whose government had legal authority from the crown, was consulted; it is presumed that a grand jury was used for the indictment and a petit jury for the trial.[2]

Plymouth's great achievement and innovation was the enactment of the code of 1636, which in itself represented a comprehensive authority of the state. The code was the first organic law made by American colonists in a voluntary association, and may rightfully be considered, as Professor Haskins regards it, the first American Constitution.[3] Revised in 1658 but issued as a new code in 1671 and 1684,[4] the code served as the basic law throughout the history of the Old Colony. It provided for the organization of government, prescribed duties of officials, codified laws and ordinances, and established a bill of rights.

Although not detracting credit due the Pilgrims for their endeavor, which undoubtedly influenced practices in other colonies and was two hundred years ahead of English statutory codification, Julius Goebel finds the Plymouth code was a compilation from imperfect knowledge of English custumals, which were in the form of codes.[5] The Plymouth code, in its substantive provisions, as Professor Goebel also notes, represents the fondness of Separatists and Puritans for the *lex scripta*—written law through express legislative enactment. The Pilgrims were aware of the successes at Calvin's Geneva, and they too believed that under stated organic law there could be but one law, the will of God.[6] In the famous foreword to the 1658 revision, the Pilgrime fathers paid their respect to the written Jewish law, for in "the mayne" it was "soe exemplary being grounded on principles of morall equitie as that all men Christians espetially ought alwaies to have an eye therunto in the framing of theire politique Constitutions."[7]

For the purposes of this study, possible motives for the codification of 1636 should be noted. Samuel Eliot Morison raises the question whether the intent and timing of the code coincided with "the near revolt of the freemen" that a few years later forced Governor Bradford and the "Old Comers" to surrender their rights under the Warwick patent to the freemen of the colony.[8] Whether or not a citizens' uprising was in the making cannot be ascertained; but undoubtedly the unsettled times—the expansion of the colony and the threat of subversion, particularly evident in the Bay Colony—contributed to the idea of making law more fixed and binding. Another motive is suggested by Roscoe Pound's observation of the Puritan tendency to enact codes of statute law. "If the Puritan did not believe in coercion," Pound states, "he did believe in instruction."[9] The conscience of the individual was free, but he would have to measure up to the abstract quality of the organic law, in which there would be little accommodation to variety and change in social behavior. It may also be noted that codification lodges fundamental law more securely within the legal authority of the state, and narrows the gap between a transgression of law and contempt for the legislator.

Distinctions in the multitudinous kinds of law and jurisdiction known in England were erased in Plymouth, although the legal system was a hybrid of English doctrine and practice, whose technicalities could only be vaguely grasped by a people who knew law from a layman's point of view. The concentration of functions is also striking, with all legal authority before 1685, except for minor actions allowed in selectmen courts, vested in the court of assistants. Scarcely any distinction was made between civil and criminal law.[10] The singularity of the legal system was also manifested in the non-recognition of a separate body of common law or equity, both of which check the legal authority of the majoritarian state.

What Mark deWolfe Howe has written of Massachusetts is largely true of Plymouth. "The old and familiar segregations became largely irrelevant," he says. "When common law, equity, admiralty, borough customs and ecclesiastical law were all administered in one tribunal, the old distinctions lost most of their operative significance." As for the common law, it was viewed in New England as a "set of unchanging principles of public law," and hence was limiting rather than creative.[11] Because the colonists considered their own statute making a "complete statement," Carl Reinsch concludes, the loose adaptation of common law doctrine was of a "rude, popular, summary kind."[12] In Plymouth, what was borrowed from the English common law was fitted into a unitary jurisprudence.

There is some truth in Roscoe Pound's assertion that "the Puritan has always been a consistent and thorough-going opponent of equity." The reasons are:

> For one thing, it [equity] helps fools who have made bad bargains, whereas he [the Puritan] believes that fools should be allowed and required to act freely and then be held for the consequences of their folly. For another thing, it acts directly upon the person. It coerces the individual free will. It acts preventively, instead of permitting free action and imposing after the event the penalty assented to in advance. For still another, it involves discretion in its application to actual cases, and that in the Puritan view, means superiority in the magistrate in that it allows him to judge another by a personal standard instead of by an unyielding, impersonal, legal rule.[13]

That a legal system based upon the fundamental laws of God excludes the need for special equity law is the argument of a New England Puritan writer at mid-century:

> there ought not to be a Court of Law or Justice, and another of Equity (Such as now are in England) maintained or suffered in

any Nation professing the Gospel . . . Nature holds forth but one
Light to men, and God gives but one Law to Christians. This is
the end of Magistry. The Execution of Justice; which in their hands,
whether Supreme or Subordinate, is that Virtue which is commonly
called, Distributive Justice, and comprehends in it Equity; and the
same likewise is called Righteousness . . . Justice and Equity are
the same thing . . . .[14]

But the Pilgrims realized that there must be some means of
equitable remedy, and they, therefore, favored leaving to the
magistracy, by virtue of their calling, a discretionary power rather
than developing a separate equity law and jurisdiction. Under
this discretionary power, equitable remedy was occasionally
administered, particularly in requiring the withdrawal of a suit
and ordering the performance of a contract without award of
damages.[15] By 1671, the court of assistants was authorized by
statute to "have power to determine all such matters of equity
as cannot be relieved by the Common Law."[16] Under the
Dominion of New England, in 1687, a court of chancery was
created along with special common law courts. After the incorporation of Plymouth into Massachusetts, an attempt was
made by colonial legislative enactment to create a court of
chancery in Massachusetts, which was disallowed by the king.[17]

In spite of the non-recognition of a separate body of common
law in Plymouth Colony, one cannot but be impressed with the
predominance of common law actions: principally actions of
breach of contract, debt, trespass, slander and defamation. But it
is worthy of note that there was also a frequency of actions on the
case (particularly action of trespass on the case or action on
the case for trespass), in which distinctions were completely
ignored between case and trespass.[18] Simple actions on (of) the
case were used, following the common law, if the matter was
intangible and the injury was consequential and not immediate.
When such a suit was brought, the litigants were encouraged to
settle the dispute outside of court. A good example of the use
of action on the case is the suit of John Williams, Jr. against
Thomas Summers for £1000 damages

for intollerable trespas, in wronging and abusing the said Williams,
by inticing his wife from him, and for unlawfull dalliance with her,
tending to, if not making of the said Summers guilty of adultery;

for whereas there was a child begotten upon the wife of the said Williams, it appeers to be begotten by the said Summers.[19]

Action for trespass involving minor damage devolved eventually upon the selectmen courts. An interesting trespass action at a selectmen court in Taunton (1690) awarded 20*s*. damages to Jonathan Harvey from John Smith for injury leading to the death of a black mare. Smith, however, appealed to the county court because; circumstantial evidence had been used, he had not been given an opportunity to clear himself, and the selectmen court had "denyed him the English Laws with Respect to a nonsuit in a book called the English Liberties."[20]

The principle that every man is responsible for his own torts was recognized in Plymouth as in other colonies. A person charged with trespass could not plead justification for his action on grounds of orders from a superior authority. Such practice would normally limit the state's legal authority because, if a person disagreed with a law or other command of the state, he could challenge its constitutionality through a suit against an official in the performance of his duty. This would implicate the law itself, and would, in a sense, give the court an implied power of judicial review.[21] However, there is no instance in Plymouth's history of a court deciding in a suit against the constitutionality of a law. As mentioned earlier, judicial review (through referendum) was the unexercised privilege of the freemen as a whole.

The abundance of slander and defamation suits (no distinction was made between the two) in the court records is amazing. An explanation may lie in several factors: the accessibility of the courts; the serious responsibility, without any levity in a Puritan state, for maintaining a good name and reputation; and, perhaps the main reason, a plaintiff could invariably count on the success of his suit—if not in amount of damages, at least vindication. An average citizen could expect an award of 18*s*.-20*s*. for a claim of damages of £100. If the plaintiff was a prominent figure in the colony, and more especially if he was a minister, awards were given usually for £100 for claims of £500-£1000.[22] Occasionally the government took upon itself to present a case of defamation or slander outside of an action, as it did when Elizabeth Randall of Scituate was presented by grand jury and fined by the court of assistants for "teling of a lye to the detterment of Gowin White."[23]

All judicial authority in civil and criminal cases originally
belonged to the General Court. In 1634 the General Court
decided that all actions either of debt or trespass under 40s. were
to be tried by the governor and assistants "without the trouble
of the whole bodie."[24] Shortly afterwards, through informal arrangement rather than by an enactment of the General Court,
the court of assistants acquired jurisdiction in trying all cases.[25]

With the expansion of the colony, provision was made by the
General Court for local courts on a limited basis. Thus, in 1640
a three man commission—one member each from Barnstable,
Sandwich, and Yarmouth—was appointed "to heare and determine all causes and controversies within the three townships" not
exceeding 20s.[26] Rehoboth was granted authority in 1647 to
choose two freemen "to be Assistants unto the magestrate then
in being" for trying all suits under the value of £10, with a
jury trial.[27] After 1666 all towns were required to choose three
to five selectmen approved by the General Court to act as
selectmen courts in determining all suits for 40s. or less and "all
Differences" between Indians and Englishmen arising in their
townships—with powers to compel testimony of witnesses.[28]
When a plaintiff and defendant lived in different towns, the plaintiff had the right to determine the jurisdiction.[29] With the establishment of counties in 1685, the county courts assumed much
of the judicial functions of the selectmen courts.

A good example of the unitary nature of the Plymouth legal
system was the complete authority of the governor and assistants
to probate wills and settle estates—functions divided among a
number of ecclesiastical and special courts in England. In the
rule of partible inheritance, Plymouth followed customary law
rather than the common law. It is also interesting to note that
the assistants exercised a discretionary power in setting aside
provisions of a will when they deemed it unjust.[30] The court of
assistants also acted on divorce cases, with divorce rarely granted,
except for desertion and conviction of sexual crime.[31]

Justice in the court of assistants, by jury trial, appears to have
been no respecter of persons. Stephen Hopkins, an assistant in
1634-5, was repeatedly fined: for permitting drinking in his
house during a meeting on the Sabbath, selling beer, liquors, and
sundry articles at excessive prices, and not honoring the indenture
of Dorothy Temple.[32] While serving as an assistant, Timothy

Hatherly had to pay damages of 50*s.* in an action of trespass and £3 18*s.* in an action of the case.[33] One instance of probable influence, however, was that of James Cudworth, who, though not an assistant at the time, secured a retrial and reversal in a case that had gone against him.[34]

As did their Massachusetts brethren, the Plymouth colonists regarded their conciliar court as the final court of justice. This position received endorsement from England during the Parliamentary interregnum. Theoretically, the Lords Committee of Trade and Plantations of the Privy Council, lasting from 1674 until it was replaced by the Board of Trade in 1696, had appellate and review jurisdiction over the colonies, but there is no evidence of the Plymouth authorities permitting appeals to England or sending legislation for review in the period before incorporation with Massachusetts.[35] Of course, on the legislative side, the investigation of the royal commissioners in the 1660's and 1670's served the purpose of getting Plymouth to inventory its laws to make sure they conformed to those in England and paid deference to royal authority.[36]

Provision for various colony law officers aided the centralization of the administration of justice, although gradually powers devolved substantially upon the localities. From time to time persons were designated by the General Court to exercise special legal functions in the towns: for example, to perform marriages, administer oaths to witnesses and jurors, bind over persons for trial, and issue subpoenas.[37] The colony appointed a chief marshal and an under-marshal to execute processes of the court of assistants, especially in the collection of fines.[38]

The General Court ratified the appointment of a constable in each township. His duties included keeping the king's peace, apprehending suspicious persons and bringing them before the court of assistants, impaneling a jury to determine cause of death, "measuring of lands, and sealing of waights and measures," convening town meetings, collecting taxes, promulgating "Instructions" of the General Court, and serving executions by selectmen.[39] Refusal to serve as constable necessitated a 50*s.* fine, and if a constable neglected to collect taxes or issue a summons, he was liable to pay himself the defaulted sums. Needless to say, an officer, who was both a plainclothes policeman and sheriff, was not entirely appreciated. William Chase, constable at Yarmouth, was censured and sentenced to find sureties for his good behavior and to leave the town within six months for his "miscarriages" against the minister, Marmaduke Matthews, and "disturbance of the proceedings of the church, Court and countrey." The sentence, however, was never executed.[40]

Another administrative arm of the judicial system was the grand jury, adopted early in Plymouth history, "to serve the king by enquiring into the abuses and breaches of such wholsome lawes and ordinances as tend to the preservation of the peace and good of the subject."[41] Chosen by the General Court and "confirmed" by the court of election,[42] the grand jury investigated crimes and "all such misdemeanors of any person or persons as tend to the hurt and detriment of societie Civillitie peace and Naighbourhood" and presented their findings to the court of assistants.[43] The grand jury, consisting of twenty-one and not more than twenty-three persons (the maximum number under common law practice), was expected to be available for hearings at all sessions of the General Court.[44] Failure to answer a summons to serve on a grand jury entailed a fine of 20s. and after 1658, 40s.[45] Plymouth followed closely the distinction in the common law between presentment and indictment, with the latter voted by the General Court. After 1685, grand juries were impaneled in the shire towns to report to the county courts, with two to four jurors from each town, depending on size of population, and one from each plantation; however, after this date the colony-wide grand jury was continued, though enlarged to twenty-seven persons from eighteen jurisdictions.[46] Grand jurymen from each township were also to meet in their respective jurisdictions once a year to "view all the measures waights and tole dishes."[47]

The grand jury in Plymouth also probed government policy and authority, thereby acting as a check upon any action that seemed to diverge from the popular will. For example, the grand jury required explanation on such topics as criteria for making land grants, contribution of the undertakers to the colony for their trade monopoly, the non-appointment of a colony treasurer when money had been allocated, the feasibility of letting areas where disorders occurred be turned over to Rhode Island, and the administration of oaths of fidelity.[48] Town implementation of statutes of the General Court was also a subject of inquiry.[49] In general, the grand jury operated on the principle of the people's right to inquire into all affairs of the colony affecting the public interest.

Only late in Plymouth's history did the colony recognize the right of a person to designate an agent in court on his behalf. As in Massachusetts, it can be presumed that if a person wished counsel from the court, he sought advice from a magistrate before trial.[50] The first mention of an attorney in Plymouth colony was John Smith of Taunton, who, in 1672, acted on power of attorney for Seth Smith of Medfield, Massachusetts, in a theft case in Taunton.[51] By 1680, the employment of attorneys was prevalent; thus, the General Court felt it necessary to fix a charge of 5*s.* for any action and no more than 2*s.* 6*d.* per diem.[52] Since judicial proceedings in Plymouth were a mixture of common sense and a collective borrowing from various forms of English law, there was little need for a specialist at law. But as time went on, the legal procedure became more technically identified with the common law, and the idea of agency became generally accepted. Even then, a lawyer had to be a versatile attorney at large.

In the course of Plymouth history, we find emerging from the enactment of codes and statutes an admiration for the fundamental rights of freemen derived from the Magna Carta. In the preamble to the 1636 code, and subsequently re-enacted, no laws could be made except by the consent of the people "according to the free liberties of the State and Kingdome of England and no otherwise."[53] The right to petition the government for redress was acknowledged.[54] The idea of popular based government, with the magistrates elected and bound by the will of the freemen, contributed to the latitude in the Pilgrim reading of the English heritage. Concerning the administration of justice, a guarantee of substantive due process is found in the sweeping clause in the preamble ("The Generall Fundamentals") to the code of 1671:

> no person in this Government shall be endamaged in respect of Life, Limb, Liberty, Good name or Estate, under colour of Law, or countenance of Authority, but by virtue or equity of some express Law of the General Court of this Colony, the known Law of God, or the good and equitable Laws of our Nation suitable for us, being brought to Answer by due process thereof.[55]

Procedural due process, although not fixed into any definite rules, fared rather well in Plymouth. Citizens were insistent that officers of the colony have special search warrants to invade a person's property.[56] Special care was taken so that more than one witness was necessary to establish guilt[57]—and persons could well fear defamation suits if they divulged information not confirmed by other witnesses.[58] Among procedural rights gaining acceptance by 1672 were the rights to bail (with such exceptions as for capital crimes) and counsel, and there was also a statute of limitations for petty crimes.[59]

It seemed to be the consensus among Plymouth leaders that confessions could not be extracted either by torture or applying an oath *ex officio*.[60] However, two of three Plymouth clergymen giving Governor Winthrop of Massachusetts advice on the subject (Chauncey and Reyner for, Partridge against) felt that when there was strong presumption of guilt in a capital case, the accused should be forced to answer all questions.[61] The records do not tell us anything direct of actual procedural due process in Plymouth, but, reading between the lines, it is reasonable to assume that the right against self-incrimination in capital cases was absolutely safeguarded. In other cases, undoubtedly the right against self-incrimination was occasionally honored in the breach; but at least there were none of the flagrant violations evidenced in the Massachusetts purge trials of Anne Hutchinson and company.

Although, as mentioned before, a statute of 1623 guaranteed a jury trial in all civil and criminal cases, the magistrates held the discretionary power to distinguish between a felony and a misdemeanor, with the latter not being considered a "crime" and hence a jury trial was not obligatory. On this matter, Julius Goebel reasonably concludes:

> The indications in the records are that a petty jury was drawn as of course only in case of a major crime. Where an offender was presented, the court proceeded apparently to sentence without further trial, the findings of the grand jury being deemed sufficient inquest. In the English leets unanimous presentment except in cases where the freehold was involved operated as a conviction, and this may have been the source of Plymouth practice. Occasionally the accused as well as witnesses were examined in open court, but apparently a

jury was impanelled for small offences only if the presentment was formally traversed. Since the bulk of offences, drunkenness and sexual transgressions and uncivil carriage, far outnumbered more serious infractions of public order, this quasi-summary method of procedure was workable, and having precedent religious and customary behind it, was not regarded as subversive of individual rights.[62]

Only the magistrates were excluded from jury duty.[63] Plymouth was the first colony to institute a desegregated jury: six Indians were added to the regular English jury in the trial of the murderers of John Sassamon in 1675.[64] In at least one incident, the bench overruled the verdict of a jury,[65] which again indicates the reach of the discretionary powers of the magistrates and that common law doctrines had not become fixed.

All capital crimes were tried in the court of assistants before 1685.[66] Capital crimes in Plymouth did not differ substantially from the Massachusetts code: treason and rebellion "against the person of the King state or Common wealth either of England or these Colonies," "Willful murder," "Solemn Compaction or conversing with the divell by way of witchcraft conjuration or the like," "willfull" arson, sodomy, rape, and buggery.[67] Such capital crimes as blasphemy, kidnapping, false witness with intent to take life, and idolatry were found in the Massachusetts code of 1641; however they were omitted in Plymouth. Interestingly, the punishment for adultery, though listed as a capital crime, was left to the discretion of the magistrates. No person was executed for adultery in Plymouth; but a Plymouth woman was put to death in Massachusetts on this charge.[68] After 1671, capital crimes were extended to selling arms and ammunition to the Indians, burglary and robbery on the highways, and piracy on the high seas.[69] Compared to the Massachusetts record of fifty-six or fifty-seven executions for eight crimes before 1692, Plymouth's ten executions (nine for murder and one for bestiality)[70] represent a more even tempering of justice with mercy.

One impressive aspect of capital cases in Plymouth was that mitigating circumstances were taken into full account. Thus an Indian tried for the murder of another Indian was convicted for manslaughter instead of premeditated murder because of mental disorder ("chaunce medley").[71] The killing of a resident at Scitu-

ate by a Negro firing a gun through a door was declared an act
of "misadventure," and the defendant was ordered to pay £5
(£3 for causing lameness and £2 for the subsequent death) to the
father of the slain man.[72] Such a recognition of a private claim
in a criminal case was not infrequent in Plymouth. In another
case, involving fatal injury during a fight, the defendant was
acquitted.[73] A very curious episode was the conviction of an
Indian for raping a white girl—though the jury considered the
death penalty proper in this case, "yett considering hee was but
an Indian, and therefore in an incapasity to know the horiblenes
of the wickednes of this abominable act, with other cercom-
stances considered," he was sentenced to be whipped and to be
exiled out of the colony.[74] A son was convicted of "stricking and
abusing his parents" and whipped; "his punishment was allevi-
ated in regard hee was crasey brained, otherwise hee had bine
put to death or otherwise sharply punished."[75] What is significant
here is not so much the leniency on the part of the court but that
the Mosaic law of putting to death a rebellious son (in effect in
Massachusetts) was seriously pondered in Plymouth.

The poor and disadvantaged were also given consideration
outside of criminal action. Indians, "by reason of their poverty,"
could sue *in forma pauperis*.[76] Indigent prisoners did not have
to pay their upkeep in prison.[77]

The Plymouth colonists preferred to follow the Old Testament
in leaving to the discretion of the magistrates the fitting of the
penalty to the crime. Thus moral and psychological factors could
be taken into account; crime and sin were synonymous, and
remission was the desired end.[78] Discretionary judgment enabled
greater flexibility in finding exactly the right punishment. Theft
could be punished in a variety of ways, in any or all of the
following: fine, whipping,[79] branding on the hand or shoulder
(with the letter "B" if a burglary), standing on the gallows,
restitution of goods (up to fourfold), and court costs.[80] Indians
convicted of theft stood in jeopardy of being sold into slavery in
order to pay the person wronged and "to free the collonies from
soe ill a member."[81] Conviction for most crimes entailed a money
payment, and if a private party was injured the offense could be
considered in the form of a trespass action rather than by
prosecution by the state—in any event the fine or damages were
roughly equivalent.[82]

Major crimes were rare in Plymouth colony. But the court of assistants was overburdened in trying suits and moral and sumptuary cases. The unitary system of justice, fusing the broad discretionary power of the magistracy with borrowings from local customary and common law in England and the Mosaic code, made law administration flexible and direct. If the individual was discomfited by the severity of the law, he could appreciate the general fairness of its human application.

NOTES

1. *PCR,* XI, 3.

2. *Bradford Hist.* (1912), II, 110-11; Goodwin, *Pilgrim Republic,* 342-43. In a reverse circumstance, the investigation of the murder by Indians of Walter Bagnall, Mass. asked advice from Plymouth. *MCR,* I, 98 (1632); Thomas Morton, *New English Canaan* (1637), ed. Charles F. Adams, Jr., *Pubs. of the Prince Society,* XIV (New York, reprint 1967), 206n.

3. George L. Haskins, "The Legal Heritage of Plymouth Colony," in David H. Flaherty, ed., *Essays in the History of Early American Law* (Chapel Hill, 1969), 123. This article is a substantial revision of Haskins, "The Legacy of Plymouth," special article pub. by Plimoth Plantation, from *Social Education,* XXVI (1962), No. 1.

4. The 1636 and 1658 codes and segments of the 1671 code are found in *PCR,* XI. The 1671 and 1684 codes were published in *The Book of the General Laws of the Inhabitants of New Plymouth* (pub. by Samuel Green, Cambridge, 1672 and 1685); and all four codes are found in Brigham, ed., *Compact . . . Laws . . . New Plymouth* (Boston, 1836): the 1636 code, the revised code of 1658, the Samuel Green edition of the code of 1671, and selections from the 1684 code differing from previous laws. Committees for codifying the laws were: 1636, besides the governor and assistants, William Brewster, Ralph Smith, John Done, Jonathan Brewster, Christopher Wadsworth, James Cudworth, and Anthony Annable; 1658—William Collier, Timothy Hatherly, John Alden, James Cudworth, and Josiah

Winslow; 1671—Gov. Thomas Prence, Thomas Hinckley, and Thomas Walley; 1684—Gov. Hinckley, Barnabas Lothrop, Capt. John Walley, Capt. (——) Lothrop, and Capt. Nathaniel Thomas. Brigham, ed. *Compact . . . Laws . . . New Plymouth,* viii-ix; Walter Whitehill, ed., "Letters of the Reverend Thomas Walley . . . to John Cotton of Plymouth," *AASP,* LVIII (1949), 247-49; *PCR,* VI, 132.

5. Julius Goebel, Jr., "King's Law and Social Custom in Seventeenth Century New England," in Flaherty; ed., *Essays . . . Early American Law,* 103-4.

6. *Ibid.,* 99-101.

7. *PCR,* XI, 72.

8. Morison, "New Light," *WMQ,* 3d Ser., XV (1958), 362; Bradford, *Of Plymouth Plantation,* ed. Morison, 308.

9. Roscoe Pound, *The Spirit of the Common Law* (Francestown, N. H., 1921), 47.

10. Goebel, "King's Law . . . Custom," in Flaherty, ed., *Essays . . . Early American Law,* 105; Charles J. Hilkey, *Legal Development in Colonial Massachusetts, 1630-86* (New York, 1910), 112.

11. Mark D. Howe, "The Sources and Nature of Law in Colonial Massachusetts," in Billias, ed., *Selected Essays,* 15.

12. Paul S. Reinsch, *English Common Law in the Early American Colonies, Bulletin of the University of Wisconsin,* No. 31 (Madison, 1899), 11-30. According to Zechariah Chafee, "Colonial Courts and the Common Law," *MHSP,* LXVIII (1947) only the problems of maturity and technical understanding hindered a full common law adaptation. Plymouth followed the practice of allowing no suits against the state; although suits could be brought against administrative officials acting beyond their authority, none were processed.

13. Pound, *Spirit of the Common Law,* 53.

14. [anon.], "Examen Legum: Or the Laws of England Examined by Scripture, Antiquity, and Reason" (1656), in M. D. Howe, ed., *Readings in American Legal History* (Cambridge, 1952), 89-90.

15. E.g., *John Bryant* v. *Humphrey Johnson* (1656), *PCR,* VII, 77-78, and *John Barker* v. *John Williams* (1677), *ibid.,* 202-3.

16. Brigham, ed., *Compact . . . Laws . . . New Plymouth,* 260 (1671 code). This may be considered a precedent for the later assumption of "equitable jurisdiction" by the common law courts. For the upholding of ante-nuptial contracts in this respect, see Richard B. Morris, *Studies in the History of American Law . . ., Columbia U. Studies in Hist., Econ., and Pub. Law,* #316 (New York, 1930),

135, 137. By an act of 1647, Indians could forgo oath taking in any of the colony courts, which "may therein acte and determine in a way of Chancery; vallueing Testimonies not sworne on both sydes according to their Judgement and Conscience." *PCR*, XI, 236.

17. Solon D. Wilson, "Courts of Chancery in the American Colonies," in Ernst Freund *et al., Select Essays in Anglo-American Legal History, 3 vols.* (Boston, 1907-9), II, 783-85. For the introduction of the English court system during Andros' administration, see M. D. Howe, "Sources . . . Law in Colonial Massachusetts," in Billias, ed., *Selected Essays,* 4-6.

18. "The fundamental [English] idea of the trespass action was that it was a remedy for the recovery of damages and not for the recovery of possession . . . trespass on the case . . . gave damages in cases stating a ground of complaint analogous to trespass but not equivalent to it . . . as where the original act was lawful and consequential damage ensued. . . . The most irregular use of the action on the case [in the colonies] was as a substitute for the real actions and for ejectment, when the surrender of the realty rather than damages was the gist of the suit. Thus, actions on the case were brought for illegally entering upon land, for unjustly detaining land and in general for the determination of title to realty." Morris, *Studies . . . American Law,* 49-51. Not only did actions of trespass in Plymouth include unjust possession or improvement of land (e. g., "entering into and detaining forcibly a certaine parcell of land") but also actions arising out of such injuries as killing a sow with pig belonging to another party, fencing of land, cutting timber on another's property, and "spoyling of his grass, pulling up his fence, and destroying his hay." *PCR,* VII, 73 (1655), 150 (1688), 155 (1669).

19. *PCR,* VII, 138 (1667).

20. Taunton Town Records, Feb. 4, 1690, 249.

21. McLaughlin, *Foundations of American Constitutionalism,* 118. Hilkey, *Legal Development in Massachusetts,* 143-44, however, takes the position that colonial courts in general resembled the medieval German Schoffen-Gericht, in that colonial juries were more independent than in England and therefore contributed to interpretation of law.

22. *PCR, VII, passim.* Cases involving Reverends Samuel Newman (*ibid.,* 58 [1652]) and Charles Chauncey (*ibid.,* 65 [1653]). Actions for slander *and* defamation brought slightly higher awards, e.g., £5 of damage claim of £500. *Ibid.,* 57 (1652).

23. *Ibid.,* III, 47 (1654).

24. *Ibid.,* I, 29.

25. *Ibid.,* I, *passim;* XI, 9.

26. *Ibid.,* I, 155.

27. *Ibid.,* 118.

28. *Ibid.,* XI, 213. From the time selectmen were first elected until the end of the colony, the General Court held the right to approve any person elected. The selectmen courts had to meet three times a year; they also functioned as local tax courts. Refusal to serve as a selectman brought a fine of 20*s.* *PCR,* XI, *passim,* 227. Failure to answer a subpoena at a selectmen's court necessitated a fine of 20*s.* "to the partie wronged." *PCR,* XI, 251 (1680). The board of selectmen were also charged with reporting persons coming into the colony without permission and to compel their appearance before the General Court. *Ibid.,* 217 (1658). The selectmen "united the functions of the modern justice of the peace (new trial justice) and partially those of the old county courts of common pleas, with a jurisdiction limited to the towns." Lysander Richards, *History of Marshfield,* 2 vols. (Plymouth, 1901), I, 56.

29. *PCR,* VI, 115 (1683).

30. Ware, "Was . . . Massachusetts . . . a Theocracy?" *PCSM,* X (1907), 153-57; Morris, *Studies . . . American Law,* 157, 162-63; Haskins, "Legal Heritage of Ply.," in Flaherty, *Essays . . . Early American Law,* 130-31; George Haskins, *Law and Authority in Early Massachusetts* (New York, 1960), 170-72; George Haskins, "The Beginnings of Partible Inheritance . . .," in Flaherty, ed., *Essays . . . Early American Law,* 205-6. "Wills and testaments" had to be proved before the court of assistants within one year. *PCR,* I, 17 (1633). Under the Dominion of New England, a Prerogative Court (Court of Probate) was established in the counties. Andros appointed Thomas Hinckley judge of this court in Barnstable County. Sir Edmund Andros' Commission to Thomas Hinckley, Mar. 10, 1687, *HP,* 150.

31. E.g., *PCR,* IV, 192 (1668); V, 21, 23 (1669), 127 (1673), 159 (1675). In all, only six divorces were granted by Plymouth Colony, but there were also fines for "disorderly marriage." See Goodwin, *Pilgrim Republic,* 596-99.

32. *PCR,* I, 68 (1637), 75, 87 (1638), 97 (1638), 111-13, 137 (1639).

33. *Ibid.,* VII, 45 (1649).

34. *Ibid.,* 168 (1671).

35. Joseph H. Smith, *Appeals to the Privy Council from the American Plantations* (New York, 1950), 46-48 and 47n., 71-72. Only twenty-six cases were appealed from courts in the American colonies to the Lords of Trade and Plantations, 1675-96, and nine of these were from other than the mainland colonies. Ralph P. Bieber, *The Lords of Trade and Plantations, 1675-96* (Allentown, Pa., 1919), 76. In theory, of course, the General Court and not the court of assistants was regarded as the supreme court of judicature in Plymouth.

36. Plymouth's care to avoid passing laws conflicting with royal authority merited praise from Charles II. Copy of a letter of Charles II to the Colony of New Plimouth, April 10, 1666, in Thomas Hutchinson, *The History of the Colony and Province of Massachusetts-Bay,* ed. Lawrence S. Mayo, vols. 1-2 (Cambridge, 1936), I, 452; *PCR,* IV, 87 (1665). For the rise of associate (county) courts and the establishment of justices of the peace, Court of Quarter and General Sessions, Inferior Court of Common Pleas, and Superior Court of Judicature, 1685-92, see Freeman, *History of Cape Cod,* I 726-28 and n.

37. *PCR,* III, 111, 172 (1659) and *passim;* IV, 22 (1662), 65 (1664); VI, 7 (1679).

38. *Ibid.,* II, 93 (1645); XI, 162-63 (1658).

39. *Ibid.,* I, 105 (1638); IV, 130 (1666); XI, 10 (1636), 88-90 (1639-40), 166 (1643).

40. *Ibid.,* I, 162 (1640); Swift, *Old Yarmouth,* 36-37.

41. *PCR,* XI, 11.

42. *Ibid.,* 157 (1658).

43. *Ibid.,* I, 85, 87 (1638); XI, 91 (1658).

44. An exception was twenty-five jurors sworn in in 1684. *Ibid.,* VI, 128.

45. *Ibid.,* II, 171-72 (1651); XI, 43, 120, 169.

46. *Ibid.,* VI, 165-66 (1685), 193 (1686); Charles F. Swift, *Cape Cod: The Right Arm of Massachusetts* (Yarmouth, 1897), 123. For county grand juries in 1685, Plymouth County had 16 jurymen; Barnstable County, 15; and Bristol County, 15. On rare occasions the grand jury did vote a true bill, e.g., for the murder indictment of John Hawes in 1661. *PCR,* III, 205.

47. *PCR,* XI, 91 (1646).

48. *Ibid.,* I, 119 (1639); II, 37 (1642); III, 41 (1653).

49. E.g., neglect in maintaining a highway (*ibid.,* III [1654]) or

failure to establish standards for weights and measures (*ibid.,* III, 82 [1655]).

50. Edwin Powers, *Crime and Punishment in Early Massachusetts, 1620-92* (Boston, 1966), 434.

51. *PCR,* V, 100. About the same time the practice of allowing Indians to be represented by attorneys in particularly technical cases, such as land ownership, was inaugurated. *Ibid.,* VII, 191 (1674).

52. *Ibid.,* XI, 251 (1680).

53. *Ibid.,* 6; Brigham, ed., *Compact . . . Laws . . . New Plymouth,* 36. See Morison, "New Light," *WMQ,* 3d Ser., XV (1958), 361 for an outline of rights in the 1636 code.

54. But the right was considered more in a quasi-judicial sense than in the context of representation. E.g., it is interesting to note that a petition of twenty-seven persons in Scituate in 1680 against enforced tax levies for building a new church was presented to the court of assistants seeking reversal of town policy, since there was no other "Court of Appeal nor higher power within our jurisdiction." Petition of John Bailey and Others of Scituate . . . to the General Court, June 1680, *HP,* 39-40.

55. Brigham, ed., *Compact . . . Laws . . . New Plymouth,* 241.

56. John Winslow to Gov. Prence, June 25, 1670, Winslow Papers, 1638-1759, 45, MHS.

57. *PCR,* XI, 93, 168 (1656). Compensation for witnesses per diem began in 1665. *Ibid.,* 214, 258 (1682).

58. E.g., see the concern of Thomas Walley for revealing information given in confidence that could be denied in public. Walley to John Cotton, Jr., Jan. 16, 1678, Whitehill, ed., "Letters of Walley," *AASP,* LVIII (1949), 261.

59. Brigham, ed., *Compact . . . Laws . . . New Plymouth,* 255, 262 (code of 1671). Except for capital offenses and "crimes that may concern loss of member" or felonies "above twenty shillings," indictments not made within a year from the time of the offense were void.

60. To tell the truth to all interrogation and thus opening oneself to self-incrimination—a practice used in the English prerogative and ecclesiastical courts.

61. Leonard W. Levy, *Origins of the Fifth Amendment* (New York, 1968), 346-47; *Bradford Hist.* (1912), II, 315-28 contains the "answers" of the three ministers. The Thomas Granger execution came shortly after the submission of this report.

62. Goebel, "King's Law . . . Custom," in Flaherty, ed., *Essays . . . Early American Law,* 113-14.

63. Also, an assistant or any other judge was barred from passing sentence in a civil case if he were related in any way to one of the parties involved. *PCR,* XI, 257 (1682).

64. *Ibid.,* V, 168.

65. *Isaac Wilder* v. *Humphrey Johnson,* "an action of trespass on the case," July 3, 1677, *ibid.,* VII, 204; John Leverett to Gov. Winslow, Nov. 29, 1677, Winslow Papers, 1638-1759, 108, MHS.

66. *PCR,* III, 60 (1654). After 1685, capital cases were tried in the Superior Court of Judicature (1687-89). For comparison with Mass. see Powers, *Crime and Punishment in Massachusetts,* 89-90; Haskins, *Law and Authority in Early Massachusetts,* 33.

67. *PCR,* II, 60 (1654); XI, 12 (1636). Cf. the "Body of Liberties" enacted in 1641 in Mass.; a convenient reprint is in Edmund S. Morgan, ed., *Puritan Political Ideas* (Indianapolis, 1965), 178-203. In 1648, cursing and striking a parent and rebelliousness of a son against his parents were added as capital offenses in Mass. Haskins, *Law and Authority in Early Massachusetts,* 145-46.

68. Powers, *Crime and Punishment in Early Massachusetts,* 291.

69. *Ibid.,* 300.

70. *Ibid.,* 294; Goodwin, *Pilgrim Republic,* 601. A breakdown of the number of Mass. executions for the period: witchcraft, 23; bestiality, 2; adultery, 2; arson, 2; rape, 4; treason, 2; Quakers defying banishment, 4; and piracy, 5 or 6. Extradition was recognized by the four Puritan colonies under the New England Confederation; it is interesting to note that Rhode Island in 1638 delivered three servants to Plymouth who had killed an Indian—these were promptly tried and executed in Plymouth; the fourth culprit had made good his escape. *Winthrop Hist.,* I, 321.

71. *PCR,* V, 156 (1674).

72. *Ibid.,* VI, 141 (1684).

73. *Ibid.,* III, 205 (1661).

74. *Ibid.,* VI, 98 (1682).

75. *Ibid.,* 20 (1679).

76. *Ibid.,* 202 (1691).

77. *Ibid.,* III, 93 (1645).

78. For reasons for emphasis upon proof of change of heart of the culprit in gauging the actual punishment (often in variance with the sentence) in Mass., see Jules Zanger, "Crime and Punishment in Early

Massachusetts," *WMQ*, 3d Ser., XXII (1965), 471-77; Haskins, *Law and Authority in Early Massachusetts*, 204-212.

79. Every township was required to have a whipping post. Ply. Col. Laws, 1636-71, 22 (1636), Boston Pub. Lib.; *PCR*, III, 60 (1654).

80. Most of these were inflicted on a Negro slave who had commited a nocturnal burglary on his master's house in Scituate. Records Sessions of the Peace, 1686-1721, Oct. 26, 1686, 11, Ply. County, Pilgrim Hall, Ply., Mass.

81. E.g., *PCR*, V, 156 (1674); VI, 98 (1682).

82. E.g., assault, "breakinge the Kinges peace," fine 3*s*. 4*d*. (*ibid.*, IV, 139 [1666]) and an action of trespass and assault, with the plaintiff being awarded only the cost of the suit (*ibid.*, VII, 56 [1651]). Of course, one can only generalize on the relation between damages and fines in comparable action and prosecution because of the obvious variation in circumstances and merits of the cases, and injury to a person in a private suit would be coupled with other wrongs. Persons arrested—with warrant served for appearance before the court of assistants—had to post "sureties" for good behavior, and for failure to do so, they were committed to jail. E.g., *ibid.*, II, 24 (1641). Thus Plymouth, as courts in the United States since, distinguished between rich and poor under the law.

Chapter Six

MORAL AND SUMPTUARY LAW

A state that promotes fairness and thrift in economic life is likely to express similarly a paternalism in relation to personal conduct.

The Pilgrims, of course, did not invent moral and sumptuary laws; they are as old as human society and reached a wide range in the medieval towns and particularly in the reformed city-states of the Reformation period. The Plymouth settlers were as liberal as any people of their time, and sumptuary legislation affecting manners and customs (for example, the wearing of apparel), as found in Massachusetts and other colonies, was totally absent in Plymouth. Nevertheless, to maintain piety and order and to bring out the greatest good in each person, it was considered necessary to restrict pleasure and wantonness in the lives of individuals.

Discipline over private conduct during the early years was exercised chiefly by the church; but, as church authority waned, not only was responsibility entrusted more to the civil government, but regulations and prosecutions in the area of individual conduct increased. The reasons for the expansion of governmental concern are at least superficially evident: the fanning out of society, making it difficult for close tribalism in the supervision of private conduct; the nuclearization of the family, hence reducing patriarchal authority; the inroads of secularization; and the anxiety over loss of faith in the mission into the wilderness.

Much of the breadth of moral and sumptuary laws in Plymouth Colony shows the concern for posterity. It was incumbent upon the older generation to keep the community along the path of reformation as envisaged by the founders. There should be no leeway for persons of weak character, who gave in easily to temptations of the flesh, to corrupt the whole of society. And it was also important, for the success of their mission, that the younger generation should not be exposed to any unpunished refractory behavior of their elders. The young, too, must be strictly disciplined to the responsibilities of carrying on the dream of the founders. There was no generation gap in Plymouth. All considered themselves young in spirit—it could not be otherwise for an undertaking in a strange new world. In a sense it was the youthful and adventurous spirit that the Pilgrims did not want to lose sight of. The Pilgrims had not sought a new home in the wilderness to grow up with the country—to reach a plateau of self-satisfaction or mature into a different people. Rather, they wanted to keep the country and themselves young forever. Rugged individualism and an idealism that called for the constant striving for perfection, to the mind of the Pilgrims, required a spartan discipline on the part of old and young alike.

Frontier people have always had an inordinate concern with vice. It would seem from their preoccupation that vice is more prevalent in the primitive society than in the more civilized and stable community. But actually vice is readily spotted in the newly established community, where everyone is intimately acquainted, and where it is considered a grave threat to the serious business of building a new way of life.[1]

Particularly the colony stressed certain areas where neglectful or excessive conduct endangered the well-being of the community: namely, Sabbath observance, sex, drinking, swearing, gambling, vagrancy, and idleness.

Keeping the Sabbath holy was taken for granted by the early Pilgrims—as a matter of fact, they came under severe criticism in 1624 for a too strict observance, to the "Neglecte of familie

duties" on the Lord's day.[2] Although persons were punished for
Sabbath breaking earlier, there was no statutory provision until
1651, when the General Court ordered that failure to attend
church by any person, whether a church member or not, and any
"prophanation" of the Sabbath, such as "doeing any servill
worke," were offenses each subject to a 10*s*. fine or whipping.
Masters were responsible for attendance by their servants.[3] It is
interesting to note, however, that the compulsory church attendance law was repealed in 1659 and not revived until the incorporation with Massachusetts.[4]

Laws on the profanation of the Sabbath, however, were expanded: for example, a 12*d*. fine was the penalty for smoking
tobacco within two miles of the meeting house, "violent ryding"
was prohibited, and constables had to report to the General Court
persons who "sleep or play about the meeting house in times of
the publicke worship of God."[5] In 1682, the towns were ordered
to appoint a person to check on Sunday travel—however, in the
same year, the fine for working or engaging in sports on Sunday
was reduced to 5*s*.[6] Ordinaries had to remain closed on the
Sabbath and during the weekly lecture.[7]

There are numerous instances in the *Records* of sentences
(sometimes at variance with the law) of whipping, the stocks, or
fines (ranging from 2*s*. to 40*s*.) for breach of the Sabbath. A jury
trial could be granted in flagrant cases.[8] "Quarreling and fighting"
on the Sabbath brought a 40*s*. fine.[9] Perhaps the most literal
enforcement of the Sabbath laws was that of Lieutenant James
Wyatt, who was "sharply reproved for his writing a note about
common business on the Lord's day, att least in the evening
somewhat to soone."[10] And the most unfortunate case was that of

> Ann, the wife of Thomas Savory, [who] was presented before the
> Court to answere for being att home on the Lords day with Thomas
> Lucas att unseasonable time, viz., in the time of publicke exercise in
> the worshipe of God, and for being found drunke att the same time
> under an hedge, in uncivell and beastly manor, was sentanced by the
> Court as followeth, viz.: for her accompanying of the said Lucas
> att an unseasonable time as aforsaid, she was sentanced to sitt in the
> stockes during the pleasure of the Court, which accordingly was
> performed and executed; and for her being found drunke as
> aforsaid, fined five shillings; and for prophaning the Lords day, fined
> ten shillings, according to the lawes in such cases provided.[11]

A great deal of time was consumed by the magistrates in deciding upon cases involving unlawful sexual relations. Although, at
the outset of settlement, the Pilgrims drew up "stringent laws and
ordinances upon the subject of fornication and adultery,"[12] the
early years were relatively "free from wickedness and vice."[13] In
the 1630's, the Pilgrims were only slightly troubled with an
occasional assault, Sabbath breaking, drunkenness, gambling, or
fornication before marriage case.[14] But after 1640, "some kind
of wickednes did grow and breake forth."[15]

The banner year for sex crime was 1642. Convictions of incest,
"lude caryages," homosexual sodomy, and fornication before
marriage brought a whipping or the stocks for the persons involved. Thomas Granger, a servant lad of sixteen years, was
executed for buggery. Bradford implies there were other reports of
sex crimes that did not reach the stage of presentment to the
court. Combined with other breaches of the law—vagrancy,
drunkenness, and the like—and a fear "of a generall conspiracy
intended by the natives to cutt of all the English in this land," it is
no wonder that the prevalence of evil "may justly be marveled at,
and cause us to fear and tremble at the consideration of our
corrupte natures, which are so hardly bridled, subdued, and
mortified."[16]

The sex crime wave of 1642 caused the Pilgrim authorities to
conduct a thorough soul-searching and to examine the whole
category of sexual offenses and punishments and the legal procedure that should be accorded the accused. The most disturbing
question of "what sodomiticall acts are to be punished with death"
was entrusted to a panel of three ministers—John Reyner, Ralph
Partridge, and Charles Chauncey. Citing scriptural and "moral
law," the ministers, in rendering separate opinions, agreed that
unnatural sex acts merited the death penalty; but they merely
confused the issue by recognizing differences between simple and
aggravated acts as well as considering the commission of concurrent
crimes. Thus adulterous or incestuous relationships, age and consent of the parties, coercion, and other factors had to be considered in gauging the weight of the offense. Chauncey argued that
each society has to adopt its own morality. The scriptures cannot
provide complete direction on every matter, and he cites, as an
example, that "there is no express [scriptural] law against destroying conception in the wombe by potions."[17] It is probably because

of this inability of the clergy to arrive at any clear definition of capital sex crimes as well as the difficulty in obtaining proof that no person after 1642 was put to death for a sexual offense—and the execution of Granger stands as the only such instance.

Considering the record in Massachusetts and the emphasis in Plymouth upon scriptural authority, the leniency in dealing with sex offenses is rather striking. Brief comment on the handling of specific sex crimes will bear out this point.

A conviction for a homosexual act brought any or all of whipping, branding, and banishment.[18] There is some indication, however, that unless complainants sought legal remedy, the state took no action.[19] A lesbian offender was ordered to make "publick acknowlidgment and [to] take heed for future otherwise greater punishment."[20] A person punished for buggery in the later years of the colony incurred a severe whipping, sitting on the gallows with a rope around the neck, and branding on the forehead "with a Roman P to signify his abominable pollution, and soe depart this government."[21]

The court failed to develop any *prima facie* case of incest, and it was reluctant to return a verdict in such a capital crime on any other grounds. Hence, when a woman gave birth to an illegitimate child, which was "suspected to be begotten" by her own father—a confession, however, which the daughter would not make—she was whipped for "whoredome."[22] The general practice was to bring acquittal on the incest charge but to return conviction for an "unclean" act, which entailed whipping.[23] Conviction for rape, a capital offense, merited whipping or exile or both.[24] It seems that the Pilgrim fathers allowed lesser pleas in capital sex cases and mitigated punishment for several reasons: the uncertainty as to the facts of a case; the hesitance to taint society with blood; and what appears to be a general belief that the crime must fit the punishment—a life only for a life. They did not share the opinion in England that a crime carried with it a greater potential danger than the act itself. Furthermore, a person should have the benefit of being warned of the gravity of his offense and have the opportunity to make retribution by future good behavior.

Most fornication cases involved birth of a child before twenty-seven weeks of marriage had passed. Conviction for this offense—"carnal coppulation before marriage, after contract"—usually brought a £3-£5 fine and occasionally the stocks for each party;

if definite proof of the facts of the crime was worthcoming, the fine
upon conviction could be £10.[25] Since fornication could seldom
be proved, unless paternity was involved or in unusual circumstances when there might be a witness or a confession, those
accused were allowed to plead to "unclean" or lewd acts. As a
misdemeanor, lewdness carrying the suspicion of fornication
merited fines of 20s.-50s. for each party.[26] Lewdness in accosting
women led to a sentence to the stocks, with the "fact" of the
crime on one's hat or a whipping.[27] A good example of changing
a fornication case—based upon the testimony of only one party—
into a lesser charge was to try a man for "lacivious and light
behaviour with Deborah Woodcocke" and being the putative
father of the girl's child; the sentence was whipping and provision
for child support of 20d. for three years.[28] Apparently the court
reasoned that the man, if not the child's father, could well have
been from his general deportment.

Guilty persons in adultery cases were sentenced to whipping,
and frequently both parties had to wear the initials "AD" on the
left sleeve. If caught without the letters, they were subject to
whipping.[29] Divorce was granted on grounds of adultery; in such
an action brought by the wife, she could be awarded one-third of
her husband's property.[30] Bigamy was simply treated as adultery.
The penalty was whipping and recognition for grounds of
divorce.[31] When an adulterous liaison was suspected, the couple
would be threatened with whipping if they continued to see each
other.[32] As in other sex cases, alleged adultery was usually treated
as a misdemeanor, which meant the magistrates could use their
discretion in disposing of the case.

Many prosecutions for sexual offenses were dropped after
presentment, probably because warning was considered a sufficient deterrent. It is also important to note that the court carefully
scrutinized the testimony of a complainant, and frequently held
him partially responsible for the crime. Thus, for example, after a
wife had been convicted of lewd conduct with another man, the
husband had to sit in the stocks "for leaveing his family, and
exposing his wife to such temptations."[33] No wonder there was a
hesitancy to make accusations.

Upon landing in the New World, the Pilgrims were worried
about their low supply of beer; but they seemed to have had
enough "strong water" (probably Dutch gin) to entertain on

several occasions that freeloading Indian sachem, Massasoit.[34] What had been "pleasant to them" in Europe and succor on the oceanic crossing, however, in the wilderness, as with other frontier folk, would turn into a demon. By the many laws and entries of cases for drunkenness, one gathers that tippling, if not outright alcoholism, posed a major social problem.

Drunkenness and to "suffer any to drinke druncke in their houses" were early made misdemeanors, punished by "the discretion of the bench."[35] It was assumed that anyone imbibing more than an hour at a tavern would become drunk, and, therefore, the tavern keeper had to send away anyone drinking beyond this period or pay a 12*d*. fine; the fine for the person continuing to drink was 4*s*. 4*d*. In 1646, drunkenness was punishable by a 5*s*. fine for the first default, 10*s*. for the second, and, if unable to pay the fine, "to be sett in the stocks." Intoxication must have been a grave problem by this time, for by the same law the General Court set up a test for drunkenness—a common sense method, which many an overzealous policeman since has found convenient:

> And by drunkennesse is understood a person that either lisps or faulters in his speech by reason of overmuch drink, or that staggers in his going or that vomitts by reason of excessive drinking, or cannot follow his calling.[36]

So that no drunkard would go unpunished, constables and grand jurymen were charged with reporting offenders to the General Court, and the towns were required to appoint two or three persons to investigate ordinaries or "any other places suspected." An ordinary keeper failing to report drunkenness on his premises was fined 5*s*. and could also lose his license.[37] Before the statutory enactment of 1646, drunkenness was punished with a 20*s*.-40*s*. fine, the stocks, or whipping.[38] With a few exceptions, such as a £5 fine for drunkenness "both in the Bay and at Scituate" or 50*s*. for a repeated offender,[39] the 5*s*. fine for the first offense and 10*s*. for the second became standard.[40] For the third offense, the Pilgrims held out incentives: for example, a sentence of whipping was suspended "until hee shalbe taken drunke the next time, and then hee is to be forthwith taken and whipt, without further presenting to the Court."[41] Also, for a three-time offender in 1681, it was required that £10 sureties be put up to guarantee good behavior until the next court session—it appears that the culprit kept sober during the period for he was released of his bond.[42] The Pilgrims gave up on the unredeemable alcoholic. Thus,

> Thomas Lucas, for being distempered with drinke, it being soe oftens, and that hee hath borne severall particular punishments gradually, and can not be reclaimed, it was ordered concerning him, that all that sell drinke be stricktly ordered and prohibited to lett him have none.[43]

Gambling did not cause concern until the later years. But in 1656

> Wheras complaint is made that some have brought Cards into some of the townes of this Jurisdiction wherby sundry young persons mens both children and servants have ben drawne together to spend their time in playing at such unlawfull games to the corrupting of youth with sundry other sadd consequences

a 40s. fine was placed upon card or dice players and anyone who permitted playing in his house; children were to be punished at their parents' discretion for the first offense and "publickly whipt" for the second.[44] The few convictions for gambling brought fines ranging from 10s. to 40s. for the first offense to £2 for repeated infractions if one's house was used.[45] Horse-racing, forbidden by statute in 1674, upon penalty of 5s. or the stocks for one hour,[46] was never the subject of prosecution by the colony.

Although the law of 1640 provided a 12d. fine for swearing and left to the magistrates' discretion whether to substitute a prison term or the stocks "according to the nature and quality of the person," penalties matched other misdemeanors—a 5s.-10s. fine and occasionally a few hours in the stocks or a day in prison. The most severe penalty was a 20s. fine for a person "detected in cursing and swearing and running away from the Court." One could be disfranchised for swearing, but none were.[47]

Combining moral law with positive law is also evident in the Pilgrims' attempt to preserve a society of like-minded and fit persons. The Colony and towns passed ordinances prohibiting the residence of undesirables, especially against those who might become a public charge. Warning out notices were given by the town selectmen for those whom the town voted exclusion. This local authority received endorsement for all the Puritan colonies from the commissioners of the United Colonies. Various criteria for excluding persons were used by the Plymouth towns: persons who owned no land, idlers, persons with a reputation for disorderly conduct, those who came without obtaining permission, "sojourners which came but for a seasone," suspicious strangers, and persons of known dissenting religious views.[48] The colony as early as 1632 gave "warning in open courte to all our people" not to receive any such persons, "but to acquainte us first therewith that we may inquire of ther certificates or dismissions." It was also declared that "we have libertie to punish shuch things at our discretions." Eventually the consent of the governor and two magistrates were required for entry into the colony.[49] In 1642, the towns were empowered to exclude persons likely to become a public charge.[50]

The most far-reaching statutory enactment against vagrants, which the Pilgrims considered to be in accordance with English law, was passed in 1661, with apparently the Quakers in mind. It gave powers to the marshal or town constable to apprehend anyone whom he deemed a "vagabond;"

> and upon examination soe appeering; hee shall whip them or cause them to be whipt with rodds; soe as it exceed not fifteen stripes; and to give him or them a passe to depart the Government and if any such person or persons shalbee found without theire passe; or not acteing according therunto they shalbee punished againe as formerly; and incase any Constable of this Jurisdiction shalbee unwilling or can not procure any to Inflict the punishment aforsaid; that then they shall bringe such persons to Plymouth to the under Marshall and he shall Inflict it.[51]

This law was in line with the recommendation of the commissioners of the United Colonies that Quakers be banished and upon a third return to a colony be put to death. The Pilgrims, of course, stopped short of enacting the capital penalty, which Massachusetts had adopted and was enforcing.

Since the warning out of persons coming into a colony devolved, in the first instance, upon the towns, it became impossible to exclude a band of "subversives" when they made up the major part of a new town. This was the trouble the Pilgrims ran across with the Quakers, and it explains the leniency of the colony toward dissenters in the later years.[52] In 1678, when much of the fears of immigration into the colony had been dispelled, the fine for ignoring a warning out order was fixed at 5s. for each week the newcomer stayed.[53] However, before this time, the penalty of whipping and forced exile, with the constable taking a person to the border of the colony, was very sparingly enforced, except during the Quaker scare of the late 1650's.[54]

The brunt of the repressive legislation against vagrants or "vagabonds" fell upon those who encouraged and abetted their stay in the colony. In the town of Plymouth no one could entertain a newcomer in his home beyond a fortnight without informing the selectmen, upon penalty of 10s. As a general practice, security had to be put up by anyone who received a visitor who had not been granted permission to enter.[55] In this area, however, town authority could be subjected to the executive order of the governor. For example, acting upon information that a Quaker troublemaker was on his way from Boston to Sandwich, Governor Bradford issued a special warrant that none could "entertain" him; several assistants, however, persuaded the old governor to allow the Quaker to remain in the colony until springtime.[56]

As would be expected, some friction developed between Massachusetts and Plymouth over passing off undesirables on each other. James Luxford, who had been whipped and had had his ears cropped in Massachusetts for defrauding his employer, John Winthrop, went to Plymouth and was the defendant in several actions for indebtedness.[57] The Massachusetts authorities considered it "a bold Act; and no smale Affront" when Plymouth sent three Narragansett Indians and a squaw with a baby to Boston.[58] One instance provoked the tempers of authorities in both colonies and involved the commissioners of the United Colonies in heated discussion. This was the sending of a poor "distracted person," Hannah Bumpas, out of the Massachusetts town of Hingham, where she had been a resident for a year, into Plymouth Colony. Such an action by the selectmen at Hingham was considered by Plymouth as a violation of Article Thirteen of the Articles of Confederation, which said that a person unwanted at a new abode had to return to the place of former residency. The woman was brought into Marshfield, which led to a suit against the conductors by three selectmen of Marshfield —the only actionable case of this sort on record. The Plymouth court of assistants fined the defendants £5. What happened to the poor woman afterwards is not known, but probably she was allowed to stay in Marshfield, where there were other persons by the same family name—and at least one of whom, as a youth, was also considered mentally deranged.[59]

In the holy commonwealth, every person was expected to have a sense of calling, which meant primarily a motivation to work. There was no reason for anyone to be idle. Early in the colony's history, therefore, the magistrates made it their business to discourage neglect of duty. In 1639, they assumed discretionary authority to deal with this problem.

> It is enacted by the Court That the Grand Jury men of every Towne shall have power within their severall Towneshipps to take a speciall view and notice of all manner of persons married or single dwelling within their severall Townes that have smale meanes to mayntaine them and are suspected to live idlely and loosely and to require an account of them how they live, And such as they fynd delinquent and cannot give a good account thereof unto them that they cause the Constable to bring them before the Governor and Assistants at Plymouth the first Court of Assistants after such delinquents shalbe found out. That such course may be taken with them as in the wisdome of the Government shalbe adjudged just and equall.[60]

The towns could also warn out idle or disorderly persons; and they could bind out poor children, whose parents "have releefe from the Towns."[61] Entertaining another man's servant without permission was an actionable offense, and, in one such case, a jury found damages of 30*s.* plus court costs for the plaintiff.[62]

The Pilgrims felt that idleness like disorderly conduct was best punished by setting a public example—namely, by whipping or prison sentence. Indeed the intent in building a house of correction was to punish idlers and young people who did not obey their parents.[63] But there is no record that anyone was convicted under the law for idleness. The reason is that the laws against disorderly conduct, such as drinking beyond a certain time or smoking in the streets, vagrancy, and Sabbath breaking amply covered most cases of idleness. Also the Pilgrims were a rural folk, with plenty of work for everyone, and, as modern sociologists have discovered, where there is opportunity for gainful employment, a person will usually choose to work. Another factor curtailing idleness was the close attention that the Plymouth authorities gave to providing strict supervision of the young. It was a common practice of the state to take charge of unruly children, orphans, and those whose parents were too poor to care for them and to place them under guardians.

If the Pilgrims in their legislation seemed to adhere too much to the ideal of a Genevan city state, the reluctance and leniency in enforcing the moral and sumptuary laws revealed a liberal and humanitarian temper. In the closed rural society of Plymouth colony, social ostracism was often sufficient in itself to bring about reform, or at least better discretion, on the part of a wayward soul. If one considers the congeries of blue codes in our own time that have accumulated on the dusty shelves of local archives, the Plymouth record of regulating the private lives of individuals appears scanty and moderate indeed.

NOTES

1. For much the same reasons, Bradford emphasized the need of a primitive community to be attentive to the moral turpitude: "I would rather thinke . . . that Satane hathe more power in these heathen lands . . . then in more Christian nations . . . it may be in this case as it is with waters when their streams are stopped or dammed up, when they gett passage they flow with more violence, and make more noys and disturbance, then when they are suffered to rune quietly in their owne chanels. So wikedness being here more stopped by strict laws, and the same more nerly looked unto, so as it cannot rune in a comone road of liberty as it would, and is inclined, it searches every wher, and at last breaks out wher it getts vente . . . here the people are but few in comparison of other places, which are full and populous, and lye hid, as it were, in a wood or thickett, and many horrible evills by that means are never seen nor knowne; wheras hear, they are, as it were, brought into the light, and set in the plaine field, or rather on a hill, made conspicuous to the view of all." *Bradford*

Hist. (1912), II, 309-10. Edmund S. Morgan contends in *The Puritan Family: Essays on Religion and Domestic Relations in Seventeenth Century New England* (Boston, 1944), 90 ff. that the Puritans were so conscious of keeping their children in the fold they were detracted from their missionary zeal. For the role of officials in enforcing moral and sumptuary laws in early New England, see David H. Flaherty, *Privacy in Colonial New England* (Charlottesville, 1972), Chapter 7.

2. *Bradford Hist.* (1912), I, 362 and 362-3n.

3. *PCR,* XI, 57-58.

4. *Ibid.,* 122. As early as 1639 the question of non-church attendance by those working or living on remote farms was considered by the Ply. Church—particularly whether a person could be represented by a substitute in church and whether servants working in a remote area should go to their master's homes for the Lord's Day. John Reyner and William Brewster to the Ply. Church, Aug. 5, 1639, Ply. Col.—Pilgrims MSS—Misc. NYPL. Eventually, as noted before, exemption from public worship was permitted by the General Court for settlers who lived at a great distance from a church provided they met in private worship. Profanation of the Sabbath seemed to be on the increase in the later years, as witnessed by the election sermons of Thomas Walley (1669) and Samuel Arnold (1674). George Shove wrote Gov. Hinckley in 1682 "that some effectual provision" should be made "against the open profanation of the Lord's Day. I must confess, it is very hard to suppress that sin in some parts of our Colony, and I fear every day will render this more difficult." Feb. 23, 1682, *HP,* 58.

5. *PCR,* XI, 224-25 (1669).

6. *Ibid.,* 258.

7. *Ibid.,* 137 (1662), 258 (1682).

8. For various kinds of breach of the Sabbath and punishments, see *ibid.,* I, 44 (1636), 92 (1638); II, 140 (1649), 156 (1650), 173 (1651); III, 47 (1654), 186 (1660); IV, 50 (1664); V, 27 (1669); VI, 178 (1686); VIII, 135 (1671), 142-43 (1674). In all, it is estimated that about sixty cases of Sabbath breaking were brought before the court of assistants.

9. E.g., *ibid.,* V, 253-54 (1678).

10. *Ibid.,* III, 150 (1658). See also Alice M. Earle, *The Sabbath in Puritan New England* (New York, 1892), 246. Cf. a ridiculous case in Mass. also involving a soldier: Jonathan Atherton was fined two weeks pay for cutting a piece from his hat and putting it in his

shoe. Petition of Jonathan Atherton, July 30, 1676, MA, Military, LXIX, 29.

11. *PCR,* III, 212 (1661).

12. Quoted from Isaac de Rasieres' letter of 1628 in *Bradford Hist.* (1912), II, 60n.

13. John Pory to the Earl of Southampton, Jan. 13, 1623, Sydney V. James, Jr., ed., *Three Visitors to Early Plymouth* (Plymouth, Mass., 1963), 11.

14. *PCR,* I, *passim.*

15. *Bradford Hist.* (1912), II, 308.

16. *Ibid.,* 309, 328-29; *PCR,* II, 35-52, *passim.*

17. *Bradford Hist.* (1912), II, 310, 315-328.

18. E.g., *PCR,* I, 64 (1637).

19. As evidenced in the proceedings of the case cited above; also that it took a number of complaints before a man who had the habit of "meddling with mens privitys" during worship at the Barnstable church was finally excommunicated by the church (no civil prosecution followed), and the disciplinary action was partially based on his being slack in the "duty of prayer." Lothrop, Diary, Sep. 5, 1641, 355-56, Yale U. Lib.

20. *PCR,* II, 163 (1650).

21. *Ibid.,* VI, 75 (1681).

22. *Ibid.,* V, 21.

23. E.g., *ibid.,* III, 199-200 (1660).

24. *Ibid.,* VI, 98 (1682).

25. E.g., *ibid.,* I, 12 (1633); II, 109-10 (1646); IV, 77 (1664), 83-84 (1665), 182 (1668); V, 27 (1669), 32 (1670); VIII, 135 (1671). A rare conviction for fornication in which paternity was not the cause of the prosecution was that of a man who had cohabited with his dead wife's sister—he was fined £20. *Ibid.,* VI, 20 (1679). In the Plymouth County Court, a man was fined 50*s.* because his wife had given birth twelve weeks after marriage, and a woman was whipped for not confessing who the father of her baby was (an Indian was suspected). Records of Sessions of the Peace (1686-1721), June 1688, 24 and 34, Pilgrim Hall, Ply., Mass.

26. *PCR,* VI, 195 (1686); IV, 50 (1664).

27. *Ibid.,* III, 159 (1659), 210 (1661); VI, 176 (1685). Although there was no law against "mixed dancing," the Pilgrims frowned on it—witness the attitude toward the carrying-on around the maypole at Morton's Merry-Mount. Only one instance seems to

have been reported to the court, in which the woman charged was "cleared with admonition." *Ibid.,* III, 5 (1652).

28. *Ibid.,* VI, 63 (1681).

29. *Ibid.,* II, 28 (1641), III, 111-12 (1657); Andrew M. Davis, "The Law of Adultery and Ignominious Punishments—with Especial Reference to the Penalty of Wearing a Letter Affixed to the Clothing," *AASP,* X (1896), 101, 103, 105, 110-11, 117-20. Wearing letters probably originated in the English ecclesiastical courts.

30. E.g., *PCR,* III, 221 (1661).

31. *Ibid.,* VI, 44-45 (1680).

32. *Ibid.,* III, 37 (1653). Kissing the wife of another and neglecting a summons led to a 20*s.* fine. *Ibid.,* IV, 50 (1664). No single women were involved in adultery cases, and the wife of an adulterer could seek no relief in the courts for the wrong that had been done her. John Demos, *A Little Commonwealth: Family Life in Plymouth Colony* (New York, 1970), 97.

33. *PCR,* 112 (1657).

34. *Mourt's Relation,* 40, 49, 51; *Bradford Hist.* (1912), I, 164, 196-97.

35. *PCR,* XI, 17, 96 (1636), 173 (1639).

36. *Ibid.,* 50, 113, 197. "Lyers drunkards swearers" could also be disfranchised. *Ibid.,* 177 (1658); see Chapter 2.

37. *Ibid.,* V, 59 (1671); XI, 123 (1659), 197 (1646); Records of Sessions of the Peace (1686-1721), 7, Pilgrim Hall, Ply., Mass. For comment on the ups and downs of the proprietors of an ordinary in Duxbury, 1638-76, see Justin Winsor, *History of the Town of Duxbury, Massachusetts* (Boston, 1849), 46-47, 76.

38. *PCR,* I, 12, 36, 44 (1636), 100 (1638), 106, 132 (1639).

39. *Ibid.,* II, 66 (1643); IV, 29 (1662).

40. E.g., *ibid.,* III, 150 (1658), 168 (1659); IV, 162 (1667), 173 (1659), 187 (1668); V, 16 (1669), 31, 39 (1670), 61 (1670), 107 (1672), 117 (1673), 254 (1678); VI, 16 (1679), 82 (1682), 125 (1684); VIII, 135 (1671), 153 (1679).

41. *Ibid.,* IV, 33 (1663).

42. *Ibid.,* VI, 78-79. In 1682 the church at Plymouth petitioned for a more rigid enforcement of laws against drunkenness. The petitioners asked Gov. Hinckley to take sterner measures: "the Lord calls upon you in your political capacity" to "be a terror to evil-doers, and therefore not to suffer such offenders to pass without due shame and punishment . . . ." It was also recommended that there be only one

ordinary in a town, whereas there were usually four or five opened at all hours. John Cotton (Jr.), Pastor, and Thomas Cushman, Elder, with the consent of the Church to the gov. and assistants, Mar. 7, 1682, *HP*, 59.

43. *PCR*, V, 169 (1675). Various laws were also passed to discourage smoking. It was punishable by a 12*d*. fine and 2*s*. for a second conviction to smoke on the streets or in and around such places as barns and haystacks—although soldiers could smoke on the streets at time of trainings. Smoking on the Sabbath was forbidden as well as within a certain radius of the meeting house. A person serving on a jury was fined 5*s*. for each time he was caught smoking. *Ibid.*, I, 106 (1639); XI, 36 (1640), 53 (1646).

44. *Ibid.*, XI, 66, 96, 173.

45. *Ibid.*, IV, 42, 47 (1663); VI, 15, 20 (1679); VIII, 152-53 (1679).

46. *Ibid.*, XI, 236.

47. *Ibid.*, I, 35 (1635); II, 9, 12 (1641), 37 (1642); III, 199 (1660); IV, 43 (1663), 52, 76-77 (1664); V, 27 (1669), 94, 107 (1672), 253 (1678); VI, 94 (1682); XI, 33-34, 95, 172-73 (1640), 101 (1658).

48. The gov. and assistants of Ply. to gov. and assistants of Mass., Feb. 6, 1632, *Winthrop Papers*, III (1943), 65; Richard L. Bowen, *Early Rehoboth: Documented Historical Studies of Families and Events in This Plymouth Colony Township,* 4 vols. (Rehoboth, Mass., 1945-50), II, 133-165; Josiah H. Benton, *Warning Out in New England, 1656-1817* (Boston, 1911), 10, 18, 26-27, 49, 155. Bowen has printed extensively the extant warning out notices for the colony.

49. *PCR*, I, 105 (1638); V, 155 (1674); XI, 26, 109 (1636), 118 (1658).

50. *Ibid.*, XI, 40. For reputable newcomers approved by a town there was a three month probation period, followed by one year as a non-inhabitant. If a person, however, became a public charge, whoever had been responsible for bringing him into the colony was liable for his upkeep. *Ibid.*, XI, 40 (1642); Jernegan, *Laboring and Dependent Classes,* 191-93.

51. *PCR*, XI, 206.

52. For the view of one who felt the brunt of the policy of treating Quakers as vagrants, see Humphrey Norton, *New England's Ensigne* (1659), copy in NYPL, *passim*. The Quaker problem, primarily one of the right to dissent, is discussed in the following

chapter. For rules proposed by Thomas Willett of Swansea for excluding persons, see Felt, *Ecclesiastical History,* II, 448-49.

53. *PCR,* XI, 248.

54. *Ibid.,* I, 163 (1640); II, 36 (1642); IV, 154 (1667); V, 156 (1674).

55. *Ply. Town Records,* I, 169 (1681); Benton, *Warning Out,* 37; Bowen, *Rehoboth,* II, 135-36; Richards, *History of Marshfield,* I, 30 (Selectmen Records, 1665).

56. George Bishop, *New-England Judged,* revised by Joseph Grove (1703), 39-40, 115.

57. *Winthrop Papers, Letters to, MHSC,* 5th Ser., I (1871), 127n.

58. Mass. Gen. Ct. to Gov. Winslow, Oct. 11, 1675, MA, Military, LXVIII, 5.

59. *PCR,* VII, 175 (1673); on Edward Bumpas, VI, 20 (1679), 155 (1685). Also see Ward, *United Colonies,* 268.

60. *PCR,* XI, 32.

61. *Ibid.,* 38 (1641); Jernegan, *Laboring and Dependent Classes,* 102; Richards, *History of Marshfield,* I, 49 (Selectmen Records).

62. *PCR,* VII, 165 (1671).

63. *Ibid.,* XI, 143-44 (1662).

Chapter Seven

DISSENT

In the little commonwealth there were no waves of protest—certainly not riots, insurgency, or other extralegal action by a large segment of the community, as took place in most of the other colonies at one time or another. But the interlocking of civil authority and religious obligation was bound to create disaffection. The Plymouth state inevitably confronted the right to conscience and its concomitant freedom, the right to expression.

Although the Pilgrims tended to regard criticism against public policy or officials as seditious conduct, unlike Englishmen at home, they did not confuse sedition with treason. Although treason was a capital crime in Plymouth, in no instance was anyone ever charged with this crime because of sedition or any other reason.

Isolated cases of blasphemy and seditious conduct occurred throughout the colony's history. Six grave confrontations, which affected the shaping of a greater toleration in religion and liberalization of civil liberty, were the Lyford, Morton, Williams, Vassall, Gorton, and Quaker affairs.

108

Not until the Quaker scare did the colony give statutory prohibition to blasphemous and seditious expression. In 1658
persons could be disfranchised for being "Apostates from the
Fundamentals of Religion" or who "manifestly appear to be dis-
affected to this Government."[1] After 1655, a law was in force
"That such as shall deny the Scriptures to bee a rule of life
shall receive Corporall punishment according to the descretion
of the Majestrates soe as it shall not extend to life or Limb."[2]

Scoffing at God and religion could be construed as having
seditious intent because of the belief that God had ordained
human society and government. Persons arraigned for blasphemy were usually let off with a reproof if they had confined
their remarks to the Deity. But fines ranged up to 20s. if they
had engaged in other misconduct or had spoken out against
duly constituted authority, such as the ministry.[3] Blasphemy was
most repugnant as a form of contempt of authority rather than
merely a vilification of God. Katherine Aines was sentenced to
wear a "B" on her right arm and to be whipped at both Plymouth
and Taunton for her "blasphemous words" compounded with
"laciviouse behavior."[4] Late examples, in the 1680's, of the
tendency to regard blasphemy as contempt were the fining of
Joseph Palmer 20s. "for speaking contemptuously of the word of
God and of the minnestry"[5] and the arraignment of James Bishop
by the Plymouth County Court "for many Railing and Blasphemous words and contemptious Carriages."[6] That there were
so few cases of simple blasphemy was probably due to the culprit
being considered demented and hence no action would be taken,
and a charge of blasphemy could be fitted into a charge for disorderly conduct, such as drunkenness.[7]

The Pilgrims took a very serious view of any disrespect toward
the magistrates. Common law as well as Mosaic law condemned
any reproach of authority, regardless whether the assertion was
true or false.

"Opprobrious speech" against lawful authority was dealt with
sternly. Hardly had the Pilgrims landed than John Billington had
his neck and heels tied together for a few hours for taking this
liberty against Captain Standish.[8] For defaming a magistrate or
the king, a person was usually warned to desist, but if the attack
was personal and vicious, there could be a heavy fine, up to £30,
whipping, or exile.[9] To call into question a government policy

could also lead to a fine or whipping.[10] Even ministers were not
exempt, as in the case of Samuel Newman, minister at Rehoboth,
who was arraigned (but not tried) for criticizing in a public
meeting the magistrates' leniency toward the Baptists.[11] In the last
years of the colony, about the only concern of the government
relating to sedition involved jurisdictional disputes with Rhode
Island. Orders went out from the governor to arrest leaders who
persuaded settlements to resist Plymouth authority; such persons
were declared public enemies.[12]

To note typical cases where seditious speech had a religious
connotation, we find Lieutenant Matthew Fuller was censured and
fined 50s. in 1650 "for speaking reproachfully of the Court, and
saying the law enacted about minnesters maintainance was a
wicked and a divillish law, and that the divell satt att the sterne
when it was enacted."[13] In 1640, upon complaint of several
ministers, a man who criticized the doctrine on baptism held by
the church at Taunton, was ordered to leave the colony,[14] and
Thomas Pope was fined 10s. in 1670 "for villifying the ministry."[15]
For "opprobrious words against the church of Marshfield, saying
they were all lyers, etc," Kenelm Winslow was imprisoned and
had to put up sureties for good behavior.[16]

Seditious libel was not much of a problem in Plymouth since
the colony had no printing press[17] (and hence, unlike Massachusetts, no censorship agency was established), and circulation of
any printed matter among the poor and unlearned settlers could
not have been very great. There were, however, several prosecutions during the Quaker crisis for possession of written materials
"both false and pernicuous to the government," which, linked
with other subversive activity, resulted in fines, imprisonment, and
whipping.[18] Arthur Howland was convicted of presenting to the
General Court a "writing" which was found "full of factiouse,
seditious, and slanderouse passages, tending to the desturbance of
the peace of this government"—but because of his advanced age
he was let go with a warning.[19] The most celebrated libel case (to
be discussed later), was that of James Cudworth, who was disfranchised for having written a critique of policy toward the
Quakers.[20]

As the old order faced the religious dissent of the "Rising
Generation," it fell to the clergy to remind the people that the
straight and narrow path of the true faith did not allow for

unlimited freedom of expression. Throwing out a salvo for repression, the Reverend Thomas Walley in his 1669 election sermon asked the question of Jeremiah 8:22: "Is there no Balm in Gilead? is there no Physician there? Why there is not the health of the daughter of my people recovered?" False ideas were spreading and in turn were breeding contempt for the authority of the magistrates and ministers.

> If a people contemn *Magistry* and *Ministry,* though they are Gods Ordinances, yet God is provoked to withhold his blessings from them, so that they cannot prevent the ruine and destruction of a proud, wilful and stubborn people, that endeavour to exalt themselves above the Lord and his Appointments. . . . those that are sick hearken to *Mountebanks,* rather then to experienced and tryed Physicians. The Jews in their sick estate held the false Prophets in high esteem, but persecuted the true; and this became the ruine of their Church and State; they looked upon the Lords Prophets as the cause of all their troubles; and hearkened to those that poisoned them in stead of healing them . . . .

In Plymouth, the people were moving out of their lethargy into a "Burning Fever" of factionalism and contentiousness. "Do your utmost for the Extirpation of Profaneness," Walley entreated, "it is a growing Evil in the Country. This is one of the great Works God hath called you that are *Magistrates* and *Deputies* unto." It is the duty of both civil and religious authorities to insure unity among the people.

> Let all Incendiaries be branded, all such as are stirrers up of Strife and Division, that are *Salamanders,* that love to live in the Fire, that are Fire-brands in Church and Common-wealth, that are Instruments of Contention in Court and Country; let such be marked in the Churches, and let them be abhorred by all that love God . . . . Let their Corruptions be kept under by good Lawes and their Manners healed.[21]

Samuel Arnold's election sermon of 1674 emphasized the obligation of the magistrates to enforce the will of God, and not to be misled by the clamor of dissension among the people.

> *God hath delivered the Custody of both Tables into your hands as Magistrates* . . . . Tollerate not things that are intollerable, a bound-

less Toleration will be found at last an intollerable thing; such as differ only in Circumstantials, *Controversal points* and are quiet, peaceable, moderate, and do not busy themselves in learning others, we may and must bear with them . . . . but when persons erre in Fundamentals . . . . such Heresies and Hereticks had need be suppressed.[22]

What seemed to weigh particularly upon the ministers' minds, besides heresy and profaneness, was the audacity of persons standing up to be counted in their refusal to support an established ministry. The dissenters were emboldened by their belief that the Pilgrim authorities dared not compel support to "a church government or ministry as is repugnant to the Church of England."[23] Thus, we find in the later years the right to dissent in religion being bolstered by an English prop. Religious dissent was considered by the government more as a factious disease rather than as sedition. The wailings of the clergy against laxity of the magistrates in tolerating religious dissent is witness that the guardianship of one's conscience in religion (but not, as already shown, in morality) was passing from the magistrates to the clergy. Let us now turn to the more aggravated cases of dissent which were regarded as serious threats to the state.

Plymouth's first encounter with formidable dissent within its ranks led the colony's leaders to charge sedition and a conspiracy to overthrow the government of the colony. It would be Plymouth's only round with what approached criminal conspiracy.

John Lyford arrived in 1624 under the best of auspices. Though a Church of England preacher, he was soon accepted into the Pilgrim church and alternated with Elder Brewster in preaching to the congregation; both he and Brewster served as consultants to the magistrates. Appearing as a humble and amiable man, the Pilgrims provided him and his wife and five children with lodging and subsistence. However, Lyford was never made the pastor of the church, which partially accounts for his holding services outside the church. He began to cater to the malcontents, especially the newcomers (the "Particulars") such as John Oldham, who felt they had not been given a fair share in lands or participation in the government. The Lyford affair is a familiar story, told by Bradford himself with vindictive relish, and hence all the details need not concern us here.[24]

A strong faction formed around Lyford and Oldham, who probably felt that if they championed all the malcontents they would have a majority to take control of the colony's affairs. The governor and several others seized letters by Lyford to persons in England whom the Pilgrims regarded as enemies; copies were made and several originals were kept as evidence of "slander and false accusations, tending not only to their prejudice, but to their ruine and utter subversion." Meanwhile, Oldham refused to perform watch duty, and was summarily put in chains by Standish, an event which would be repeated.

The gist of the letters were the charge against the colony of excluding newcomers from church and society and contemptuous observations on the Pilgrim leaders. Tried by the whole "company," both Lyford and Oldham were sentenced to exile. Lyford, however, was allowed to stay six months before departure, and he used this time to ingratiate himself once again into the good graces of many of the colonists. His change of heart was short-lived; "notwithstanding all his former confessions, convictions, and publick acknowledgments, both in the face of the church and whole company, with so many tears and sadde censures of him selfe before God and men," he wrote a letter to the adventurers, again intercepted, justifying everything he had said before. Lyford's reputation was further tarnished by his wife's revelations that he had fathered an illegitimate son in Ireland and by Edward Winslow's report upon returning from England that the adventurers, facing "like bickering," had conducted a hearing and decided that Lyford was unfit to be pastor at Plymouth. Thus ostracized and still under the sentence of banishment, Lyford, with others of his faction, joined Oldham at Nantasket (the town of Hull); later he became an Anglican pastor in Virginia.

As William Bradford's biographer has noted, Lyford was a convenient scapegoat, serving as a "guilt symbol" of a primitive community, which had the effect of aiding the consolidation of the social order.[25]

Thomas Morton's Merry Mount (or Mount Wollaston), at the present site of Quincy, posed only an external threat to the security of Plymouth, but as such involved the right of persons living beyond the limits of the colony to pursue their interests unmolested by a neighboring established society. The "vilanie" of selling guns to the Indians in order to quicken the supply of furs, the anarchy among the Merry Mount ex-bound servants who had followed Morton's advice to mutiny against Captain Wollaston, the "riotous prodigallitie and profuse excess," the maintaining "(as it were) a School of Atheism," and simply the competition against Plymouth's own fur trading enterprise were reasons that moved the Plymouth authorities to uproot these impediments to a good society.[26]

But Plymouth did not take the initiative in breaking up the settlement. Not until 1628, three years after Morton's arrival, when "sundrie of the cheefe of the stragling plantations,[27] meeting togither, agreed by mutuall consente to sollissite those of Plymouth (who were then of more strength then them all) to joyne with them, to prevente the further growth of this mischeefe, and supress Morton and his consorts before they grew to further head and strength," did Plymouth act. The colony dispatched its fiery military chieftain at the head of a company of eight to arrest the "Lord of Misrule." Morton was brought to Plymouth, and was sent on the next boat to England, only to return the next year. He established himself in his old haunts, now under Salem's jurisdiction and soon to be part of Massachusetts. But being dealt with highhandedly by the Puritan authorities, he again returned to England, where he tried to create disfavor for both Massachusetts and Plymouth, but was effectively countered by the colonies' agent, Edward Winslow. During the next decade not much is known about Morton, but he did serve a jail term in England. When eventually he returned to Massachusetts, he was put into the stocks and imprisoned. In 1644, we find Morton back in Plymouth, where he could have stayed unmolested ("for we are diversely minded"), but the "odium of our people" was too much for him[28] and he removed to Rhode Island. Somehow he soon turned up a prisoner in Massachusetts, charged with having "set forth a book against us" and having complained against Massachusetts to the Privy Council. He was kept in jail a year without trial and fined £100; unable to pay the fine he could have been whipped, but because he was now "old and crazy," he was allowed to go to Acomenticus (in Maine), where he died two years later.

Perhaps no New Englander suffered more for ill-fame (except a few of the Quakers) than did Morton. He had all his property taken away; he was whipped, imprisoned, banished, and scandalized. Whatever was the true character of the man is not important; that he was victimized for living the life of a raucous frontiersman too close to the community and writing and speaking against the New England oligarchy is a black mark upon the history of liberty in early New England. In his condemnation of the Pilgrims, he tended to forget, however, the economic base for his persecution. To Morton, Plymouth was a true conformist state:

> So that, when they finde any man like to proove an enemy to their Church and state, then straight the meanes must be used for defence. The first precept in their Politiques is to defame the man at whome they aime, and then hee is a holy Israelite in their opinions who can spread that fame brodest, like butter upon a loafe: no matter how thin, it will serve for a vaile: and then this man (who they have thus depraved) is a spotted uncleane leaper: hee must out, least hee pollute the Land, and them that are cleane.[29]

Roger Williams never ruffled the Pilgrims during his assistant pastorate at Plymouth, 1632-34, as he did the Puritans of the Bay Colony; the Pilgrims never really felt unkindly towards him. His rigid Separatism was no more offensive to the Pilgrims than the Puritanism of other New England ministers. But Williams did slightly prick the conscience of the Pilgrims and soon his services were not so much desired. He berated his congregation for not disciplining members who had attended Anglican worship while visiting in England, which would be similar to his later criticism of the Massachusetts churches for not being truly reformed. Also, Williams's chief reason for coming to America, to save "Native Soules," did not strike a response among the conservative Pilgrims.[30]

Probably Williams argued for limiting magisterial authority to civil affairs in Plymouth; but, in any case, Bradford simply cites the contention he began to breed in the churches and says nothing about his views on church and state. After his return to Salem, Williams's denouncing of land acquired by patent and charter did not set well with the Pilgrims, even though they agreed with him that land should be purchased from the Indians.[31] Writing from hindsight, Nathaniel Morton indicates that the Pilgrims followed Williams's errors in the Bay Colony with misgiving. When Williams went into exile from Massachusetts, the

Pilgrims advised him—and to their relief he agreed—to settle beyond the Plymouth bounds.[32] Though the Plymouth authorities had avoided a direct confrontation with Williams, they sought to avoid the displeasure of Massachusetts by supporting his banishment.

With the suppression by the Massachusetts authorities of the Hutchinson-Wheelwright faction, Samuel Gorton, a clothier by trade and lay preacher, who had resided less than a year in Boston, hurried off to Plymouth. His unorthodox opinions on religion—akin to the beliefs of the Familists and Levellers—soon brought suspicion, especially when he "began to leaven that jurisdiction" with his "atheistical" views. Although keeping his political doctrines to himself, he was known to hold that magisterial power belonged only to God, which, in the mind of the Pilgrims, would make each person a judge of each other and thereby produce anarchy. Ralph Smith, pastor of the Plymouth Church, fanned the controversy when he ordered Gorton and his family to leave his house, where they had been living, because of offensive remarks by Gorton. This Gorton refused to do; and to complicate matters, his maid, a widowed woman named Ellen Aldridge, received a summons to appear in court for smiling in church. Gorton, however, went in her stead. At the informal hearing, he spoke contemptuously of magisterial power over private conscience: "If Satan [Bradford, who was presiding] will accuse the breathren, let him come downe from Jehoshuahs right hand and stand here." Then turning to the spectators, he stretched his arms, and declared: "Yee see good people how yee are abused! Stand for your liberty; And let them not bee parties and judges, with many other opprobrious speeches of that kinde." When he had finished, several elders present called upon the court to dispense some "condign punishment" upon Gorton for his "seditious carriage."[33]

As a result, for his "misdemeanors in the open Court towards the elders, the Bench, and stirring up the people to mutynie in the face of the Court," Gorton was fined £20 and had to put up sureties for his good behavior for fourteen days, after which time he was to be banished.[34] Gorton would probably have not been exiled from Plymouth for his religious opinions alone at this time; but contempt for constituted authority was more than the Pilgrims could endure.

From Plymouth, Gorton went to a disputed area claimed by both Rhode Island and Massachusetts. His misfortune increased; he was whipped in Rhode Island, and later he was abducted by agents from Massachusetts and detained in Boston under rough treatment. Finally he was sent to England. His accusations there, embodied in his famous pamphlet, served to discredit the New England governments; but England, at the height of civil war, paid little attention to his ordeal in New England. His views, however, later influenced the investigation of the royal commissioners in 1665.[35]

Legitimate dissent is exercised in a free society through the right to be heard in legislative assembly or in petition. William Vassall of Scituate joined with the Presbyterian faction in Boston to test this right. Vassall was a respected man in the colony, having served as a deputy and a member of the colony's war council.[36] Formerly he had been one of the original assistants of the Massachusetts Bay Company. Up to the time of his controversial petition, he had been embroiled only in the internal factionalism of his church.[37]

In the petition of 1645, submitted to both the Massachusetts and Plymouth General Courts, Vassall called for complete religious toleration for all faiths—"Turk, Jew, Papist, Arian, Socinian, Nicholaytan, Familist, or any other"—provided they "preserve the civil peace and submit unto government." The petition also asked for establishment of English laws. Meanwhile, Vassall supported a similar petition in Boston "much enlarged" from his own, the famous "Child Remonstrance."

When Vassall's petition came up at the October session of the Plymouth General Court, the magistrates were heatedly divided. Winslow "utterly abhorred" the petition and said its acceptance "would make us odious to all Christian commonweales." Governor Bradford and Thomas Prence sided with Winslow, and William Collier probably would have joined them had he been present. Three other assistants—John Browne, Timothy Hatherly, and Edmund Freeman—"applauded it as their Diana." Miles Standish apparently remained neutral. A majority of the deputies favored the petition. Governor Bradford, however, refused to put the petition to a vote, and so the matter was unresolved; a similar fate met Vassall's petition in Boston. Next Vassall sent his petition to Parliament, which was too busy with the internal civil strife to pay much attention to it; and Winslow's agency in England effectively combated the petition and the other charges against the New England Puritans. Vassall soon moved to the Barbados; his counterpart in Massachusetts, Robert Child, was forced to return to England.[38]

While in England, Winslow took up his pen to defend the Massachusetts and Plymouth actions. Answering the "notorious" charges of Child that persons were imprisoned for petitioning the government, Winslow said that he knew of no one imprisoned for exercising this right, but the detainment in Massachusetts of Child and his followers resulted from "their Remonstrance and the many false charges and seditious insinuations tending to faction and insurrection sleighting the government, etc."[39]

One casualty of the affair in Plymouth was the turncoat, as Bradford thought of Edmund Freeman, for his stance during the debate over Vassall's petition. He was denied his seat as an assistant in 1646, an action which left Winslow somewhat puzzled: "I suppose the countrey left [him] out in regard of his professed Anabaptistry and separation from the Churches."[40] For the next decade, the ship of state would rest on relatively quiet waters, until the Quakers rolled in with the tide.

The Quaker problem caught the Pilgrims by surprise. When complaints reached the General Court in early 1657 of persons in Sandwich holding their own worship service, which "they used to invey against minnesters and majestrates, to the dishonor of God and contempt of government," warnings went out to the offenders without any awareness that they were Quakers.[41] But soon "great was the uproar, hearing that we who were called by such a name as quakers, was come into those parts: A great fire was kindled, and the hearts of many did burn within them . . . but the most Part knew not what was the matter." Then began the Quakers' ordeal: orders were given to use force to remove them from the colony—including whipping and imprisonment, if necessary.[42] The new governor was the tough-minded Thomas Prence, who already had a long reputation as a relentless foe of toleration. "Like unto a mad Dog, ready to bite at every one that crosseth his way," he would follow a policy of severe repression until, so he thought, the Quakers would be only too glad to leave the colony. Thomas Hinckley and William Collier were the staunchest supporters of the governor.

Between 1657 and 1660 numerous laws were passed against the Quakers, providing penalties of disfranchisement, imprisonment, fines, whipping, the stocks, seizure of property, and banishment; abetting Quakers such as entertaining them and allowing meetings in one's house were punishable by fines.[43] A resolution of the commissioners of the United Colonies, September 1658, propounded to the General Courts that as the Quakers

> arrogantly and presumptuously do presse into severall of the Jurisdictions and there vent their pernisious and Divellish oppinions which being permited leads mannifestly to the disturbance of our peace, the withdrawing of the hearts of the people from there subjection to Government and soe in issue to cause devision and rueine if not timely prevented

they should be banished, imprisoned on their return, and put to death upon their third entry into the colony.[44] The Plymouth authorities, however, elected not to inflict the extreme penalty.

Yet in Plymouth Quakers faced arbitrary punishment without regard for civil rights. Search and seizure took place without warrant, persons were detained incommunicado without being informed of the charges against them, and penalties were meted out merely at the discretion of a single magistrate. Those allegedly ridiculing the magistracy were instantly whipped. William Brend, an old man, was whipped "for saying unto one of them who accused them for being false prophets, told him he lyed; and the other for signing a Paper wherein it was said John Alden's head shook, and his knees trembled."[45] The maximum penalty inflicted for openly professing Quakerism in the colony was thirty-eight stripes. Fines for Quakers refusing to take oaths of fidelity at Marshfield, Sandwich, and Duxbury ranged as high as £27 but usually were £12-£14.

Because of the "extraordinary circumstances" of the Quaker crisis, the General Court in 1658 appointed a special marshal to serve the towns of Sandwich, Barnstable, and Yarmouth. This was the notorious George Barlow, who was so overzealous in manhandling the Quakers and taking their property that the Court finally censured and fined him 10s.

The harsh treatment of the Quakers and their steadfastness for the cause of freedom of conscience turned public opinion towards them. The influx of Quakers continued unabated to Marshfield,

Scituate, Duxbury, and the Cape towns. After 1660, except for the denial of political privileges and rarely a fine for holding an unauthorized public meeting, the Quakers enjoyed religious liberty in Plymouth.

The *cause célèbre* of the Quaker scare of 1657-60 was the persecution of one of the most respected leaders of the colony. Since 1632 James Cudworth had resided in the colony, and in 1634 he was admitted a freeman of Scituate. He served in various high posts: militia captain from Scituate, deputy to the General Court (1649-56), assistant (1656-8), and commissioner of the United Colonies (1657). For entertaining Quakers, Cudworth was discharged as captain of the militia company, which probably did not offend him since he was inclined to pacificism. But Cudworth could not sit idly by while persons in Plymouth were being beaten and deprived of liberty, a policy instigated by his fellow magistrates. With the aid of Hatherly he got hold of court depositions, which he personally turned over to the Quakers.[46]

But what brought on the full fury of the other magistrates was the writing of a letter, addressed to "Mr. Browne," a former assistant who was in England, exposing and condemning the excessive repression of Quakers in Plymouth. The letter was immediately published in England. Cudworth lashed out against the self-preservation practices of the oligarchy: "All is well, if we can but keep the people ignorant of their liberties and Priviledges then we have liberty to act in our own wills what we please, wee are wrapped up in a Labyrinth of confused Laws," and "the free mens power is quite gone . . . ." Citing a passage from *Lamentations,* Cudworth said, "The Daughter of my people is become cruel, like the Ostriches in the Wilderness."[47] It was one thing to fight for a change of policy within the Plymouth government; but, in the view of his colleagues, it was an unpardonable breach of public trust to broadcast at home the repression of the liberties of His Majesty's subjects in Plymouth.

Because of the ill-fame Cudworth brought to the colony, he was removed as a commissioner of the United Colonies in 1658 and the next year deprived of his office as assistant. Scituate, however, returned him as a deputy, but the General Court refused to seat him. Not until Prence's death and Josiah Winslow's election to the governorship in 1673 did Cudworth's rehabilitation begin. When he took the oath of fidelity in 1673 he was restored to the freemanship; subsequently he was an assistant (1674-80), captain of troops for the Dutch War (1673), commander-in-chief of the army (1675-81), and a member of the committee of three (including Hinckley and Southworth) to revise the laws (1678).[48]

Although Baptists were lumped with Quakers as a subversive element, their infiltration was gradual and less obvious than the Quakers. They were willing to take the oath of fidelity, unlike the Quakers, which made them less conspicuous.[49] Some sharp penalties were meted out to Baptists, but these were mainly fines for holding unauthorized public meetings.[50] As the Baptists made further inroads at Rehoboth and Dartmouth in the late 1660's, the General Court allowed a group to take up lands at Wammamoiset (Swansea). Mitigating against the repression of the Baptists were the presence of such prominent men as Thomas Willett and John Butterworth,[51] and the fact that the colony still had to live down the reputation for religious intolerance, which the royal commissioners had made the most of in the 1660's. Most Baptists, however, preferred to go to Rhode Island; not until after the Great Awakening did their sect appreciably spread elsewhere in New England.

In spite of the condemnation by the Synod of 1679 of Quakers and Baptists as "false Worshippers," who were evidence "that God hath a Controversy with his New-England People,"[52] Plymouth Colony continued the policy of limited toleration inaugurated by Winslow. Hinckley, as Governor after 1680, did a turnabout from his earlier bitterness toward dissenters. As long as persons behaved civilly, they were allowed to go their own way. Such persistent critics as Edward Randolph would not let the issue of intolerance against the Quakers die out,[53] but the wrongs were of the past. The policy of the colony in the 1680's was to allow a town to select its faith as well as its own church and pastor, a sort of minim of *cuius regio, eius religio*. Though a church could be of a dissenting faith, the matter of support of the established church of the colony was an unresolved question. Ministers still proclaimed jeremiads against a generation forsaking the true church, but religion became more and more irrelevant to actual civil policy.[54] As agent for Plymouth and Massachusetts, Increase Mather in England insisted that Puritan New England acknowledged "Liberty in matters of Religion to serve God according to our Consciences."[55] Even Cotton Mather considered the disuse of infant baptism by some of the "unhappy sectaries" on the fringes of Plymouth Colony not a serious threat to the true religion.[56]

As Plymouth moved away from the frontier march type of society, greater latitude was given to the freedom of expression. As mentioned before, cases for sedition decreased; and religious toleration was beginning to be a reality. But it is also important to note that the broadening of the right to dissent accompanied the weakening of political authority; much of the gains in individual freedom by Plymouth in the later years would be lost under the incorporation with Massachusetts. Nevertheless, Plymouth was showing the way that a free society cannot be based merely upon the negative limitation of governmental authority, but it must also recognize the positive right to express one's conscience with impunity.

NOTES

1. *PCR,* XI, 177. Treason did receive some definition in 1684, when the General Court made it a felony to serve under a foreign power "in America in an hostile manner" against any foreign power allied with England. *Ibid.,* VI, 137.

2. *Ibid.,* XI, 64, 175.

3. E.g., *ibid.,* I, 35 (1635); III, 190 (1660); IV, 168 (1667); VI, 81 (1682).

4. *Ibid.,* III, 112 (1657). See Chapter 6 for reference to the same case.

5. *Ibid.,* VI, 81 (1682).

6. Records of Sessions of the Peace (1686-1721), June 1688, 28, Pilgrim Hall, Ply. Mass.

7. E.g., concerning Abraham Sutliffe, *PCR,* IV, 168 (1667).

8. Extract (March 1621) made from early Ply. records by Thomas Prince, Young, *Chronicles,* 149n., 199. Similarly an old man

in 1659 was sentenced to have his heels and neck tied together, but because of his "infirmitie" he was released, though with a warning that a second offense would lead to exile. *PCR,* III, 175.

9. E.g., *PCR,* II, 17 (1641), 70 (1643); IV, 140 (1667); VI, 41 (1680), 114 (1683). As noted in reference to blasphemy, if a person accused of seditious conduct was considered demented, he was not held responsible for his action. E.g., John Cowin was acquitted in 1671 for making a statement that there was no king in England "but one crooked back Richard," whom the court noted resembled a deformed man in Scituate. *Ibid.,* V, 61.

10. E.g., concerning Indian policy—fine of £5 or a whipping. *Ibid.,* V, 61 (1671).

11. *Ibid.,* II, 140 (1649), 150 (1650); Felt, *Ecclesiastical Hist.,* II, 25.

12. Thomas Hinckley to [Gov. Phips], [Dec. ?], 15, 1692, MA Colonial, III, 50; A Declaration of Sundry the Inhabitants of Plymouth [Against Nathaniel Clark], April 22, 1689, *HP,* 197.

13. *PCR,* III, 150. Although not going as far as other Puritans in believing that man's conscience led him to act according to God's will, the Pilgrims could agree in principle with Increase Mather's statement on freedom of conscience: "God alone is Lord of the Conscience, and hath left it free from the Doctrines and Commandments of men, which are in any thing contrary to his Word, or not contained in it; so that to believe such Doctrines, or to obey such Commands out of Conscience, is to betray true liberty of Conscience, and the requiring of an implicit faith, and an absolute and blind obedience, is to destroy Liberty of Conscience; and Reason also." (Increase Mather), *A Confession of faith owned and consented unto by the elders and messengers of the churches . . . May 12, 1680* (1680), Evans #280.

14. Lechford, "Plaine dealing" (1642), *MHSC,* 3d Ser., III (1833), 95-96.

15. *Ibid.,* V, 39.

16. *PCR,* II (1646).

17. Under the Dominion of New England, an imprimatur of Joseph Dudley, censor appointed by Governor Andros, was required for all publications in New England, and no printer could be licensed until he put up £500 not to print unauthorized "papers, books or Pamphlets." Mass. inaugurated censorship under a committee, consisting of Daniel Gookin and Jonathan Mitchell, in 1662. See Clyde

A. Duniway, *The Development of Freedom of the Press in Massachusetts* (New York, 1906), 17, 41, 55; Toppan, ed., *Andros Records, AASP,* XIII (1901), 249, Jan. 28, 1687.

18. See Borden, *Bristol County,* 22-23.

19. *PCR,* III, 129 (1658), 139 (1658).

20. *Ibid.,* 189 (1660); XI, 121; James Thacher, *History of the Town of Plymouth, 1620-1832* (Boston, 1832), 150. Isaac Robinson, son of John Robinson, and James Cudworth were disfranchised for writing letters critical of the government. Both men were restored to the freemanship shortly after Josiah Winslow's election as governor in 1673. It has been alleged that Timothy Hatherly was also disfranchised for his views on Quakers, but, except for not being sworn in as an assistant, I find that Hatherly kept his posts as a member of the council of war and performer of marriages and that there is no record of his disfranchisement.

21. Walley, *Balm in Gilead,* Evans #146, 3-14.

22. Arnold, *David serving his generation,* (1674) Evans #185, 4-16.

23. Edward Wanton, Joseph Colman, Nathaniel Fitsrandel, William Allen to the governor and magistrates . . . of New Plymouth, June 1678, *HP,* 18-20.

24. *Bradford Hist.* (1912), I, 380-403, 414-20; *Plymouth Church Records,* I, 54-6; George F. Willison, *Saints and Strangers* (New York, 1945) gives a lively account of the whole affair, 242-53.

25. Smith, *Bradford,* 64-65.

26. See *Bradford Hist.* (1912), II, 45-48, 77, 201; Morton, *New English Canaan,* ed. C. F. Adams, Jr., Introd., 1-98; Francis Baylies, *An Historical Memoir of the Colony of New Plymouth,* 2 vols. (Boston, 1830), I, 136-39; Charles F. Adams, *Three Episodes of Massachusetts History,* 2 vols. (Boston, 1903), I, 162-211, 244-45, 282-84, 346-50.

27. "Pascataway, Namkeake, Winisimett, Weeagascusett, Natascot, and other places."

28. Edward Winslow to John Winthrop, Feb. 7, 1964, *Winthrop Papers,* IV (1944), 428.

29. Morton, *New English Canaan,* ed. C. F. Adams, 338-39.

30. Roger Williams to John Winthrop, July 1632, *Winthrop Papers,* III (1943), 86; Morgan, *Roger Williams,* 24-26.

31. Irwin H. Polishook, ed., *Roger Williams, John Cotton and Religious Freedom* (Englewood Cliffs, N. J., 1967), 8-9. Williams

essentially differed from the Calvinist political theory of the Pilgrims and Puritans that the magistrates should be Godly persons; he felt that duty to the magistrates was obligatory regardless of their religious standing. See T. H. Breen, *The Character of the Good Ruler: A Study of Puritan Political Ideas in New England,* 1630-1730 (New Haven, 1970), 44-46.

32. *Bradford Hist.* (1912), II, 162-64; Morton, *New-England's Memorial,* 96-100; Samuel H. Brockunier, *The Irrepressible Democrat: Roger Williams* (New York, 1940), 89-90. John Cotton justified Williams' banishment as a proper punishment for a dissenter: "the Jurisdiction (whence a man is banished) is but small, and the Countrey round about it, large, and fruitfull: where a man may make his choice of variety of more pleasant, and profitable seats, then he leaveth behind him. In which respect, Banishment in this Countrey, is not counted so much a confinement, as an enlargement, wher a man doth not so much loose civill comforts, as change them. And as for spirituall liberties, (liberty of Church Ordinances) they were a burden and bondage to his spirit here." John Cotton, *A Reply to Mr. Williams his Examination; And Answer of the Letters . . .* (1647), *Pubs. of the Narragansett Club,* 1st Ser., II (1867), 18-19.

33. Edward Winslow, *Hypocrisie Unmasked A True Relation of the Proceedings . . . Against Samuel Gorton of Rhode Island* (1646), ed. Howard M. Chapin (Providence, reprint 1916); Hubbard, *General History of New England* (1682), *MHSC,* 2d Ser., VI (1848), 663; Morton, *New-England's Memorial,* 125-28; Felt, *Ecclesiastical Hist.,* I, 604-5; Charles Deane, "Notice of Samuel Gorton," *NEHGR,* IV (1850), 201-3; Osgood, *American Colonies,* I, 344-53.

34. *PCR,* I, 100, 105-6 (1638); Samuel Gorton to Nathaniel Morton, June 30, 1969, in *Bradford Hist.* (1912), II, 393-94n.

35. Reply to the interview with His Majesty's Commisioners . . . Vindication of Treatment towards Samuel Gorton, May 30, 1665, MA, Ecclesiastical, I, 341; see Ward, *United Colonies,* 137-45.

36. *PCR,* II, 46-47 (1642).

37. *Bradford Hist.* (1912), II, 306n. The Familist doctrines seem to have threatened the Barnstable and Scituate churches, for which Vassall may have had a share in the responsibility. Otis, ed., "Scituate and Barnstable Church Records," *NEHGR,* X (1856), 38, June 10, 1641.

38. Edward Winslow to John Winthrop, Nov. 24, 1645, *Winthrop Papers,* V (1947), 55-56; *Winthrop Hist.,* II, 319-20; Winslow

Warren, "Governor Edward Winslow," *MHSP, LII* (1919), 328; Walker, *Creeds and Platforms,* 163-64.

39. Winslow, *New-England Salamander* (1647), *MHSC,* 3d Ser., II (1830), 119-20.

40. Edward Winslow to John Winthrop, June 4, 1646, *Winthrop Papers, Letters to, MHSC,* 4th Ser., VI (1863), 178.

41. *PCR,* III, 111, 113.

42. See Norton, *New England's Ensigne* (1659), 22-25.

43. *PCR,* XI, *passim.*

44. This is from a transcription of the resolution in the Winthrop Papers, Sep. 23, 1658, MHS.

45. *PCR,* III-IV, *passim;* Norton, *New England's Ensigne* (1659), 25-49; [anon.], *New-England A Degenerate Plant who having forgot their former Sufferings, and lot* (London, 1659), photostat, NYPL, 10-16; Bishop, *New-England Judged* (1703 rev. ed.), 202ff; Rufus M. Jones, *The Quakers in the American Colonies* (New York, reprint 1966), 60-62; also see Freeman, *History of Cape Cod,* concerning Barnstable and Sandwich, I, 215-42 and II, 57-65, 265-66.

46. *PCR,* III, 130 (1658); Nathaniel Morton to Gov. Thomas Prence, April 2, 1658, *MHSP,* LI, 201-2; Samuel Deane, *History of Scituate, Mass.* (Boston, 1831), 244-48; Felt, *Ecclesiastical Hist.,* II, 234.

47. "A true Copy of a Letter which was sent from one who was a Magistrate in New-England, to a Friend of his in London," in *New-England A Degenerate Plant* (1659), 19-20. This was the first printing of Cudworth's letter (unsigned). It also had contemporary publication in Bishop, *New-England Judged;* numerous extracts of it have been published, e.g., in Deane, *Scituate,* 246-48.

48. *PCR,* V, 124, 136 (1673), 175 (1675), 263 (1678).

49. *Ibid.,* II, 150 (1650). Obadiah Holmes won a case in slander against the Rev. Samuel Newman for being falsely accused of having taken "a false oath."

50. *Ibid.,* 162 (1650); IV, 175-76 (1668).

51. Reed, *Church and State in Massachusetts, 1691-1740,* 44-45, 285-86; Isaac Backus, *A History of New England with Particular Reference to . . . Baptists,* 2 vols. (Newton, Mass., 1871), I, 454. In 1685, the colony allowed the formation of the first Baptist church at Dartmouth. Most of these Baptists were from Wales.

52. See Walker, *Creeds and Platforms,* 426-28.

53. E.g., Edward Randolph to Thomas Hinckley, Nov. 24, 1683, *HP*, 96.

54. See "The humble Petition and Address of. the Governor and Council . . . of New Plymouth (to King Charles II)," Nov. 1683, *HP*, 102. However, the Plymouth authorities considered the issuance of James II's Declarations of Indulgence as a dangerous opening for popery. See Arthur Riley, *Catholicism in Colonial New England, 1620-1788* (unpubl. Ph. D. diss., Catholic University, 1936), 42-43.

55. Address of Increase Mather and the colony of New Plymouth [in pen of Gov. Hinckley], June 1688, *Letter-Book of Samuel Sewall, MHSC,* 6th Ser., I (1886), 59-60n.

56. Mather, *Magnalia Christi Americana,* I (1820 ed.), 59.

Chapter Eight

MILITARISM

"Our Military Strength is, under God, the appointed means for our preservation, therefore it is a duty to encourage Souldiers," spoke Samuel Nowell in an election sermon to the Massachusetts General Court in 1678. "God can work miracles, but when ordinary means may be had, he will not . . . . There is such a thing as Liberty and Property given to us, both by the Laws of God and Men, when these are invaded, we may defend our selves."[1] God would not have given men arms could they not be used for the working of His Providence.

Military preparedness was a constant fact of life in Plymouth. The Pilgrims had been led to the promised land, and God expected that they clear it of enemies; they had to be on guard and ready to strike out against any one who might threaten their existence. Throughout the history of the colony, the Pilgrims faced war emergency: three Dutch wars, two Indian uprisings, war with France, and always an uneasy Indian truce. It would be expected, therefore, that a degree of militarism would pervade Plymouth life. In the sense that the war crises temporarily enlarged the powers of the executive over the lives of the people and called upon an obligation of each male adult, this is true. Acceptance of war as an instrument of policy and the fear psychology generating from the insecurity of a majoritarian government—so discernible in our own time—had origins in the experience of Plymouth Colony and other early settlements.

But there is a difference between militarism in the seventeenth century and the twentieth. The early settlers had more important things to do than to provide for a warfare state. They were not involved in imperialist enterprise; there were enough jobs so that there was no necessity to have a war machine to absorb surplus labor; no heavy industry stimulated war preparation. Fear of standing armies and agrarian pursuit also worked against any thorough-going militarism.

Militarism may be said to exist when the state has a strong military spirit and policy, when it regards military efficiency as a paramount end, and when it subordinates other interests to those of the military. Plymouth Colony could qualify only as a limited military state. Military action had definite and restricted goals, more often improvised for an occasion rather than fixed. Again the obligation was more on each individual instead of the state. Civil liberty never really became suppressed in the interest of national security. Yet the pervasiveness of military policy and the fusion of civil and military authority is significant.

The colony was seldom without a military commander even in time of peace. One of the first acts of the Pilgrims in assembly was to choose a military leader. Troubled by Indians lurking around and pilfering tools, the body politic in February 1622 voted to establish "military orders among ourselves" and to commission Miles Standish captain and chief military commander of the colony.[2] Standish soon had a reputation as a zealous officer, always eager to lead a Plymouth band to teach interlopers upon Plymouth trade a lesson or to overawe the Indians. He held his military office until he died in 1656.

To succeed Standish, in 1658 the General Court named Josiah Winslow major and commander of the colony's troops. Winslow's specific duties included acting as a superior officer over the various town military companies, supervising operations and logistics, and in general having responsibility for keeping the militia in readiness to ward off any invasion.[3] Winslow would retain his commission even during his governorship, but after his election William Bradford (Jr.) was named, with the rank of major, to be the commandant for training the colony's troops.[4] As a very popular governor, Winslow served as general and commander-in-chief of the army of the four confederated colonies during King Philip's War—an office, however, which was encumbered by the commissioners of the United Colonies themselves acting as a joint war executive.[5]

James Cudworth had the distinction of being appointed commander of the colony's forces on two occasions: first to lead an expedition against the Dutch in 1673 and later, when Winslow had the chief command of the intercolonial army, to field the colony's troops in King Philip's War. Cudworth, however, declined his commission during the Dutch War. Undoubtedly, the sudden switch from persecution to conferring upon him every high office, as an expiation for the wrongs done him by his countrymen, must have struck Cudworth as utter hypocrisy. In refusing the command in the Dutch War, Cudworth also displayed his qualms against offensive war. To him war was morally justified only if the enemy had committed depredations upon the lives and property of his people. Cudworth's letter to Governor Winslow declining the appointment is indeed a rarity in military annals:

> So being persuaded to myself of my own insufficiency, it appears clearly and undoubtedly unto me, that I have no call of God thereunto; for *vox populi* is not always *vox Dei;* and therefore I cannot, in any thing give a more full and real demonstration of my loyalty and faithfulness unto my king and country, than in declaring my unfitness for the acceptation of the management of such a design; and should I embrace and accept of the call, knowing of my own insufficiency for the work, what should I less than what in me lies, but betray the lives of men into the hands of the enemy.

Cudworth also pleaded that his wife was sick, and at sixty-seven years old he had only an Indian boy of thirteen to help him manage his livestock.[6] In King Philip's War, though chosen commander of the colony's forces by the Plymouth General Court, Cudworth had to accept the seniority of the command of Captain

James Savage of Massachusetts when Savage and his troops were sent to operate within Plymouth's bounds.[7]

After Governor Winslow's death in 1680, the colony did not choose a military commander until 1689 when Benjamin Church was given the chief command in the war against the northern Indians.[8] Thereafter, when Plymouth became part of Massachusetts, full military authority was bestowed, by the royal charter, upon the governor, who had powers to appoint officers (including a commander), train and govern the militia, arm the inhabitants, establish martial law, and build forts. Two important restrictions, however, would hamper the governor's war powers: he could exercise martial law only during wartime—and then only with the consent of the council—and he could not send troops out of the colony except with their consent or that of the General Court.[9]

Since the Pilgrims regarded war primarily as defense, local military commanders had important authority. The Indian scare of 1642 led to the General Court's ordering the towns to select military commanders. Each town nominated two or three persons "above the degree of Sergeants (to exercise their men in armes)," from whom the General Court made the final appointment. Besides training men, the town military commander had power "in time of feare and danger or suddain assault of an enemie" to call out the soldiers of a town "and put them into a posture of warr." He had complete authority in the disposition of troops for the defense of the town.[10]

Although local trainbands could elect their own sergeants, the colony government, because of an occasional tendency to choose persons of "unworthy carriages" and who held government "in contempt," soon exercised review of these appointments.[11] Votes for officers were certified to the General Court, and the one with the most votes named the company commander of the town. Typically, in 1689 at Rehoboth, soldiers and the "rest of the householders" gave Lieutenant Peter Hunt eighty-seven votes and Ensign Nicholas Peck fifty-five votes. The authorities at Plymouth, therefore, named Hunt captain and Peck lieutenant.[12] If a town refused to choose a military commander, the General Court, through the Council of War, made the choice for the town.[13] Thus military command was essentially decentralized and democratic. But ultimate authority, in every respect, rested with the central government.

Although activated only in time of war crises, the Council of War exercised control over the resources of manpower and materiel. The Council had its origins in the Pequot War when the General Court ordered two persons each from Plymouth, Duxbury, and Scituate to join the governor and assistants "to assesse men towards the charges of the souldiers that are to be sent forth for the ayde of the Massachusetts Bay and Connecticut."[14] The Council named during the Indian threat of 1642 set the pattern for later councils: a mixed board of assistants and chief military officers. Probably a major factor in erecting a Council of War at this time was distrust of Standish's ability to keep a cool head with the Indians. The expedition planned was primarily to back up negotiations. As a matter of fact, Standish was not allowed to take the Plymouth force into the field alone; Thomas Prence was appointed to accompany him, "to be his counsell and advise in the warrs."[15] In the following year, the Council of War was again established, consisting of Governor Bradford, three of the assistants, and Captain Miles Standish. The Council was empowered "to order all things concerning the generall warrs for the government," especially in impressing men, arms, and provisions from the towns, to act as a court martial, and to recommend to the General Court the selection of commanders of town companies from persons nominated.[16] During the Indian scare of 1646, the Council consisted of all the assistants (except William Thomas) and several military officers. Three of the members could "make orders for matters of Warr," but if only two met, "approbation" from the governor was required.[17]

In 1653, the Council of War received the permanence of a standing committee. The Council (now made up of nine persons, including all the assistants and the governor) had been reconvened to meet the threat of the Dutch War. In addition to overseeing preparations, the Council became embroiled in a debate over the "ground and reasons" for declaring war—an issue which, on the intercolonial level, left the commissioners of the United Colonies irrevocably split. Nevertheless, the Plymouth Council of War voted in 1654 to send a contingent to aid a British expeditionary force against New Netherland,[18] which proved to be unnecessary because the war came to a quick end. The proceedings of the Council of War of 1653-54 served as guidelines for future meetings.

The Council of War was gradually enlarged. In 1657-58 it consisted of eleven persons (including the assistants), five of whom could be a quorum.[19] Chief business of the council in the 1660's dealt with policy concerning the accountability of King Philip's actions.[20] In 1667, the council met to revamp the whole military system. It propounded regulations for defense to the towns and created local councils of war from each of eleven towns—each council included one or several civilians along with the commissioned officers. Articles of discipline for soldiers on watch were also issued.[21] Moreover, a special council of war, in addition to the regular body and consisting of town officers, was arranged to consult with Josiah Winslow, as commander-in-chief. Of the nineteen officers on this field council, six had to meet in order for a decision to be made.[22] In a few years, officers selected from the towns were brought into the regular council of war along with the governor and assistants. As new towns were incorporated, additional officers were placed on the council of war. In 1671, an oath was required of all members:

> You shall reddily appeer on any summons directed unto you by the president of the councell of war, att such place or places as you shalbe ordered unto by the said summons, unlesse any inevitable providence shall or may hinder youer said appeerance, on which occations and meetings you shall faithfully, with respect to the glory of God and the good and welfare of this jurisdiction, afoard youer best advice and councell in all matters of importance and waighty concernment (or soe seeming) that may or shalbe presented before you; in reference to the continuance of peace or nessesitated warr, as occation may require; you shall faithfully keep cecrett all such expeditions and achievements as may or shalbe ordered and contrived by the councill of warr, tending to the generall peace and good of this collonie of N. Plymouth; you shall with like cecresye conceale all other matters that may be agitated and transacted by the said councill, in reference to the premises, that shalbe thought meet by the president and councell aforsaid to be concealled. Soe healp you God, whoe is the God of truth, and the punisher of falsehood.[23]

Until the outbreak of King Philip's War, the Council continued to concern itself with negotiations with the Indians. During the Dutch War in 1673, however, the Council of War and the gov-

ernor were empowered to make war preparations in conjunction
with the United Colonies.[24]

During King Philip's War the Council met in almost un-
interrupted session, with meetings held at Plymouth, Marshfield,
and Duxbury. In matters affecting civil liberty, it condemned
Indian captives to slavery, proclaimed the death penalty for any
Indians coming near Plymouth and for anyone who traded guns
and ammunition with the Indians, and ordered all residents not
to depart from their towns upon penalty of forfeiture of their
estates. Again the Council coordinated the work of the town
councils of war and issued numerous orders for impressment of
men and supplies. Costs for the war were assessed the towns.[25]
The Council of War, therefore, in the interests of the security
of the colony, performed in a legislative and executive capacity.

The Council of War was continued in the 1680's, except during the period of the Dominion of New England. When Plymouth was incorporated into Massachusetts, the governor, with
strong war powers invested by the royal charter, and his Council
could act as a council of war; and, especially if the Assembly
was not in session, they could raise and dispose militia as they
saw fit.[26]

In Plymouth, the Council of War was a matter of expediency.
It did not represent the interests of a military establishment;
rather it was used as a means for military administration whenever the occasion dictated. The idea of a mixed, military-civilian
board would become embedded in the colonial experience, and
it would be the type of military administration tried by the
Continental Congress during the American Revolution.

All able-bodied, male adults, between the ages of sixteen and
sixty, faced a military obligation. As early as 1633, the General
Court voted "That all and every person within the colony be
subject to such military order for training and exercise of armes
as shall be thought meet, agreed on, and prescribed by the Governor and Assistants."[27] Servants were excluded; but foreigners
were eventually made eligible.[28]

Plymouth had a rudimentary system of universal military
training. "Inhabitants of every Towne within the Government fitt
and able to beare armes" had to attend training at least six times
a year. If a town was deficient in this obligation, extra training
days were added.[29] After King Philip's War, training days were
reduced to four a year.[30]

Beginning in 1662, one day a year was set aside for mustering all the trainbands at one place. The first general training was held at Plymouth, and afterwards, alternately, at Duxbury and Yarmouth. Absentees were subject to a 5*s*. fine. After 1669, general trainings were conducted triennially at Plymouth, Taunton, and Yarmouth on a rotating basis.[31]

Participation in the exercises on the training days was taken for granted as a necessary duty. In the stern Puritan society, where there were no holidays except for the dreary Sabbaths, the citizen soldiers must have looked forward to the parades and the fraternization with their neighbors.

It was considered an honor to be a member of a military company. Only freemen "of honest and good report" were admitted upon election by the whole company. The inductee also had to take the oath of fidelity. Exercises were tended to with prayer by the clergy. There must have been some sense of competition and pride in mastering the manual of arms, which all members of a trainband were required to learn. If a soldier or veteran died, he was entitled to full military honors at the funeral. "Membership dues" in the form of 6*d*. quarterly were required. Although there were statutory penalties for absenteeism and for possessing faulty equipment, the supreme humiliation was to be "put out of the list"—tantamount to a dishonorable discharge.[32] Flogging was not permitted.[33] But it can be assumed that consciousness of one's peer group and dread of censure were sufficient for maintaining basic discipline in a trainband.

For a field force, a pool was usually drawn from each of the local companies, unlike militia mobilization in England where trainbands took to the field as units. As population increased in Plymouth, the proportion of men taken from any one company decreased, thus making a town company even more a unit of defense—and as Archibald Hanna, Jr. has noted, "Militia became more and more an administrative and training organization, not a tactical one."[34] Company commanders, who were salaried, were concerned chiefly with instruction at arms.[35]

Frontier towns, such as Taunton and Rehoboth in 1645, did not have to draft men for field service, but they bore a substantial share of the financial burden.[36] Pressing of soldiers for the field was done in ratio to the population of a town.[37] When a town considered its quota unfair, it simply neglected to honor the full requisition—and the colony generally preferred not to make an issue of it.[38] Normally it was the duty of town constables to see that the town's field quota was filled, but in King Philip's war "press masters" were sent into the recalcitrant town of Scituate.[39] An individual refusing field service in King Philip's War faced the stiff fine of £10 and, if he were without property, six months in prison. If a person sought not to chance active military duty by moving to another town in the colony, he was to be immediately pressed into service.[40] Draft-dodgers have met a similar consequence in our own time! But not many soldiers were called out of the towns; the largest levy at any one time (and presumably most of these were volunteers) was that of October 4, 1675 when 182 men were ordered up from twelve locations.[41] Men were called out of the towns in 1689 for an expedition against the Maine Indians and for the land and sea operations in the Canadian invasion of 1690.[42]

Several obligations were required of all able-bodied men other than the militia trainings and field service. Servants as well as freemen were expected to own a firearm with adequate powder, shot, and "other appurtenances"—upon penalty of 10s.[43] Massachusetts ordered that no one could travel between Plymouth and Massachusetts without arms.[44] In times of emergency, members of trainbands had to bring their weapons to Sabbath meeting.[45] They were also subject to watch duty up to twenty-four hours.[46]

Soldiers who fought in the big war (King Philip's) received compensation. The colony awarded them lands and assessed the towns for £1000 to pay soldiers "whose needy condition may call for other supplyes more suitable for their families than lands, and such other smale dues to others of them as may be by them desired."[47] The Massachusetts government gave Narragansett lands to veterans, including soldiers from Plymouth Colony.[48] Part of Plymouth's debt from the war—totalling £11,743 3s. 11d.— was defrayed by the sale of lands. The Mount Hope lands brought £1100 from a Boston syndicate, and towns were allowed to dispose of other "conquered lands" to help meet their share of war costs.[49]

War was not inimical to the morality of the Pilgrims, despite Pastor John Robinson's entreaty to Christianize the inhabitants of the New World, not to conquer them. The Pilgrims, however, were willing to coexist with the Indians, even though they had been preserved "to be thorns in our sides,"[50] and foreign neighbors, as long as no peril immediately threatened the security of the colony. But given provocation by the enemy any war was justifiable.

When the Pequot War erupted, Plymouth delayed as long as it could from sending aid to Massachusetts, and when a band of fifty troops was dispatched, the war was over. Explaining the delay, the Plymouth authorities first accused Massachusetts of provoking a needless war,[51] a view not well taken in the Bay Colony since a year before Massachusetts had agreed to send men and arms to help Plymouth drive out the French at Penobscot.[52] Winthrop's warning, however, that Plymouth might need Massachusetts aid in the future finally convinced Plymouth to contribute to the winning of the Pequot War.[53] Once the colony made up its mind to assist its neighbors, full measure was to be exacted from the enemy; the army should "take such revenge as may be a service to after times for any of the barbarians to rise against us."[54]

After the Pequot War, Plymouth became more susceptible to the idea of preventive war to ward off potential Indian aggression. "Haveing intelligence of a generall conspiracy intended by the natives to cutt off all the English in this land" prompted the General Court in 1642 "to make speedy preparation" for "a defensive and offensive warr against them" and to hasten the establishment of the New England Confederation for this purpose.[55] In 1645, the colony raised a punitive force to march into the Narragansett Country and, in 1654, Massachusetts troops were permitted to move through Plymouth territory to overawe one of the sub-tribes of the Narragansetts who had given cause for alarm;[56] for the 1654 expedition Plymouth voted to contribute fifty-one soldiers,[57] but the troops were not needed. The fascination the Puritan colonies now seemed to have for "offensive war" as a means of defense led Roger Williams to comment: "All men of Conscience or Prudence, ply to the Windward and wisely labour to mainteine their Wars to be defensive."[58]

The idea of a punitive expedition against the Indians, again broached in 1660 by Massachusetts, was acceptable to the Plymouth government, provided that such action was sanctioned by the commissioners of the United Colonies and there was sufficient evidence of Indian conspiracy.[59]

Amidst persistent rumors in 1667 that King Philip was plotting with the French or Dutch (the lack of specificity here itself proves the groundlessness of the charge) to recover Indian lands sold to the colonists and "to inrich themselves with there goods," a cavalry band was dispatched to Wampanoag country—the expense of £40 had to be borne by King Philip.[60] Similarly, one hundred troops were pressed from the towns in 1671 to form an expedition to disarm the Indians.[61] Plymouth joined Massachusetts in preparation for war against the Dutch in 1673 on grounds of defense and because of the "Insolent and Injurious Carriage" of the Dutch "in takeing our vessells and Goods on our Coastes. . . ."[62]

King Philip's War might not have been more than a coercive action instigated by the Plymouth authorities to enforce disarmament of the Indians had not some of Philip's rash warriors killed settlers in a raid, which gave the colony complete justification for going to war.[63] Even Roger Williams immediately condoned Plymouth's making war: King Philip "broke all laws, and was in armes of rebellion against that Colony, his ancient friends and protectours" and he was the "author" of the murder of John Sassamon.[64] Massachusetts quickly responded with troops, fearing for its own security and a general Indian insurrection.[65] Meanwhile, the Indian conflagration spread to within the borders of Massachusetts and Connecticut. The story of King Philip's War, however, is better told elsewhere. Suffice it to say the attack on the Narragansetts, involving Plymouth forces, late in the war was strictly a preventative action: to hit a tribe, which was not at war with the colonists, but which was held "deeply accessory in the present bloody outrages of the Barbarous Natives" before they could launch an attack. Josiah Winslow's intercolonial army caught the Narragansetts by surprise at their camp; the massacre that ensued would go down in New England annals as the "Great Swamp Fight."[66] Once the New England Puritans had been drawn into war, they were bent upon the annihilation of the enemy, whose ranks included not only hostiles but those guilty by association. King Philip's War is perhaps early proof of Alexis De Tocqueville's observation that once a democratic people makes up its mind to go to war there is no peace short of total victory.

Opposition to war in Plymouth did not proceed beyond debating the abstractions of offensive versus defensive war. When war was in progress, there was no room for dissent. Of course, the Indian Uprising of 1675-6 was a clear-cut war to the Pilgrims whose lives were jeopardized, and no one cared to protest against it. This was not the case in Massachusetts, where Daniel Gookin and others were persecuted for their insistence upon protection of peaceable Indians within that colony. No voice was lifted in Plymouth over the massacre of the Narragansetts. Only from outside of Plymouth were doubts expressed on the justice of King Philip's War. Wrote a Connecticut resident:

> this unhappy war [of] . . . our friends of Plymouth parts . . . it proved very difficult, dissatisfying, and uncomfortable to conscientious parents and other Relations, to send out their children, and other dear relations unto the war, where many of them were slain, and all in danger of their lives . . . the dishonor would redound to the Name of God, if New England should go to war in a bad cause, or not every way justifiable in the sight of God and all the world.[67]

If anti-war sentiment[68] was lacking, the Calvinist conscience was pricked to self-accusation for the causes of such a holocaust as the Indian War of 1675-6. Before the deterioration of Indian relations that led to war, days of humiliation and thanksgiving had been directed to the blessings that God had bestowed on his people in the enjoyment of "civill and religious liberties" and deliverance from the tribulations of the Old World.[69] As the Reverend William Hooke declared in 1640: "Neither let this be forgotten, that of all the Christian people this day in the World, wee in this Land enjoy the greatest measure of peace and tranquillity. . . . Wee have beaten our swords into plough-shares and our speares into pruning hooks. . . ."[70] But King Philip's War evoked a sense of guilt that God had humbled his people for their sins. In the midst of the war, the colony, therefore, entered into its first written covenant with God.[71]

Threat of war generates a fear psychology, which in turn justifies militarism. To what extent did fear affect the lives of the Plymouth settlers? Again it is necessary to look at the eve of the Great War rather than the brief alarms of the earlier period. By 1671, rumors of Indian conspiracy had Plymouth settlers in a "great Stirre." Undoubtedly crop failures due to a "strange blasting and mildew" and other signs of Providential disfavor added to the anxiety.[72] Yet until the actual outbreak of the war, the Plymouth government did no more than to order "a Militia Watch" in all the frontier towns and all persons to keep their firearms at hand.[73] When war did come, Plymouth did not feel that it had to inculcate a martial spirit among the people—the war was too close for such action to be necessary. In Boston, however, it was a different situation; the severed head of an executed Indian spy was placed over the governor's door—certainly a suitable insignia for a Puritan war department.[74] In Plymouth after the war, the head and hands of King Philip would be conspicuously exhibited to remind citizens of the horrors of rebellion.

Settlers fled Dartmouth, Middleboro, and Swansea, which were hardest hit by the Indians. Many refugees went to the Cape towns. Sandwich granted displaced persons use of common lands until it was safe for them to return.[75] For other exposed towns, the General Court sought to prevent a wholesale evacuation and ordered that no one could leave except by permission. Fortunately, there was no panic and almost everyone stayed. "God encouraged them to keep their Stations notwithstanding the extream danger then presented."[76]

Although very little is recorded of the actual fears of the settlers—the Pilgrims were not ones to indulge in their emotions for the sake of posterity—the treatment of the vanquished reflected a choleric bitterness. Like Southern planters of later generations, the Pilgrims wanted full insurance against any future insurrection of a people of color. The General Court, therefore, decreed that all of the defeated Indians over fourteen years of age were to be sold into slavery, and a majority were. Children were to serve as indentured servants until age twenty-four. Volunteers in the war were given first preference in acquiring slaves or servants.[77] Many captives were sent to the slave ports of Spain.[78]

Supposedly enslavement was meted out only to those Indians who had rebelled, but, since it was difficult to weigh individual cases, generally all those who had remained in tribal association during the war were considered disloyal. Some Indians had demonstrated their allegiance to the colony government during the war, and they were allowed their freedom—most of them, however, were placed under the Old Testament system of one being responsible for the behavior of nine others.[79] One faithful Indian guide did not fare so well. His daughter was made a slave and when the father brought his claim to the General Court for her freedom, she could not be found—therefore, to assuage the honor of the colony, he was given an indemnity of two English coats, two pairs of stockings, two pairs of shoes, a white shirt, and 4*s*.[80]

If the enslavement of Indians seems to have been too severe a punishment, it should be pointed out that the Pilgrims thought they were acting out of leniency. Two of the influential clergy in the colony, Arnold and Cotton, went so far as to recommend that the Indian children be put to death—a fitting sentence for the progeny of "notorious traitors, rebels and murderers," whose sins and "horrid villainies" would visit their children for generations to come.[81] Plymouth could well have harkened back to one of its own prophets, whose words would be echoed two centuries later in the strains of Walt Whitman. Pastor John Robinson had admonished:

Brethren! Liberty is more precious than life . . . seldome is it, that cruelty rests satisfied with bondage, but makes his progressions to further degrees of blood. . . . If any say, How are we concerned in the miseries of other men, so long as we are free. I say, it toucheth us. . . .[82]

Except for denying rights to a conquered enemy and a frail attempt of the colony to restrict frontier movement, civil liberty in wartime was not infringed upon. Nevertheless, a subjective fusion of civilian and military authority would leave its imprint on the American character. A standing militia and the right to impress men into service against their will were accepted facts of life. The militia establishment provided a unifying tie for the community at large. Though professionalism in the modern sense was lacking in Plymouth's military affairs, the idea of a democratic soldiery, ready to respond at a minute's notice, enhanced the military arm of the state probably to a greater degree than if a small regular army had been maintained entirely separate from civilian life.

NOTES

1. Samuel Nowell, *Abraham in Arms; Or the first religious General with his Army Engaging in a War For which he had wisely prepared* . . . (1678), Evans #256, 10-11. The same view is stated in Johnson, "Wonder Working Providence" (1654), *MHSC,* 2d Ser., II (2d ed., 1826), 59-60.

2. *Mourt's Relation,* 49.

3. *PCR,* III, 149, 152-53; XI, 102.

4. George M. Bodge, *Soldiers in King Philip's War* (Baltimore, reprint 1967), 457.

5. E. g., see Gov. Winslow to Gov. of Mass, July 28, 1675, MA, LXVII, 229; *ibid.,* LXVIII, 53, Nov. 1675, for Winslow's selection by the commissioners as commander in chief; Josiah Winslow to John Winthrop, Jr., July 29, 1675, *Winthrop Papers, Letters to, MHSC,* 5th Ser., I (1871), 149.

6. James Cudworth to Josiah Winslow, Jan. 16, 1673, "Letters to Josiah Winslow," *MHSC,* 1st Ser., VI (1800), 81-82. It may be presumed that the Dutch taking goods "of our confederates" at New York partially overcame Cudworth's moral opposition to the war. *PCR,* V, 135-36 (1673).

7. Josiah Winslow to Capt. Cudworth and Council, June 27, 1675, Misc. Bound MSS, III, MHS; *PCR,* V, 175 (1675).

8. Thomas Church, *The History of the Great Indian War of 1675 and 1676* (1716), ed. Samuel G. Drake (New York, 1845), 156.

9. Archibald Hanna, Jr., *New England Military Institutions, 1693-1750* (unpubl. Ph. D. diss., Yale University, 1951), 161-62.

10. *PCR,* XI, 39 (1642).

11. *Ibid.,* III, 89 (1655).

12. *Ibid.,* VI, 89-90. To resign, as in Peck's case, required approval from the General Court. *Ibid.,* 234.

13. E. g., *ibid.,* 109 (1683). Or if there appeared to be irregularities in the voting for officers (such as persons under twenty-one voting or less than a majority of soldiers voted), the colony intervened. (E.g., at Swansea, 1689; see John Walley to Thomas Hinckley, Aug. 13, 1689, *HP,* 208-9.)

14. *PCR,* I, 61 (1637).

15. *Ibid.,* II, 47. Prence had also been a "counsell of warr" to the Plymouth force raised in the Pequot War. *Ibid.,* 60 (1637).

16. *Ibid.,* 64-66.

17. *Ibid.,* 100.

18. *Ibid.,* III, 54-55.

19. *Ibid.,* 138.

20. *Ibid.,* IV, 25.

21. *Ibid.,* 142-47.

22. *Ibid.,* III, 153.

23. *Ibid.,* V, 64. This oath was slightly abridged in the July session, 1671. *Ibid.,* 73.

24. *Ibid.,* 134.

25. *Ibid.,* 173-210; Douglas E. Leach, *Flintlock and Tomahawk: New England in King Philip's War* (New York, 1966), 187-88; George Howe, *Mount Hope: A New England Chronicle* (New York, 1959), 41, 52; Pratt, *Early Scituate,* 172. The town council of war dealt primarily with garrisoning, scouting, relief for neighboring towns, and other defensive measures. They also fined persons delinquent in military duty.

26. Act of June 28, 1962, MA, LXX, 70. At the beginning of King Philip's War, Plymouth favored the use of an inter-colonial war council, consisting of commissioners of the United Colonies and commissioners from New York, and more than willingly cooperated —in view of the fact that any revival, in any form, of the New England Confederation, would demonstrate the political integrity of the colony and its ability to act in concert with the other colonies. MA, Intercharter, XXV-XXVI, *passim.*

27. *PCR,* I, 22.

28. *Ibid.,* XI, 65 (1655).

29. *Ibid.,* 36 (1640). Scituate, because of its negligence, was required to have eight trainings in 1644. *Ibid.,* II, 70. The New England Confederation endorsed six trainings for all the Puritan colonies. *Ibid.,* IX, 12 (1643).

30. *Ibid.,* XI, 246 (1677).

31. *Ibid.,* IV, 38-39 (1663), 64-65 (1664); XI, 137, 208 (1662), 185 (1664), 220-221 (1668). The general training was suspended in 1686. *Ibid.,* 194.

32. *Ibid.,* III, 60-62. Bodge, *Soldiers of King Philip's War,* 456-57.

33. See Hanna, *New England Military Institutions* (Ph. D. diss.), 230-31.

34. *Ibid.,* 18-19, 232.

35. E.g., £20 was allotted to Capt. Standish and Lt. Holmes for

training troops. Warrants for soldiers sent "abroad" were to be issued by the governor and assistants in the king's name; for such an occasion in 1653, when troops were sent to join a British expeditionary force at Boston, the warrants, because of the change of government in England, bore "in the name of the State of England." *PCR,* III, 28 (1653); XI, 13 (1636).

36.   *Ibid.,* II, 91, 93.

37.   In Massachusetts, every eighth man was taken from the train-bands for the projected New England-British invasion of New Netherland. MA, Military, May 14, 1653, LXVII, 137. A contemporary estimate gives 20,000 men as capable of bearing arms in the New England colonies. "Answer of Edward Randolph to several heads of enquiry concerning the present state of New England," Oct. 12, 1676, *CSP,* (1675-76), #1067.

38.   See Pratt, *Early Scituate,* 176.

39.   *PCR,* V, 183 (1675).

40.   *Ibid.,* 185 (1675).

41.   *Ibid.,* 175-177. Breakdown of the force is as follows: Plymouth, 15; Duxbury, 8; Scituate, 23; Sandwich, 16; Taunton, 20; Yarmouth, 15; Barnstable, 16; Marshfield, 13; Rehoboth, 15; Eastham, 8; Bridgewater, 8; troops pressed into garrison duty at Mt. Hope, 25; total—182. The force that Plymouth put into the field was always very small; for example, an expedition against the Narragansetts raised in 1645 consisted only of 40 men from six towns. *Ibid.,* II, 90-91.

42.   *Ibid.,* VI, 216 (1689), 231 (1690). In 1692, Cotton Mather wrote John Cotton, Jr.: "What a filthy stir do they keep at Taunton, about their military Affairs; whereof, you and I bear most of the blame! Is it Reasonable?" W. C. Ford, ed., *Diary of Cotton Mather (1681-1708),* MHSC, 7th Ser., VII (1911), 143.

43.   *PCR,* XI, 14, 17 (1636); *Ply. Town Records,* I, 14 (1643). As early as 1638 persons at Sandwich were fined 10*s.* each for having defective arms. *PCR,* I, 107.

44.   *MCR,* I, 85 (1631).

45.   *PCR,* III, 24 (1653); V, 77 (1671), 176 (1675).

46.   *Ibid.,* XI, 43 (1644), 180 (1642); *Ply. Town Records,* I, 15 (1643).

47.   *PCR,* V, 191 (1676).

48.   See Bodge, *Soldiers in King Philip's War,* 198.

49.   The total cost for all the colonies was estimated as high as

£100,000; the Massachusetts share was £46,292 6s. Plymouth's expenses for the war were met by the towns. *PCR,* V, 240 (1677); VI, 19 (1679); X, 392 (1678); "Answer . . . Randolph," Oct. 12, 1676, *CSP,* #1067. Contributions of each individual town are as follows:

Plymouth	£ 601.01.06	Eastham	£ 500.00.00
Yarmouth	497.12.08	Sandwich	1099.08.04
Barnstable	800.17.09	Scituate	1200.00.00
Taunton	1000.00.00	Rehoboth	1100.00.00
Swansea	500.00.00	Bridgewater	244.10.08
Duxbury	300.00.00	Marshfield	600.00.00
Dartmouth	200.00.00	Middleborough	100.00.00

Treasurer's Disbursements £3000.00.00

Total sum £11,743.10.11

50. Thomas Walley to John Cotton, Feb. 16, 1676, Whitehill, ed., Letters of Thomas Walley," *AASP,* LVIII, 252; Nowell, *Abraham in Arms* (1678), Evans #256, 14.

51. *Winthrop Hist.,* Oct. 22, 1636, I, 238. For rationalization of the Pequot War, see Alden T. Vaughan, "Pequots and Puritans: The Causes of the War of 1637," *WMQ,* 3d Ser., XXI (1964), 256-69.

52. *MCR,* I, 160 (1635).

53. Winthrop to Bradford, May 20, 1737, *Bradford Hist.* (1912), II, 244-46.

54. Edward Winslow to John Winthrop, June 5, 1637, *Winthrop Papers,* III (1943), 428.

55. *PCR,* II, 46-47.

56. See *ibid.,* X, 435 for the expedition in context of the New England Confederation.

57. *Ibid.,* III, 67 (1654).

58. Roger Williams to Commissioners of the United Colonies, Oct. 5, 1654, *ibid.,* X, 439.

59. Josiah Winslow to John Winthrop, Jr., July 17, 1660, *Winthrop Papers, Letters to, MHSC,* 5th Ser., I (1870), 388-89.

60. *PCR,* IV, 164-65.

61. *Ibid.,* V, 74-76. R. I. promised to send aid if necessary. R. I. Colony to Gov. Prence, June 16, 1671, Winslow Papers, (1638-1759), 62, MHS.

62. Gen. Ct. of Ply. to Mass., Dec. 18, 1673, MA, Military,

LXVII, 186; Edward Rawson for Gen. Ct. of Mass. to Gov. Winslow, Sept. 19, 1673, *ibid.,* 187.

63. King Philip did not send his defiant reply to a Ply. summons reiterating an order to lay down arms and to account for his actions to the Gen. Ct. until after the outbreak of hostilities. Misc. Bound MSS, July 1675, III, MHS. Plymouth's justification for taking up arms in King Philip's War "A Breif Narrative of the beginning and progresse of the present trouble . . ." is printed in *PCR,* X, 362-64.

64. Roger Williams to John Winthrop, Jr., June 25, 1675, *Winthrop Papers, Letters to, MHSC,* 4th Ser., VI (1863), 300-1.

65. Order of Mass. Council, June 24, 1675, MA, Military LXVII, 205; Mass. Gen. Ct. to John Winthrop, Jr., July 5, 1675, *ibid.,* 209½ (copy); Benjamin Batten to Sir Thomas Allin, Account of the Indian Insurrection, July 1675, *CSP,* (1675-76), #614.

66. *PCR,* X, 357; *MCR,* V, 69; John Winthrop, Jr. to Robert Treat, Dec. 18, 1675, *Winthrop Papers, Letters to, MHSC,* 5th Ser., VIII (1882), 174-75; Gov. Leverett to Sir Joseph Williamson, Dec. 18, 1675, *CSP,* (1675-76), #745; for a contemporary report, see "A Continuation of the State of New-England . . ." (1676), Samuel G. Drake, ed., *The Old Indian Chronicle* (Boston, 1867), 178ff; of many general accounts, see Elisha R. Potter, *The Early History of Narragansett* (Providence, 1835), 189-92.

67. John Bishop to Increase Mather, July 8, 1676, *Mather Papers, MHSC,* 4th Ser., VIII (1868), 300.

68. Anti-military sentiment, of course, earlier had been prevalent among Quakers and others. E.g., James Cudworth took the General Court to task for appointing Josiah Winslow permanently a major. See Cudworth's letter in *New-England A Degenerate Plant* (1659), 20.

69. *PCR,* III, 5 (1652); V, 7 (1668); Lothrop, Diary (1653), Yale U. Lib.

70. William Hooke, "New Englands Teares, for Old Englands Feares . . ." (1641) in Samuel Emery, *The Ministry of Taunton,* 2 vols. (Boston, 1853), I, 96-97.

71. John Freeman to Gov. Winslow, June 3, 1675, in Mather, *Magnalia Christi Americana,* II (1820 ed.), 497.

72. Hubbard, *General History, MHSC,* 2d Ser., VI, 642; "Simon Bradstreet's Memoires" (Journal), *NEHGR,* IX (1855), 45-46, June, 1671. See Morton, *New-England's Memorial,* for the numerous "manifestations" of God's "displeasure," 1664-76, 176-202.

73. *PCR,* V, 76-78; William Hubbard, *The History of the Indian Wars in New England . . .* (1677), ed. Samuel G. Drake (Roxbury, Mass., 1865), 58.

74. Benjamin Batten to Sir Thomas Allin, July 1675, *CSP,* (1675-76), #614.

75. Letter of William Bradford *et al.,* June 24, 1675, MA, Military, LXVII, 203; *Sandwich and Bourne Colony and Town Records,* Feb. 28, 1675, 28.

76. Hubbard, *Indian Wars,* 189. For the extent of destruction of the towns and comment on numbers and losses of Indians and Whites, see [Nath. Saltonstall?], "A New and Further Narrative of the State of New-England" (1676), in Charles H. Lincoln, ed., *Narratives of the Indian Wars, 1675-99, Original Narratives of Early American History Series,* (New York, reprint 1959), 97-98, 98n.; William Harris to Joseph Williamson, Aug. 12, 1676, *CSP* (1675-76), #1021.

77. *PCR,* V, 207, 210, 223, 253. The average price per Indian sold into slavery on one occasion brought over £3 each. "Diary of Samuel Sewall," July 2, 1676, *MHSC,* 5th Ser., V (1879) 14; John Easton, "A Relacion of the Indyan Warre" (1675), in C. H. Lincoln, ed., *Narratives of the Indian Wars, 1675-99,* 13.

78. [Nathaniel Saltonstall?], "The Present State of New-England with Respect to the Indian War," in Lincoln, ed., *Narratives of the Indian Wars, 1675-99,* 30.

79. See Leach, *Flintlock and Tomahawk,* 187-88.

80. Thomas Walley to John Cotton, Jr., April 17, 1676, Whitehill, ed., "Letters of Thomas Walley," *AASP,* LVIII (1949), 254.

81. Felt, *Ecclesiastical Hist.,* II, 639.

82. William Hooke, "New-Englands Sence, of Old-England and Irelands Sorrowes . . ." (1645), in Emery, *Ministry of Taunton,* 123.

Chapter Nine

TERRITORIAL IMPERATIVE

The state is the corporate body of a people in a given territory. Take away jurisdictional authority, the state—if not the nation—ceases to exist. The right of the Plymouth settlers to establish government over the territory in which they lived went to them by default of higher authority to grant incorporation. The patents of 1621 and 1630, however, gave proprietary rights to the soil but recognized no right to form corporate government. This the Pilgrims took upon themselves, and could they have done, hypothetically, the impossible of divesting themselves of citizenship of England or any other parent state, their self-incorporation would have been valid. But as transplanted Englishmen, without conferral of a charter from the crown of England, their act of self-determination would always be in question. Nevertheless, the Pilgrims thought of themselves as bound in a corporate state, which had full authority over a definite territory.

It is not the purpose here to probe the landholding system of Plymouth Colony—it was a rather routine pattern similar to the other New England colonies and was a natural working out of property holding in a new community. But it is pertinent to raise the question of the relation between holding real property and the status of the individual as a member of the state and to examine the territorial authority of the colony government, which would virtually disintegrate in the last years of the colony.

Whether land was granted through the adventurers (to 1630), Bradford and his associates (1630-39), or, after the patent was surrendered in 1641 through "the whole Body of the Freemen to be Disposed of either by the whole Body . . . or such as those they may assign,"[1] all land was held subject to the interests of the colony as a whole; therefore, any grant was "conditional, and not absolute."[2] The usual means for acquiring land in Plymouth—other than individual purchase of common lands from town boards of proprietors—was for persons, as a company, to apply to the General Court for confirmation of lands already purchased from the Indians.[3] The purchasers then were constituted pro-, prietors with the right to determine future alienation of the lands of the grant. As Roy Akagi writes:

> The ordinary process in the creation of proprietors under the Plymouth practice was, with slight variations, as follows: (1) the application to the Court for a permission to purchase; (2) the authorization of purchase by the Court, often appointing a committee to supervise the transaction; (3) the purchase from the natives by the adventurers, always with a deed but very ambiguous in boundaries; (4) the confirmation of the purchase by the Court; (5) the actual occupation of the territory. Often purchases were made before the authorization of the purchase and the confirmation followed. This was particularly true in the period before the orders were passed prescribing the Court's permission for any purchase. After such a procedure the purchasers became the sole proprietors of the territory thus purchased and managed the affairs as any other proprietaries, though under the territorial jurisdiction of the General Court. The shares in the propriety were regulated in proportion to the money advanced in the purchases.[4]

After the incorporation of a town, the board of proprietors continued to hold the right to dispose of town lands, subject to the approval of the General Court. In most towns, until towards the end of the colony's history, proprietors were at least near the majority of freemen in a town, and demands for equal shares in the common lands by new freemen were warded off.[5] After 1682, the General Court compelled all towns to have proprietors' meetings and that their decisions govern entirely the disposition of unassigned town lands.[6] The General Court early required that all lands be held according to "the most free Tenure of East Greenwich in the County of Kent in the Realm of England"[7] and that all titles be recorded in the towns.[8] Throughout most of the colony's history titles were recorded in both the colony and town records. By developing a recording system for landholding and placing it under the supervision of the colony government, Plymouth, as did its neighbors, "acknowledged the desire manifest by the New England community to preserve its exclusive and homogeneous character."[9]

The General Court legislated on many matters relating to landholding, such as regulations for fencing, herding cattle, punishment for trespass, and the like that need not be of concern here, except to note that these regulations came from the colony level, with local ordinances more of a supplementary nature; only in the last years were the towns and counties expected to deal almost exclusively in these areas, when relative uniformity had already been achieved. The relationship of landholding, residency and the franchise has been discussed in an earlier chapter. But mention of a few other colony laws will indicate the reach of the central government in land policy.

As noted before, no person technically could be "admitted to live and inhabite within the Government of New Plymouth without the leave and likeing of the Governor or two of the Assistants at least."[10] Precautions were taken by the General Court to prevent persons unorthodox in religion or otherwise undesirable from receiving lands. Proprietors were ordered from time to time not to grant lands to those "unfitt for church societie."[11] The overall reluctance to sell lands to outsiders served to prevent troublemakers from disrupting the stability of the community. When a town seemed to be negligent in this respect, the General Court sent an assistant to sit on the town board of proprietors, to serve as a watchdog.[12] Also, the whole town and the church had to approve a sale of land to a newcomer.[13] Persons selling lands to newcomers not approved by the town or the proprietors faced confiscation of their lands.[14] "Old Comers" always had the right to find new lands, and titles were approved without much trouble providing that the purchasers "do not to much straiten the Indians."[15] In order to insure equality of land distribution as much as possible and to prevent depopulation, an early practice of the colony was to require persons to forfeit lands on which they were not residing or improving.[16] The colony also forbade the building of "cottages remote from prompt protection."[17] Aiding community ties was the right of every householder of a town to use perpetually the commons and outlying meadows and to gather fire wood at large. But by 1673 a differential in this privilege was recognized. Thus the General Court ordered that a person with a ratable estate of £20 could keep one horse upon the commons; of £40, two; and of £60, three.[18]

As lands were taken up beyond the immediate vicinity of Plymouth town, the General Court followed the practice of entrusting the determination of the bounds of land grants and the judgment as to a bona fide purchase from the Indians to a committee of four assistants. The committee visited areas in question and its decision, "according to justice and equitie," was considered "as authenticall and effectual . . . as if same had been done in the publicke Court."[19] When a town was already established, a town committee joined with the committee appointed by the General Court to reach an agreement concerning a land dispute.[20]

Maintenance of territorial sovereignty was a test of legitimacy of the Plymouth state. From time to time the Plymouth government reached out to claim frontier settlements that had repudiated jurisdiction of the colony, but attempts of this sort met with meager success. Orders for allegiance from Shawomet (Warwick), Gorton's refuge on the west side of Narragansett Bay, and Aquidneck Island—both part of Providence Plantations—were not enforced, even though the commissioners of the United Colonies upheld Plymouth's right to Gorton's lands. The Rhode Island charter was a stumbling block to Plymouth's expansion to the southwest.[21] Whereas Plymouth at one time claimed jurisdiction over most of Rhode Island Colony, the colony was willing from the outset to recognize Roger Williams's right to sanctuary at Providence.[22] Although Plymouth stayed out of the muddle over the contest for the "Narragansett Country" after King Philip's War, the colony was awarded lands south of Swansea by the king, who used the occasion to announce that, since

Plymouth had "only a general Grant from the old Councill of Plymouth," the "Peace and Happiness" of the whole colony might soon be confirmed by a charter from the crown[23]—of course, a promise never realized.

One continued dispute between Rhode Island and Plymouth—although considered of minor consequence by both colonies—was the jurisdiction over Hog Island (Chassawanuck) in Narragansett Bay. Contending parties each claimed to be under different colony government. At first Plymouth turned the dispute over to the colony's two commissioners of the United Colonies joined by a special committee to treat with commissioners from Rhode Island; no decision, however, was reached.[24] The Hog Island controversy flared up again in the 1680's. The colony was accused by the Rhode Island authorities of enticing several inhabitants into Plymouth jurisdiction and then arresting them for unlawfully "detaining of lands" at Hog Island.[25] Yet no force of arms was resorted to by Plymouth—the affair remained much as it had been, a private matter between two sets of claimants. In 1683 royal commissioners were given the authority to hear all boundary disputes between Plymouth and Rhode Island or elsewhere, and the court of assistants in response to this order named Governor Hinckley, by himself, or with Daniel Smith or John Walley "as opportunity may present, to make plea in defence of the rights of this Colony as to their jurisdiction or tittle to any lands granted by our patent. . . ."[26]

Several earlier boundary disputes between Plymouth and Massachusetts were settled by boards of arbitration composed of commissioners of both colonies, most notedly: the boundary at Mount Wollaston, near Dorchester;[27] jurisdiction over Pawtuxet and Shawomet (first allowed to Massachusetts and then reassigned to Plymouth);[28] and the boundary of the marsh at Cohasset (between Hingham and Scituate), which generated a good deal of ill-feeling but was finally settled with assistance from the commissioners of the United Colonies.[29]

If Plymouth showed a reluctance to extend its boundaries or to make a determined fight to assert sovereignty over disputed areas, it was because of the continued awareness of the lack of a charter giving the Plymouth government a right to exercise authority over a definite territory. Yet before the royal commissioners began snooping around the New England colonies in

1664, the colony leaders showed little interest in securing incorporation of the colony from the home government.

Particularly not much was done to establish an agency in London to lobby in behalf of the colony. An agency in itself entailed too high costs for a colony as poor as Plymouth to maintain, and when representatives for the colony had gone to England, they had bungled whatever opportunity there had been to obtain a charter. Miles Standish in 1625 sojourned in England when the council of New England was not meeting, and even then his task was merely to seek more favorable economic terms from the council. With London in the midst of a plague, he returned, having accomplished nothing.[30] Isaac Allerton's visits in 1626 and 1627 also were not intended for winning political rights for the colony. Much of the time of Edward Winslow's first agency for Massachusetts (1634) was spent in jail, on the orders of Archbishop Laud because Winslow had performed marriages in the place of a clergyman—and as Bradford wrote: "and this was the end of this petition, and this business."[31] His second agency (1646-52) was primarily to defend Massachusetts (and indirectly Plymouth) against charges brought by Samuel Gorton, John Greene, Randall Holden, Robert Child, and Samuel Maverick. Plymouth showed slight interest in joining with Massachusetts to support Winslow's agency.[32]

Plymouth tried to take advantage of other New England agents going to England. For example, in 1661 Governor Prence asked John Winthrop, Jr. to present "our humble petition" to the king, "which untell now we have not been able to do, wanting an opertunety and menes to present it . . . let not our low condishon discouridg you . . . any labor of love or exspenc you may be at in persuance of an answer from his Majesty" would be acknowledged. Winthrop, however, embarked from New Amsterdam in order to avoid last minute calls for help from Plymouth and the other New England colonies.[33]

It seemed as if no time had been apropos for Plymouth to secure a charter: in the 1630's the scheme of Sir Ferdinando Gorges almost prevailing in establishing one dominion for all of New England, then the Civil War and the Cromwellian period; in the 1660's having to face the charges of persecuting the Quakers, and then, in spite of the good will won from the home government during Josiah Winslow's administration, the

revival of attacks on the independent charters. In the early
1680's Governor Hinckley was reluctant to take an initiative.
As Governor Cranfield of New Hampshire noted after a meeting
with Governor Hinckley and Barnabas Lothrop, an assistant:
"I find them weak men and very unfit to be concerned in
Government. It is true that the inhabitants are generally low in
estate, but their greatest lack is able men to govern the colony."[34]
An effort was made to establish an agency in London, when
James Cudworth went to England, but he died shortly after his
arrival in 1682. Thereafter the colony sent several pleas to the
king for a charter, "such as you have granted to Connecticut and
Rhode Island."[35] But without an agent in England, these petitions
attracted almost no attention.

The policy of the later Stuarts to effect a complete royalization
of the colonies and the *quo warranto* proceedings against the
Massachusetts charter threatened the separate status of Plymouth as an independent colony. The first indication of what
was in store for the future was the order from the king that
Edward Cranfield, Lieutenant Governor and "commander in
chief" of New Hampshire should give aid to neighboring colonies "and particularly to our Colony of New Plymouth, in case
of any insurrection or rebellion, or of any attempt or invasion of
any of our enemies" and "that we do in the same manner
expect and require that a mutual assistance be readily given" by
Plymouth Colony if the same conditions existed in New Hampshire.[36]

After a long period of silence from the Secretary of State,
William Blathwayt, and the king's investigator in the colonies,
Edward Randolph,[37] Plymouth decided in 1683 to send another
agent to England—Ichabod Wiswall, pastor at Duxbury. Wiswall's church was asked to "lend him to the Lord for a little
season, to give up himself to a service wherein not only your
own, but the weal of all these churches and this whole Colony
together . . ." but the church voted twenty-three to fifteen against
releasing him.[38] With the Dominion of New England soon to be
established, Wiswall did not become an agent for the colony
until 1689.[39] Meanwhile, upon James II's accession to the throne,
the colony again petitioned for a royal charter.[40]

To Plymouth Colony, the Dominion of New England was a
sobering experience, which made an alternative of annexation

to Massachusetts under a royal charter a lesser of two evils. Plymouth was proportionately represented on the Dominion Council with six members.[41] All local officers—civil and miiltary —were confirmed by Andros, and laws of the colony were upheld,[42] yet liberty in the colony was curtailed. Town meetings could be held only at designated times and then only to elect selectmen and officials. All land titles had to be derived from grants from the king.[43] Shadrach Wildbor, town clerk at Taunton, was fined and spent a good part of a three month sentence in jail for signing "a modest paper" protesting taxation without representation.[44] The Plymouth councilors bided their time in the Andros regime; only the old secretary of the colony, Nathaniel Clark, collaborated—for which he was imprisoned when the Dominion government was toppled.[45]

The Revolution in New England left the Plymouth authorities at a loss which way to turn. A defeatist attitude seemed to prevail that the colony's independent status would be eliminated regardless of whatever decision was made at Whitehall.[46] Governor Hinckley's son-in-law, writing from Sandwich in the spring of 1689, expressed the general disillusionment:

> I fear whether or not the matter of settling things under a new Government may not prove far more difficult than the getting from under the power of the former, except the Lord eminently appear in calming and quieting the disturbed spirits of the people, whose duty certainly now is to condescend, comply. . . .[47]

Hopes of preserving the political integrity of the colony were pinned on a revival of the United Colonies of New England— that somehow the crown would recognize the separate status of each member of the Confederation[48]—and that Ichabod Wiswall, Plymouth's agent now in London, and the Massachusetts agents,[49] supposedly friendly to Plymouth's interests, would convince the British government to continue the corporation of Plymouth Colony.

Various addresses were sent by the General Court to the king and queen justifying the reestablishment of colony government after Andros's fall and reminding the sovereigns that Plymouth was the oldest New England colony and therefore deserved "confirmation of our former rights and liberties."[50] Particularly Governor Hinckley entrusted Plymouth's destiny to Increase

Mather, who initially petitioned for separate, independent charters for Plymouth, Massachusetts, Rhode Island, and Connecticut.[51] Hinckley apparently had little faith in the ability of the colony's own agent, so much so that Wiswall in London complained that he had not heard from the governor for a year and a half.[52] The reason was probably that Mather was the recognized leader of the delegation and Wiswall was counted as a member of the Massachusetts theocrat party; as Hinckley himself says, he was "never so much our friend." But Wiswall had a different view, blaming his lack of contact with the Plymouth authorities upon the apathy of the colony:

> When some consider the spirit which animated the first planters to venture their all, in attempting so great hazards for the enjoyment of civil and religious privileges in that day, and also reflect upon the demurs or neglects of those who so lately were providentially snatched as brands ... That Plymouth under its present circumstances, should sit silent so long ... is a great riddle. If you desire to return to the late experience of the miseries of an arbitrary commissioned Government, a little longer neglect of your opportunity may hasten it. I know not any one here that hath opened his mouth in your behalf, either to the king or others concerned.[53]

Efforts to restore Plymouth as an independent colony were sidetracked by the proposal to annex the colony to New York, for which a provision was actually inserted in Henry Sloughter's commission as governor of New York; but through Mather's intervention this clause was stricken out.[54] It was also proposed to combine Massachusetts and Nova Scotia—and from interchange of correspondence between the agents and the Plymouth authorities the position was taken that if a separate colony status could not be obtained, then the second best arrangement would be to unite Massachusetts and Plymouth.[55] Indeed by the fall of 1691 Hinckley had given up all hope for a charter:

> I see little or no likelihood of obtaining a charter for us, unless their majesties, out of their royal bounty and clemency, graciously please to grant it, *sub forma pauperis,* to their poor but loyal subjects of this Colony, whose fathers and predecessors, to enjoy the liberty of their consciences ... did, at their own proper cost and charge . . . settle the first English plantation in New England, then a howling wilderness, a land not sown. . . .[56]

The royal charter incorporating Plymouth into Massachusetts, recognizing religious toleration and taking the appointment of the governor and council out of the hands of the theocrat party, represented an effort to win popular appeal rather than to appease the leading faction in Massachusetts. The charter came closer to the principles of the political leadership in Plymouth Colony than in Massachusetts.

The subsequent delay in the imperial reordering of the New England governments after the collapse of the Dominion of New England had proved more disruptive to the Plymouth government than to the other colonies, even though the former colony government had been reestablished ad interim. Settlers at Little Compton and Dartmouth refused to acknowledge the authority of the colony to require taxes for support of soldiers in King William's War, and they engaged in "riotously assembling" to resist collection by the constables. As Governor Hinckley saw it, there would possibly be bloodshed.[57]

During this period of uncertainty, the ministry discerned the judgment of God in the looseness of morals and the failure to enforce sumptuary codes in the churches and government.[58] A letter from the elders meeting in Plymouth to the churches took note of the demoralization:

> Wee in this colony are brought exceeding low as to our civill Government, many openly casting off the yoke of subjection to our civill rulers, and there being noe strong rod for a scepter to rule, whereby wee are in great danger of being given into the hands of strangers to manage us at their pleasure, and soe of loosing the liberty of those most pretious enjoyments for the sake of which our blessed fathers followed God into this wilderness.[59]

In the end, with the new charter soon to be sent over, there was a sense of relief that the long insecurity had been resolved, since, as Cotton Mather observed, Plymouth had been "so wonderfully Sottish, as to take no Care of itself."[60] In May 1692, William Phips arrived in Boston with the new charter and his commission as governor. The Plymouth General Court met for the last time on the first Tuesday in July; its final act was to order that the last Wednesday in August should be a day of public humiliation and fasting.[61]

Even after the establishment of the new royal colony, some force had to be used to bring law and order to several of the Plymouth towns: Bridgewater, Taunton, and the border towns of Little Compton and Bristol, which preferred Rhode Island jurisdiction.[62]

In the last years of the colony, those cohesive elements that make for a strong state were lacking. Political authority had shifted from central control to a fragmentation of town democracies. The people, caught in an economic vise of subsistence farming and local fishing and without capital or a developed industry or commerce, were concerned for their immediate needs. The newer generations had lost the zeal of the original mission into the wilderness. The colony had long endured the shadow of dominance of the Bay Colony in every phase of life. The insecurity and fading hopes for recognition of a legal base of the political corporation, dating from the 1660's, added to the disillusionment. The last governor of the colony spent much of his time at his home in Barnstable. The colony was disintegrating, and there was no unified feeling to make any great effort to pull the body politic up by its bootstraps. Annexation to Massachusetts was the best palliative in restoring political and territorial integrity.

NOTES

1. Act . . . of the Gen. Ct., March 8, 1640, Misc. Bound, MSS, I, 24, MHS. See Chapter 1.

2. "An answer to the Proprietors made by Mr. Leveridge and others, of Sandwich," June 1638, *Sandwich and Bourne Colony and Towne Records,* 1.

3. Roy H. Akagi, *The Town Proprietors of the New England Colonies* (Philadelphia, 1924), 25; see Freeman, *History of Cape Cod,* II, 579-80 for the slight complications in W. Nickerson securing confirmation for his purchase of Indian lands, 1665-72 or Bowen, *Rehoboth,* I, 179-80 concerning purchase of lands at "Freetown" in 1656 by James Cudworth and associates.

4. Akagi, *Town Proprietors,* 25-26; Baylies, *Historical Memoir . . . New Plymouth,* I, 241-42.

5. Osgood, *American Colonies,* I, 464-66.

6. *PCR,* XI, 257; Akagi, *Town Proprietors,* 55. For the diminishing of opportunity for new settlers, without capital, to obtain a share in undivided lands, see Langdon, *Pilgrim Colony,* 45-47.

7. Taunton Town Records, Jan. 18, 1674, 37; *PCR,* XI, 12 (1636); Akagi, *Town Proprietors,* 37. For practices governing alienation and partible inheritance, see George L. Haskins, "The Beginnings of Partible Inheritance in the American Colonies," in Flaherty, ed., *Essays . . . Early American Law,* 205-7, 227-29.

8. *PCR,* XI, 63 (1654).

9. See Morris, *Studies . . . American Law,* 69.

10. *PCR,* XI, 26 (1637).

11. *Ibid.,* I, 84 (1638), 131 (1639); *Sandwich and Bourne Colony and Towne Records,* Dec. 4, 1638, 2.

12. E.g., *Sandwich and Bourne Colony and Towne Records,* Oct. 3, 1639, 3.

13. See Brockunier, *Irrepressible Democrat,* 164-65; Deyo, *History of Barnstable County,* 267.

14. E.g. see Otis O. Wright, *History of Swansea, Mass., 1667-1917* (Swansea, 1917), town records, Feb. 12, 1670, 53.

15. *PCR,* XI, 60 (1652); e.g., grant to Thomas Willett and associates, *ibid.,* IV, 175 (1658).

16. *Ibid.,* XI, 18 (1636); "History of Plympton . . .," *MHSC,* 2d Ser., IV (1816), 283-84.

17. "Notes on Plymouth, Massachusetts," MHSC, 2d Ser., III

(1815), 163. For immigrating into Scituate and building a home without permission from the authorities, the colony levied a 10s. fine. *PCR*, VIII, 140 (1673).

18. *PCR*, XI, 4-5 (1636), 235 (1673); e.g., April 5, 1670, *Barnstable Town Records, Library of Cape Cod History and Genealogy*, #105, 8.

19. E.g., concerning the bounds of Yarmouth and Barnstable (*PCR*, II, 19 [1641]), enlargement of bounds of Taunton (*ibid.*, IV, 28 [1662]), and grant to Thomas Willett of lands north of Rehoboth near the Mass. boundary (Taunton Town Records, Oct. 1665, 35).

20. E.g., May 17, 1686 and June 9, 1686, *Plymouth Town Records*, I, 186; Winsor, *History of Duxbury*, 14-15.

21. *PCR*, IV, 44 (1663); IX, 28 (1644); Roger Williams to John Winthrop, Jr., Sept. 23, 1648, *Winthrop Papers*, V (1947), 258-59. For the controversy also see Samuel Gorton, *Simplicities Defence against Seven-headed Policy* (1646), #6 of Peter Force, ed., *Tracts and Other Papers*, IV (Washington, 1846), 19; *Winthrop Hist.*, II, 270, May 14, 1645; Arnold, *History of R. I.*, I, 159-62; Adelos Gorton, *The Life and Times of Samuel Gorton* (Philadelphia, 1907), 45-68; Brockunier, *Irrepressible Democrat*, 195.

22. Roger Williams to Major Mason, June 22, 1670, *MHSC*, 1st Ser., I (1792), 276-77; Dana, "Account of Plymouth Colony Records," *ibid.*, 3d Ser., II (1830), 267; Potter, *Early History of Narragansett*, 165-66; Roderick Terry, "The Early Relations between the Colonies of New Plymouth and Rhode Island," *Bulletin of Newport Historical Society*, #34 (1920), 6-11.

23. Quoted in Bowen, *Rehoboth*, I, 70 (1685).

24. *PCR*, III, 142 (1658), 157 (1659); Emily Easton, *Roger Williams: Prophet and Pioneer* (Boston, 1930), 335; Arnold, *History of Rhode Island*, I, 266, 477-78.

25. *PCR*, VI, 93 (1682); the Gen. Assembly of . . . R. I. to . . . New Plymouth, June 24, 1684, *HP*, 127.

26. S/ William Bradford [for the court of assistants], Aug. 7, 1683, *ibid.*, 90.

27. *MCR*, I, 196, 217, 271 (May-Nov., 1637).

28. *Ibid.*, III, 216 (1650); IV, 15 (1650); *PCR*, III, 198 (1650).

29. *MCR*, II, 68 (1640); III, 380 (1655); IV, 285, 294 (1656); *PCR*, IX, 1-2; William Bradford to John Winthrop, April 11, 1638,

Winthrop Papers, Letters to, MHSC, 4th Ser., VI (1863), 156; *Bradford Hist.* (1912), II, 274-82; E. V. Bigelow, *A Narrative History of the Town of Cohasset* (Boston, 1898), 120-28.

30. Bradford to Council of New England, June 28, 1625, "Bradford's Letter Book," *MHSC,* 1st Ser., III (1794, reprint 1816), 38.

31. *Bradford Hist.* (1912), II, 198-204.

32. *MCR,* III, 79 (1646); Clyde M. Ferrell, *The Massachusetts Colonial Agents in England* (unpubl. Ph. D. diss., University of Wisconsin, 1923), 8-31; James J. Burns, *The Colonial Agents of New England* (Washington, D. C., 1935), 25-26, 30-31.

33. Thomas Prence to John Winthrop, Jr., Sept. 29, 1661, *Winthrop Papers, Letters to, MHSC,* 5th Ser., I (1871), 392; Richard S. Dunn, *Puritans and Yankees: The Winthrop Dynasty of New England, 1630-1717* (Princeton, 1962), 124.

34. Gov. Cranfield to Lords of Trade and Plantations, Mar. 27, 1683, *CSP,* (1681-85), #1024.

35. Gov. and Council of New Plimouth to the King, Nov. 1683, *ibid.,* #1389.

36. Charles II to the Governor and Council of the Colony of Plymouth, June 5, 1682, *HP,* 71.

37. Thomas Hinckley to William Blathwayt, May 26, 1682, *ibid.,* 65-66, 74n. and Nov. 22, 1683, *ibid.,* 94-95. Blathwayt, upon Cudworth's death, however, did request Plymouth to send another agent or to "fully instruct Mr. Randolph with all particulars of your business, that upon his return to England . . . we may join our endeavours in behalf of your Colony . . . .," Blathwayt to Thomas Hinckley, Sept. 27, 1683, *ibid.,* 91-92.

38. Gen. Ct. of New Plymouth, S/ Nathaniel Morton, Feb. 8, 1683, *ibid.,* 84-86.

39. Thomas Hinckley to Sir Henry Ashurst, Feb. 4, 1690, *ibid.,* 226.

40. Petition and Address of the Gen. Ct. . . . of New Plymouth [to James II], June 4, 1685, *ibid.,* 138.

41. Plymouth councilors were: Thomas Hinckley, William Bradford, John Walley, Barnabas Lothrop, Nathaniel Clark, and Daniel Smith.

42. "Papers Relative to the Period of the Usurpation," *MHSC,* 3d Ser., VII (1838), 168; Randolph to the Lords of Trade and Plantations, Sept. 2, 1685, *CSP* (1685-89), #350; Toppan, ed., "Andros Records," Dec. 30, 1686, *AASP,* XIII (1901), 242-44;

Viola F. Barnes, *The Dominion of New England* (New York, reprint, 1960), 73.

43. Everett Kimball, *The Public Life of Joseph Dudley, Harvard Historical Studies,* XV (New York, 1911), 49-50.

44. [anon., several former councilors of Dom. of N. E.], *The Revolution in New-England Justified* (1691), *Force Tracts,* IV, #9 (1846), 14.

45. Nathanael Byfield, "An Account of the Late Revolution in New-England," in Andrews, ed., *Narratives of the Insurrections,* 175n. For a discussion of Plymouth's grievances against the Andros government, see Langdon, *Pilgrim Colony,* 212-33.

46. E.g., see Thomas Hinckley to Sir Henry Ashurst, June 6, 1689, *HP,* 202.

47. "Letter of Samuel Prince," April 22, 1689 in Andrews, ed., *Narratives of the Insurrections,* 190.

48. Only Mass. and Plymouth seemed ready to revive the Confederation. See "Order of commissioners for the Colonys" concerning dismissal of soldiers on the frontier, Oct. 1689, MA, Intercharter, XXXV, 63; Simon Bradstreet to Thomas Hinckley and the Council of the Colony of New Plymouth, July 17, 1690, *HP,* 266; Ward, *United Colonies,* chapter 15.

49. Increase Mather, Sir Henry Ashurst (an Englishman influential at the court), and two Mass. assistants—Elisha Cooke, Sr. and Thomas Oates.

50. Address of the Gen. Ct. of New Plymouth to the King and Queen, June 6, 1689, *CSP,* (1689-92), #183.

51. Thomas Hinckley to Increase Mather, Feb. 4, 1690, *HP,* 229; Kenneth Murdock, *Increase Mather: The Foremost Puritan* (Cambridge, 1925), 215.

52. Ichabod Wiswall [Wiswall] to Thomas Hinckley, (Dec. ?) 1691, *HP,* 299-300.

53. Ichabod Wiswall to Thomas Hinckley, July 6, 1691, *ibid.,* 285. Late 1691, Wiswall was back in the good graces of the colony and it was decided to pay him for his troubles (and the Mass. agents as well); the colony became appreciative of the work of the agents after the decision to unite Plymouth with Massachusetts. Plymouth, however, was unable to raise much of the £200 voluntary subscription to pay the agents. Wiswall was also in the pay of Massachusetts. John Walley to Ichabod Wiswall (?),—1691, *HP,* 286; *PCR,* VI, 260 (1691); Ferrell, Mass. *Agents* (Ph. D. diss.,), 127-28.

54. *PCR,* VI, 259 (1690); Cotton Mather to Thomas Hinckley, April 26, 1690, *HP,* 248; John Cotton to Thomas Hinckley, Feb. 6, 1691, *HP,* 279.

55. Increase Mather, "A Brief Account of the Agents . . . 1691," Andrews. ed., *Narratives of the Insurrections,* 285; Journal of the Lords of Trade and Plantations, Sept. 7, 1691, *CSP,* (1689-92), #1738. Wiswall had been responsible for having the unification of Ply. and Mass. stricken from the Mass. Charter. According to Cotton Mather, Wiswall told his fellow agents, if such a charter had cleared, Plymouth "would all curse him for it; at which the sollicitor Generall being extremely moved, presently dash't it out." Cotton Mather to Gov. Thomas Hinckley, Feb. 26, 1691, facsimile, Columbia University Special Collections.

56. Thomas Hinckley to Increase Mather, Oct. 16, 1691, *HP,* 288.

57. Thomas Hinckley to Ichabod Wiswall, Oct. 17, 1691, *ibid.,* 293-97.

58. Oberholzer, *Delinquent Saints,* 235.

59. Letter from the Elders of this Colony to the severall churches, Mar. 1692, *Plymouth Church Records,* I, 167.

60. *Diary of Cotton Mather,* ed. Ford, *MHSC,* 7th Ser., VII (1911), 142, Mather to John Cotton, Jr., Sept. 14, 1691.

61. Sewall, *Diary, MHSC,* 5th Ser., V (1879), 361; William T. Davis, *History of the Town of Plymouth* (Philadelphia, 1885), 73. Persons appointed from Plymouth to the Mass. Council, which first met on May 24, 1692, were: John Freeman, Daniel Smith, Barnabas Lothrop, John Thatcher, John Walley, and John Cushing. Deputies were elected from nineteen Plymouth towns. For a general and uncritical discussion of the civil rights and liberty of conscience in the new charter, see Martin L. Colbert, *The Rise of the Legislative Assembly in Provincial Massachusetts* (unpubl. Ph. D. diss., Iowa University, 1939), chapter 2.

62. Samuel Gookin to Gov. William Phips, Dec. 3, 1692, MA, Colonial I, 63; Mass. Council letter to Samuel Gookin, Dec. 8, 1692, *ibid.,* 65; John Walley to Gov. Phips, Dec. 13, 1692, *ibid.,* 67.

AFTERWORD

If the Pilgrim experience is viewed as a gradual secularization and politicization of a religious mission into the wilderness, one misses the central theme of the significance of the Old Colony. Rather, the greater meaning of Plymouth's history is the shaping of institutions from a primitive frontier condition. Originally a loose and informal congregation, the Pilgrims faced the necessity of creating upon a blank slate a community and an operative political corporation. They were guided by a common sense regard of human nature tempered by an imperfect knowledge of tradition and precedent. Government was formed for self-preservation and to serve practically the needs of the people. The closeness of government to the people gave it a simplicity and flexibility that in turn aided the growth of political liberalism.

One may argue that the Plymouth commonwealth was isolated from the mainstream of life in the other colonies. Be that as it may, the Pilgrim experience probably had some modifying effect upon the excessive Puritanism of its neighbors. At least, it set an example of a humble yeomanry going about their business, seeking merely law and order from government and willing to accommodate change in order to preserve harmony.

It is true that the Pilgrims believed in forcing one to act according to one's conscience, whether in exerting the responsibility of citizenship or in living up to the moral principles of the scriptures. But such coercion, sanctioned by the will of the majority under the sovereignty of God, was not merely intended to force men to be free but was necessary for survival of the commonwealth.

164

The Pilgrim state belonged to the people—even though the body politic was willing to delegate law making and executive powers to the magistrates and the General Court. If the majority was silent and apathetic, there at least did not develop a full dichotomy between an oligarchic control of the state and the constituency—virtually everyone was a landholder and had nearly an equal stake in society, and the colony had not lasted long enough for the state to build up an immunity against the people. The purpose of the Plymouth state was to provide justice, not to exercise power. Although the interest of the covenanted community was primary, the Pilgrim state was mindful of the rights of the individual. As much freedom of choice and action was permitted as did not conflict with the interests of the whole.

There was enough fluidity in Plymouth society to give freedom a dimension that mitigated efforts to enhance a dull conformity. If good government is measured by Edmund Burke's later dicta of "political convenience" then Plymouth was a paragon of good government. Certainly the settlers of Plymouth Colony had means of self-realization and protection of their interests.

Economic restrictions and monopoly grants were intended to insure the survival of the colony; once this was achieved the colony eased restrictions and left to localities economic controls. Restrictions were most severe when the security of the colony was threatened—hence trading in arms and ammunition with the Indians was a capital offense and force was used to break up rival trading posts.

Intolerance of political and religious dissent appeared from time to time, but always led to resolution by recognizing pluralistic elements.

The Pilgrims came close to maintaining a separation of civil and religious affairs. Of course, there were laws such as prohibiting Sabbath breaking or reproach of God, but they were confined primarily to the area of social action. Like Roger Williams the Pilgrims felt matters of conscience, good morals, and respect for the Divinity should be dealt with by the churches, while crimes threatening peace and order of society should be the province of the magistracy. But as the authority of the church relaxed, the civil government increased its role over the private life of the individual.

It is true that both church and state worked towards a com-

mon end of furthering the design of a holy commonwealth. But
the Pilgrims were not proselytizers of the faith and hence were
lacking in inquisitorial zeal; nor did they feel as strongly that
competition from dissenting views posed a threat to the established order as did the Puritans of the Bay Colony, who sought
to use religion as a test of authority of the state. There were
instances of turmoil over religious doctrines and support of an
orthodox ministry; occasionally there was a denial of civil liberty
on religious grounds but none of the untoward persecutions witnessed in Massachusetts. What repression there was in religion
was aimed primarily at preventing critics from casting the wrong
aspersions on the civil government to Englishmen back home
and to guard the established law and order; by the same token
the later laxity toward religious subversion may be attributed to
the desire of external approval from the home authorities as much
as to any principles of congregationalism or freedom of conscience. Nevertheless a basic toleration—even if at times veering
off course—was something that could not be taken away from
the Pilgrims. They themselves had too long been despised and
alienated in Europe not to appreciate the dignity and responsibility of each individual's conscience. Thus Miles Standish—
military leader and assistant—was never required to join the
church, and James Cudworth and Timothy Hatherly, though
experiencing brief ostracism for their dissent, were thoroughly
vindicated in having full freedom of conscience. Religion never
became an explicit condition of the franchise, except for the
Quakers, and this exclusion was short-lived. Indirect means of
admitting freemen according to religious belief eventually fell
into disuse.

Uneducated and inexperienced in the technicalities of law and
government, it is amazing that the Plymouth colonists so rapidly
created a workable and comprehensive legal system—and one
that embraced the substance of English jurisprudence without the
complexities or details. Justice in Plymouth was swift and direct,
and because of its informality, extenuating circumstances could
be taken into account. A habitual offender, such as a local town
drunk, would be simply given up as a lost cause. Persons were
convicted only upon clear proof of a specific crime with testimony of witnesses—and circumstantial evidence was used sparingly. Of course, when it was hard to distinguish between a crime

and misconduct, a culprit would be tried on a vague charge, such as "lewdness" or the like. The centralization of judicial proceedings in the court of assistants during most of the period aided uniformity and disinterested justice. Punishments fitted the crime, and although certain sex crimes were capital offenses, except for the lone execution for buggery when the colony was in the midst of an Indian scare, the extreme penalty was never inflicted in this area—punishment for rape, for example, was far milder than the standards of our own time. For a first offense, a person was given the benefit of the doubt and an opportunity for restitution and to seek remission for his sin; repeating offenders were subsequently dealt with more harshly. In meting out penalties the interests of the individual, family, and society were taken into consideration rather than the gravity of the offense alone—if some of the penalties were severe, it was because a person had to learn responsibility and the difference between right and wrong and an example had to be made.

Although the Plymouth state is instructive in the origins of authority and the natural desire to maintain that authority, there was no urge to exercise power for power's sake. Thus ferreting out sedition was not an active concern of the government. The absence of a printing press in the colony, relative immunity from an initial reception of knowledge from abroad, and the lack of an urban population lessened the threat of sedition. Sedition was viewed primarily as refusal to recognize an act of constituted authority rather than as subversive ideas or expression. The colony drew a sharp distinction between treason and sedition, unlike the mother country, with treason never being the subject of punitive action in Plymouth. Attempts to repress criticism against the state were aimed not so much at the danger to internal authority of the colony but to the disrepute that might be brought on the colony in England.

One of the marvels of Plymouth Colony is that, faced continually with Indian unrest and intermittently with the threat of war with a foreign neighbor, the state did not seek aggrandizement through military affairs. If, when the colony did go to war, there was no room for dissent and excessive cruelty was inflicted upon the enemy, war—and militarism—was nevertheless distasteful. Once engaged in war, the Pilgrims sought its immediate termination by complete victory and the extirpation of its causes, that the citizens might get back to their normal routine.

It was Plymouth's fortune to have men of moderation and wisdom to lead the colony. The only governor of intemperate disposition was Thomas Prence—but even he, in spite of his bitterness towards Quakers, only slightly stepped beyond the bounds of propriety. Hardly more able men could have been found in the gubernatorial seats in any of the colonies at any time than William Bradford and the two Winslows—and even if Hinckley did not possess the leadership qualities he made up for this deficiency in his sense of moderation.

Plymouth provides a microcosm in the construction of society by man in a state of nature. Through a continuing convention of the people, the colony dealt effectively with the necessity of the bare minimum for law and order. Though it was inevitable that a fairly sophisticated state would develop, it still rested on the consensus of the whole. If there were elements of elitism and the electorate was apathetic, conditions of freedom prevailed.

And remarkably, individual liberty had a breadth that was novel for the time. The Pilgrims believed in the sovereignty of God and not the institutions of man. Though they did not develop theories of fundamental law and were unfamiliar with the debates over the social compact in Cromwellian England, they believed the dignity and respect of each individual was inviolable. If the later generations lamented, as did Jeremiah, that "The fathers have eaten sour grapes, and the children's teeth are set on edge," as they saw the religious mission of their fore-fathers fade, they could nevertheless survey the howling wilderness and know that they had succeeded not only in surviving but in building a free society.

ABBREVIATION IN NOTES

AASP	*Proceedings of the American Antiquarian Society*
AHR	*American Historical Review*
CSP	*Calendar of State Papers, Colonial Series, American and West Indies,* ed. W. N. Sainsbury and J. W. Fortescue
HP	*The Hinckley Papers, MHSC,* 4th Ser., V (1861)
MA	Massachusetts Archives
MCR	*Records of the Governor and Company of the Massachusetts Bay in New England,* ed. N. B. Shurtleff
MHS	*Massachusetts Historical Society*
MHSC	*Collections of the Massachusetts Historical Society*
MHSP	*Proceedings of the Massachusetts Historical Society*
NEHGR	*New England Historical and Genealogical Register*
NYPL	New York Public Library
PCR	*Records of the Colony of New Plymouth in New England,* ed. N. B. Shurtleff and D. Pulsifer
PCSM	*Publications of the Colonial Society of Massachusetts*
WMQ	*William and Mary Quarterly*

SELECTED BIBLIOGRAPHY

The student of the history of the Old Colony should consult George D. Langdon, Jr., "Bibliographic Essay," *Occasional Papers in Old Colony Studies,* #1 (1969), 41-50 for an evaluation of the sources and particularly the local records. John M. Bumsted has prepared an exhaustive inventory of church, town, and parish records to 1775, which is available in mimeographed form from Plimoth Plantation, Inc. For a broad introduction to most of the published sources and a representation of the secondary works (pre-1945), the general reader will find the bibliographies in George F. Willison's *Saints and Strangers* (1945) and *The Pilgrim Reader* (1953) useful.

A vast reservoir of vital, land, and proprietary records remain in manuscript form, and only recently have been mined to produce several significant demographic studies, but there still is need for further work in these sources, especially in order to trace economic development and social patterns and structure. Town meeting and selectmen records, which come under the purview of this study, however, are scant for the period before 1690—many of the towns were founded late in the colony's history and some records have been destroyed. Most of these records before 1690 have been published either *in toto* or in extracts in the numerous town and county histories and elsewhere.

I. MANUSCRIPTS

Boston Public Library
Plymouth Colony Laws, 1636-71
Columbia University
Cotton Mather to Gov. Thomas Hinckley, Feb. 26, 1691, facsimile
Massachusetts Archives, State House, Boston
Colonial Series, I-III
Ecclesiastical Series, IX-XI
Intercharter Series, XXXV-XXXVII
Judicial Series, XL
Military Series, LXVII-LXX
Massachusetts Historical Society, Boston
Winslow Papers (1638-1759)
Miscellaneous Bound Manuscripts
Records of the West Parish of Barnstable, Massachusetts, photostats
New York Public Library
Plymouth Colony: Pilgrim Manuscripts, Miscellaneous—assorted collection of photostats, typescripts, etc.—mainly items used in 1921 library exhibit
Bancroft Transcripts. New England Letters of Governors and Others, 1607-83. 2 vols.
Chronicles of the Indians. Transcripts (by Samuel G. Drake) of documents relating to the Indians. 1 vol.
Pilgrim Hall, Plymouth, Massachusetts
Records of the Sessions of the Peace, 1686-1721, Plymouth County
City Hall, Taunton
Records of the Town of Taunton, 1642-1816. Vol. I
Yale University Library
John Lothrop, Diary, copied from the original in 1769 by Ezra Stiles, in Extracts from John Winthrop's manuscript History of New England

II. UNPUBLISHED THESES

Bumsted, John M. The Pilgrims' Progress: The Ecclesiastical History of the Old Colony, 1620-1775. Brown University, 1965.

Colbert, Martin L. The Rise of the Legislative Assembly in Provincial Massachusetts. University of Iowa, 1939.

Ferrell, Clyde M. The Massachusetts Colonial Agents in England. University of Wisconsin, 1923.

Hammelef, John C. British and American Attempts to Coordinate the Defenses of the Continental Colonies to Meet French and Northern Indian Attacks, 1643-1754. University of Michigan, 1955.

Hanna, Archibald, Jr. New England Military Institutions, 1693-1750. Yale University, 1951.

Johnson, Harry W. Moral Discipline in Early New England Churches. Bachelor of Divinity Thesis. University of Chicago, 1915.

Preston, Richard A. Colonial Schemes of Sir Ferdinando Gorges. Yale University, 1936. (Pub., Toronto, 1953).

Riley, Arthur. Catholicism in Colonial New England, 1620-1788. Catholic University, 1936.

Roberts, William C. The Fur Trade of New England in the Seventeenth Century. University of Pennsylvania, 1958.

III. PRINTED SOURCES

Arnold, Samuel. *David serving his generation, or a Discourse wherein is shewed that the great Care and Endeavour of every Christian ought to be . . . Serviceable unto God . . . . a Sermon preached to the General Court of the Colony of New-Plimouth . . .* (June 3, 1674) *Being the Day of Election there* (1674). Evans #185.

Ashton, Robert, ed. *The Works of John Robinson.* 3 vols. London, 1851.

Barnstable Town Records. Library of Cape Cod History and Genealogy, #105. Yarmouthport, 1910.

Bishop, George. *New-England Judged, by the Spirit of the Lord.* Revised edition, by Joseph Grove, of work originally published in 1661. London, 1703.

Bradford, William. *History of Plymouth Plantation, 1620-1647.* Ed. Worthington C. Ford *et al.* 2 vols. Boston, 1912.

———— *Of Plymouth Plantation, 1620-1647.* Ed. Samuel E. Morison. New York, 1967.

———— "A Dialogue, or the Sum of a Conference between Some Young Men Born in New England and Sundry Ancient Men that Came out of Holland and Old England, Anno Domini, 1648." *Old South Leaflets.* II, #49.

———— "Letter Book," *MHSC.* 1st Ser., III (1794), 27-84. Reprinted by the Society of Mayflower Descendants (Boston, 1906) and "Correspondence between the Colonies of New Netherlands and New-Plymouth" from the "Letter Book" is reprinted in *N. Y. Hist. Soc. Colls.* I (1841), 355-368.

"Extract from the Records of the Town of Bridgewater," *MHSP.* XIII (1875), 68, Feb. 22, 1660.

Brigham, William, ed. *The Compact with the Charter and Laws of the Colony of New Plymouth.* Boston, 1836.

Byfield, Nathanael. "An Account of the Late Revolution in New-England. Together with the Declaration of the Gentlemen Merchants . . . April 18, 1689." *Narratives of the Insurrections, 1675-1690.* Ed. Charles M. Andrews (New York, 1915), 170-182.

Church, Thomas. *The History of the Great Indian War of 1675 and 1676 Commonly Called Philip's War* . . . (1716). Ed. Samuel G. Drake, New York, 1845.

Clarke, John. "Ill Newes from New-England or A Narrative of New-Englands Persecution" (1652), *MHSC.* 4th Ser., II, 1-113.

A Letter of Mr. John Cottons . . . to Mr. Williams (1643). *Publications of the Narragansett Club.* 1st Ser., I.

Cotton, John. *A Reply to Mr. Williams his Examination; And Answer of the Letters sent to him by John Cotton* (1647). *Publications of the Narragansett Club.* 1st Ser., II (1867).

———— *Gods Promise to His Plantations* (1636). *Old South Leaflets.* III, #53.

———— "The Way of Congregational Churches Cleared" (1648), Extract. Adams, C. F., ed. *Antinomianism in the Colony of Massachusetts Bay, 1636-38. Publications of the Prince Society.* XXI (1894), 337-91.

Cotton, John (Jr.). *Poem upon the Death of . . . John Alden . . .* (1687). Portsmouth, N. H., 1806. Evans #426.

Crouch, Nathaniel. *The English Empire in America: Or a Prospect of His Majesties Dominions in the West-Indies, Namely, New-foundland, New-England . . .* London, 1685.

A Declaration of the Warrantable grounds and proceedings of the first Associates of the Government of New-Plymouth In their laying the first foundations . . . with the General Fundamentals of their Laws. Boston, 1773.

Deane, Charles, ed. "Records of the Council of New England, 1622-38." *AASP,* V, Minor Publications #4 (1867), 51-131.

Drake, Samuel G., ed. *The Old Indian Chronicle; being a Collection of Exceeding Rare Tracts, written and published in the Time of King Philip's War.* Boston, 1867.

Easton, John. "A Relacion of the Indyan Warre." *Narratives of the Indian Wars, 1675-99.* Ed. Charles H. Lincoln. New York, reprint 1959.

"Examen Legum: Or the Laws of England Examined by Scripture, Antiquity, and Reason" (anon., 1656). Howe, Mark D., ed. *Readings in American Legal History* (Cambridge, 1952), 86-95.

"The First Plymouth Patent." *MHSC.* 4th Ser., II (1854), 156-63.

Gookin, Daniel. "Historical Collections of the Indians in New England." *MHSC.* 1st Ser., I (1792), 141-227.

"Samuel Gorton's Letter to Nathaniel Morton, June 30, 1669." *Force Tracts.* IV, #7 (1846).

Gorton, Samuel. *Simplicities Defence against Seven-headed Policy . . .* (1646). *Force Tracts.* IV (1846).

Hazard, Ebenezer, ed. *Historical Collections: consisting of State Papers . . . .* Vol. I. Philadelphia, 1792.

Higginson, Francis. *New-Englands Plantation. Or, A Short and True Description of the Commodities and Discommodities of that Countrey* (1630). New York, reprint, 1943.

The Hinckley Papers. MHSC. 4th Ser., V (1861), 1-308.

Hooke, William. "New Englands Teares, for Old Englands Feares. Preached in a Sermon on July 23, 1640 being a day of Publicke Humiliation . . . (1641)." Emery, Samuel. *The Ministry of Taunton* (Boston, 1883), 75-98.

———— "New-Englands Sence, of Old-England and Irelands Sorrowes. A Sermon Preached upon a day of generall Humiliation in the Churches of New-England (1645)." Emery, Samuel. *The Ministry of Taunton* (Boston, 1883), 99-129.

Hubbard, William. *A General History of New England from the Discovery to 1680* (1682). *MHSC.* 2d Ser., V and VI (1848).

———— *The Happiness of a people In the wisdome of their Rulers directing and in the obedience of their brethren attending unto what Israel ought to do: Recommended in a Sermon before the Honourable Governour and Council, and the respected Deputies of the Mattachusets Colony in New-England. Preached at Boston, May 3d, 1676, being the Day of Election there . . . (1676).* Evans #214.

———— *The History of the Indian Wars in New England from the First Settlement to the Termination of the War with King Philip in 1677.* Ed. Samuel G. Drake. Roxbury, Mass., 1865.

James, Sydney V. Jr., ed. *Three Visitors to Early Plymouth.* Plymouth, Mass., 1963.

Jameson, J. Franklin, ed. *Narratives of New Netherland, 1609-1664.* New York, 1909.

Johnson, Edward. "Wonder Working Providence of Sions Saviour in New-England (1654)." *MHSC.* 2d Ser., II, 49-96; III, 123-61; IV, 1-51; VII, 1-58; VIII, 1-39.

Lechford, Thomas. "Plaine dealing: or Newes from New-England (1642)." *MHSC.* 3d Ser., III (1833), 55-128.

Lee, Samuel. *The Great Day of Judgement handled in a Sermon preached at the Assizes at New Bristol, October 7, 1687.* Boston, 1672. Evans #614.

Mason, John. "A Brief History of the Pequot War." *MHSC.* 2d Ser., VIII (2d Ed., 1826), 120-53.

Mather, Cotton. *Diary* (1681-1708). *MHSC*. 7th Ser., VII (1911).
———— *Magnalia Christi Americana: or, the Ecclesiastical History of New England* . . . 1620-1698 (1702). 2 vols.
Mather, Increase. *A Confession of faith owned and consented unto by the elders and messengers of the churches assembled at Boston in New-England, May 12, 1680. Being the second session of that Synod* (1680). Evans #280.
———— "A Brief Account concerning Several of the Agents of New-England, their Negotiation at the Court of England . . . (1691)." *Narratives of the Insurrections, 1675-90*. Ed. Charles M. Andrews (New York, 1915), 269-97.
The Mather Papers (chiefly letters to Increase and Cotton Mather). *MHSC*. 4th Ser., VIII (1868).
Morgan, Edmund S., ed. *Puritan Political Ideas*. Indianapolis, 1965.
Nathaniel Morton to Gov. Thomas Prence, April 2, 1658. *MHSP*. LI (1918), 201-2.
Morton, Nathaniel. *The New-England's Memorial* (1669). Plymouth, Mass., 1826.
Morton, Thomas. *New English Canaan* (1637). Ed. Charles F. Adams, Jr. *Publication of the Prince Society*. XIV (reprint, 1967).
Mourt's Relation [by Edward Winslow and William Bradford?] (1622). Ed. Heath, Dwight. The American Experience Series. New York, 1963.
[anon.] *New-England A Degenerate Plant who having forgot their former Sufferings, and lot* (1659). Photostat, NYPL.
Norton, Humphrey. *New-England's Ensigne* (1659). NYPL.
Nowell, Samuel. *Abraham in Arms; Or the first religious general with his Army Engaging in a War For which he had wisely prepared, and by which, not only an eminent Victory Was obtained, but a Blessing gained also. Delivered in an Artillery Election Sermon, June 3, 1678.* (1678). Evans #256.
Otis, Amos, ed. "Scituate and Barnstable Church Records." *NEHGR*. IX (1855), 279-87 and X (1856), 37-43.
"Papers Relative to the Period of Usurpation in New England." *MHSC*. 3d Ser., VII (1838), 150-91.
"Petition of John Prince and Nathaniel Bosworth to the Government of Plymouth, June 8, 1671." *MHSC*. 1st Ser., VI (1800), 127-28.
Pierce, Ebenezer W. *Civil, Military and Professional Lists of Plymouth and Rhode Island Colonies, 1621-1700*. Baltimore, reprint 1968.
Plymouth Church Records. 2 vols. New York, 1920-23.

Polishook, Irwin H., ed. *Roger Williams, John Cotton and Religious Freedom.* Englewood Cliffs, N. J., 1967.

"Letter of Samuel Prince [to his wife to be forwarded to Gov. Thomas Hinckley]." *Narratives of the Insurrections, 1675-90.* Ed. Charles M. Andrews. (New York, 1915), 186-90.

Records of the Town of Plymouth. 3 vols. I (1636-1705). Plymouth, 1889.

Robinson, John. "A Manumission to a Manuduction Or Answer to a Letter Inferring Publique communion in the parrish assemblies upon private with godly persons there (1615)." *MHSC.* 4th Ser., I (1852), 165-94.

(anon.—"several Gentlemen who were on his Council [Andros].) *The Revolution in New-England Justified* . . . (1691). *Force Tracts.* IV, #9 (1846).

Sainsbury, W. Noel and Fortescue, J. W., eds. *Calendar of State Papers, Colonial Series, America and West Indies.* Vols. I-VII (1574-1692). London, 1893-1901.

[Saltonstall, Nathaniel?]. "A Continuation of the State of New-England (1676)." *Narratives of the Indian Wars, 1675-99.* Ed. Charles H. Lincoln. (New York, reprint 1959), 53-74.

———— "A New and Further Narrative of the State of New-England (1676)." *Narratives of the Indian Wars, 1675-99.* Ed. Charles H. Lincoln. (New York, reprint 1959), 75-99.

———— "The Present State of New-England with Respect to the Indian War (1675)." *Narratives of the Indian Wars, 1675-99.* Ed. Charles H. Lincoln. (New York, reprint 1959), 19-50.

Sandwich and Bourne Colony and Towne Records, Library of Cape Cod History and Genealogy. #104. Yarmouthport, 1910.

Diary of Samuel Sewall. Vol. I (1674-1700). *MHSC.* 5th Ser., V (1879).

Letter-Book of Samuel Sewall. MHSC. 6th Ser., I (1886).

Shurtleff, Nathaniel B., ed. *Records of the Governor and Company of the Massachusetts Bay in New England.* 5 vols. (1628-1686). Boston, 1853-54.

———— and Pulsifer, David., eds. *Records of the Colony of New Plymouth in New England.* 12 vols. Boston, 1855-61.

"Simon Bradstreet's Memoires [Journal]." *NEHGR.* IX (1855), 43-51.

Smith, John. *The Generall Historie of Virginia, New-England, and the Summer Isles, with the names of the Adventurers, Planters, and Governors . . . 1584 to . . . 1624.* Facsimile ed. Cleveland, Ohio, 1966.

Toppan, Robert N., ed. "Andros Records (Minutes of the Council,

Dec. 29, 1686-April 25, 1687)." *AASP*. XIII (1901), 237-268 and 463-499.

Walker, Williston, ed. *The Creeds and Platforms of Congregationalism.* Boston, reprint 1960.

Walley, Thomas. *Balm in Gilead to heal Sions Wounds: Or a Treatise wherein there is a clear discovery of the most prevailing sicknesses of New-England, both in the civill and ecclesiastical state; as also sutable remedies for the cure of them: Collected out of that Spirituall directory, the word of God. Delivered in a sermon preached before the Generall Court of the Colony of New Plimouth on the first day of June 1669. Being the day of Election* (1669). Evans #146.

Whitehill, Walter M., ed. "Letters of the Reverend Thomas Walley of Barnstable to the Reverend John Cotton of Plymouth." *AASP*. LVIII (1949), 247-62.

Whitfield, Henry (pub.) "Strength out of Weaknesse; Or a Glorious Manifestation of the further Progresse of the Gospel among the Indians in New-England (1652)." *MHSC*. 3d Ser., IV (1834), 149-96.

Roger Williams to Major Mason, June 22, 1670. *MHSC*. 1st Ser., I (1792), 275-83.

Willison, George F., ed. *The Pilgrim Reader.* New York, 1953.

Winslow, Edward. "Good Newes from New England (1624)." Abridgement. *MHSC*. 2d Ser., IX (1832), 74-104.

———— *Hypocrisie Unmasked A True Relation of the Proceedings of the Governor and Company of the Massachusetts Against Samuel Gorton of Rhode Island* (1646). Introd. by Howard M. Chapin. Providence, 1916.

———— "New-Englands Salamander Discovered by an Irreligious and Scornful Pamphlet, called New-Englands Jonas Cast Up ,at London &c Owned by Major John Childe . . . (1647)." *MHSC*. 3d Ser., II (1830), 110-45.

"Letters to Josiah Winslow." *MHSC*. 1st Ser., VI (1800), 80-94.

Winthrop, John. *The History of New England from 1630-49.* Ed. James Savage. 2 vols. 2d edition. Boston, 1853.

The Winthrop Papers (1498-1659). 5 vols. Boston, 1929-47.

The Winthrop Papers, Letters to John Winthrop, John Winthrop, Jr., Fitz-John Winthrop et al. MHSC. 4th Ser., VI (1863); VII (1865); 5th Ser., I (1871); VIII (1882).

"The Winthrop Papers [John Winthrop, Jr.]." *MHSC*. 3d Ser., X (1849), 1-126 and IX (1846), 226-301.

Young, Alexander, ed. *Chronicles of the Pilgrim Fathers of the Colony of Plymouth, 1602-25.* Boston, 1844. Includes Robert Cushman's sermon of 1621: "The Sin and Danger of Self-Love," 255-62.

IV. SECONDARY SOURCES

Adams, Charles F. *Three Episodes of Massachusetts History*. 2 vols. Boston, revised ed., 1903.

Akagi, Roy H. *The Town Proprietors of the New England Colonies*. Philadelphia, 1924.

Andrews, Charles M. "British Committees, Commissions, and Councils of Trade and Plantations, 1622-75." *Johns Hopkins Univ. Studies in Hist. and Pol. Science*. Ser. XXVI, Nos. 1-3. Baltimore, 1908.

———— *The Colonial Period of American History*. Vol. I. New Haven, 1934.

Archer, Gleason L. *With Axe and Musket at Plymouth*. New York, 1936.

Arnold, Samuel G. *History of the State of Rhode Island*. Vol. I. New York, 1878.

Backus, Isaac. *A History of New England with Particular Reference to the Denomination of Christians Called Baptists*. 2 vols. I. Newton, Mass., 1871.

Bailyn, Bernard. *The New England Merchants in the Seventeenth Century*. New York, 1964 ed.

Barnes, Viola F. *The Dominion of New England: A Study in British Colonial Policy*. New York, reprint 1960.

Bartlett, J. Gardner. "John Peirce of London and the Merchant Adventurers." *NEHGR*. LXVII (1913), 147-53.

Battis, Emery. *Saints and Sectaries: Anne Hutchinson and the Antinomian Controversy in the Massachusetts Bay Colony*. Chapel Hill, N. C., 1962.

Baylies, Francis. *An Historical Memoir of the Colony of New Plymouth*. 2 vols. Boston, 1830.

Becker, Carl. *Freedom and Responsibility in the American Way of Life*. New York, 1958 ed.

Benton, Josiah H. *Warning Out in New England, 1656-1817.* Boston, 1911.

Bieber, Ralph P. *The Lords of Trade and Plantations, 1675-96.* Allentown, Pa., 1919.

Bigelow, E. V. *A Narrative History of the Town of Cohasset.* Boston, 1898.

Billias, George A., ed. *Selected Essays: Law and Authority in Colonial America.* Barre, Mass., 1965. The essays: Howe, Mark D., "The Sources and Nature of Law in Colonial Massachusetts," 1-16; Shipton, Clifford K., "The Locus of Authority in Colonial Massachusetts," 136-48; Rutman, Darrett B., "The Mirror of Puritan Authority," 149-67.

Bodge, George M. *Soldiers in King Philip's War.* Baltimore, reprint 1967.

Bonfanti, Leo. *Biographies and Legends of the New England Indians.* #1. Wakefield, Mass., 1969.

Borden, Alanson. *Our County and its Peoples; A Descriptive and Biographical Record of Bristol County, Mass.* Boston, 1899.

Bowen, Richard L. *Early Rehoboth: Documented Historical Studies of Families and Events in This Plymouth Colony Township.* 4 vols. I-III, Rehoboth, Mass., 1945-50.

Breen, T. H. *The Character of the Good Ruler: A Study of Puritan Political Ideas in New England, 1630-1730.* New Haven, 1970.

Brewster, Dorothy. *William Brewster of the Mayflower: Portrait of a Pilgrim.* New York, 1970.

Brockunier, Samuel H. *The Irrepressible Democrat: Roger Williams.* New York, 1940.

Burns, James J. *The Colonial Agents of New England.* Washington, D. C., 1935.

Burrage, Champlin. *The Church Covenant Idea: Its Origin and Development.* Philadelphia, 1904.

Byington, Ezra. *The Puritan as a Colonist and Reformer.* Boston, 1899.

Chafee, Zechariah, Jr. "Colonial Courts and the Common Law." *MHSP.* LXVIII (1947), 132-59. Also reprinted in Flaherty, *Essays* (1969), Chapter 3.

Channing, Edward. *Town and Country Government in the English Colonies of North America. Johns Hopkins Univ. Studies in Hist. and Pol. Science.* 2 Ser., X. Baltimore, 1884.

Cotton, John. "An Account of the Church of Christ in Plymouth, the First Church in New-England, from its Establishment to the Present Day (1760)." *MHSC.* 1st Ser., IV (1795), 107-141.

Cushing, John D. "Notes on Disestablishment in Massachusetts, 1780-1833." *WMQ.* 3d Ser., XXVI (1969), 169-90.

Dale, R. C. "The Adoption of the Common Law by the American Colonies." *American Law Register*. XX (1882), 553-74.

Dana, Samuel *et al.* "Account of Plymouth Colony Records." *MHSC*. 3d Ser., II (1830), 258-71.

Davies, A. Mervin. *Foundation of American Freedom*. New York, 1955.

Davis, Andrew M. "The Law of Adultery and Ignominious Punishments—with Especial Reference to the Penalty of Wearing a Letter Affixed to the Clothing." *AASP*. X (1896), 97-126.

Davis, Joseph S. *Essays in the Earlier History of American Corporations. Harvard Economic Studies*. XVI. Cambridge, 1917.

Davis, William T. *History of the Town of Plymouth*. Philadelphia, 1885.

Day, Clive. "Capitalistic and Socialistic Tendencies in the Puritan Colonies." *Annual Report of the Amer. Hist. Association for the Year 1920*. (Washington, 1925), 223-35.

Deane, Charles. "Notice of Samuel Gorton." *NEHGR*. IV (1850), 201-21.

Deane, Samuel. *History of Scituate, Massachusetts*. Boston, 1831.

Demos, John. *A Little Commonwealth: Family Life in Plymouth Colony*. New York, 1970.

———— "Families in Colonial Bristol, Rhode Island: An Exercise in Historical Demography." *WMQ*. 3d Ser., XXV (1968), 40-57.

———— "Notes on Life in Plymouth Colony." *WMQ*. 3d Ser., XXII (1965), 264-86.

Dexter, Henry M. *The Congregationalism of the Last Three Hundred Years as Seen in its Literature*. New York, 1880.

———— and Dexter, Morton. *The England and Holland of the Pilgrims*. Boston, 1905.

Deyo, Simeon L. *History of Barnstable County, Massachusetts*. New York, 1890.

Duniway, Clyde A. *The Development of Freedom of the Press in Massachusetts*. New York, 1906.

Dunn, Richard S. *Puritans and Yankees: The Winthrop Dynasty of New England, 1630-77*. Princeton, 1962.

Eames, Wilberforce. "Early New England Catechisms." *AASP* XII (1899), 76-182.

Earle, Alice M. *The Sabbath in Puritan New England*. New York, 1892.

Easton, Emily. *Roger Williams: Prophet and Pioneer*. Boston, 1930.

Eliot, John. "Ecclesiastical History of Massachusetts and the Old Colony of Plymouth." *MHSC*. 1st Ser., VII (1792), 262-80; IX (1804), 1-49; X (1809), 1-37; 2d Ser., I, 194-210.

Emery, Samuel H. *The Ministry of Taunton.* 2 vols. I. Boston, 1853.

Ernst, James E. *The Political Thought of Roger Williams. University of Washington Pubs. in Lang. and Lit.* VI. Seattle, 1929. (Reprinted, Port Washington, N. Y., 1966).

Evans, Charles. "Oaths of Allegiance in Colonial New England." *AASP.* XXXI (1921), 377-438.

Felt, Joseph B. *The Ecclesiastical History of New England.* 2 vols. Boston, 1855-62.

Flaherty, David H., ed. *Essays in the History of Early American Law.* Chapel Hill, N. C., 1969.

———— *Privacy in Colonial New England.* Charlottesville, 1972.

Freeman, Frederick. *The History of Cape Cod: The Annals of Barnstable County and of its Several Towns.* 2 vols. Yarmouthport, reprint 1965.

Freund, Ernst *et al.,* eds. *Select Essays in Anglo-American Legal History.* 3 vols. Boston, 1907-9.

Goebel, Julius, Jr. "King's Law and Local Custom in Seventeenth Century New England." *Columbia Law Review.* XXXI (1931), 416-48. Also reprinted in Flaherty, *Essays* (1969), chapter 4.

Golob, Eugene O. *The "ISMS": A History and Evaluation.* New York, 1954.

Gooch, G. P. *The History of English Democratic Ideas in the Seventeenth Century. Cambridge Historical Essays.* No. 1. Cambridge, Eng., 1898.

Goodwin, John A. *The Pilgrim Republic.* Boston, 1888.

Gorton, Adelos. *The Life and Times of Samuel Gorton.* Philadelphia, 1907.

Hale, Nathaniel C. *Pelts and Palisades: The Story of Fur and the Rivalry for Pelts in Early America.* Richmond, Va., 1959.

Hale, Robert L. "Force and the State: A Comparison of 'Political' and 'Economic' Compulsion." *Columbia Law Review.* XXXV (1935), 149-201.

Haller, William. *The Rise of Puritanism.* New York, reprint 1957.

Haller, William, Jr. *The Puritan Frontier: Town-Planting in New England Colonial Development, 1630-1660.* New York, 1951.

Haskins, George L. *Law and Authority in Early Massachusetts.* New York, 1960.

———— "The Legal Heritage of Plymouth Colony." Flaherty, *Essays* (1969), 121-134. Revision of "The Legacy of Plymouth." Special Article published by Plimoth Plantation, Inc., reprint from *Social Education.* XXVI (1962).

———— "The Beginnings of Partible Inheritance in the American Colonies." Flaherty, *Essays* (1969), 204-44.

Hatheway, Mary E. "The Early Hatheways of Taunton." *Old Colony Historical Society Collections.* #6 (1899), 76-81.

Haynes, George H. *Representation and Suffrage in Massachusetts, 1620-91. Johns Hopkins Studies in Hist. and Pol. Science.* 12th Ser., VIII-IX (1894).

Heller, Francis H. *The Sixth Amendment to the Constitution.* Lawrence, 1951.

Hilkey, Charles J. *Legal Development in Colonial Massachusetts, 1630-86.* New York, 1910.

"History of Free Schools in Plymouth Colony, and in the Town of Plymouth with Incidental Notes." *MHSC.* 2d Ser., IV (1816, reprint 1846), 79-96.

"History of Plympton, Carver and a Part of Halifax inclusive." *MHSC.* 2d Ser., IV (1816, reprint 1846), 283-85.

Hollister, William W. *Government and the Arts of Obedience.* New York, 1948.

Holmes, Abiel. "Biographical Memoir of Rev. John Lothrop," including letters of John Lothrop to Gov. Prence. *MHSC.* 2d Ser., I (1838), 163-78.

Howe, George. *Mount Hope: A New England Chronicle.* New York, 1959.

Howe, Paul S. *Religious and Legal Constitution of the Pilgrim State.* Cape May, N. J., 1923.

Hunter, Joseph. "Concerning the Early History of the Founders of New Plymouth." *MHSC.* 4th Ser., I (1852), 52-85.

Hutt, Frank W., ed. *A History of Bristol County, Massachusetts.* 3 vols. New York, 1924.

Jernegan, Marcus W. *Laboring and Dependent Classes in Colonial America, 1607-1783.* New York, reprint, 1960.

Jones, Rufus M. *The Quakers in the American Colonies.* New York, reprint 1966.

Kimball, Everett. *The Public Life of Joseph Dudley: A Study of the Colonial Policy of the Stuarts in New England. Harvard Historical Studies.* XV. New York, 1911.

Krabbe, H. *The Modern Idea of the State.* New York, 1927.

Langdon, George D., Jr. *Pilgrim Colony: A History of New Plymouth, 1620-91.* New Haven, 1967.

———— "The Franchise and Political Democracy in Plymouth Colony." *WMQ.* 3d Ser., XX (1963), 513-26.

Leach, Douglas E. *Flintlock and Tomahawk: New England in King Philip's War.* New York, 1966 ed.

Levy, Babette M. *Preaching in the First Half of New England History.* Hartford, 1945.

Levy, Leonard W. *Origins of the Fifth Amendment.* New York, 1968.

Lombard, Percival H. "The Seal of the Plymouth Colony." *The Mayflower Descendant.* XXIX (1931), 1-9.

Lord, Arthur. "The Mayflower Compact." *AASP.* XXX (1920), 278-94.

———— "The Pilgrims' Church in Plymouth." Marshall, George N., ed. *The Church of the Pilgrim Fathers.* (Boston, 1950), 46-66.

Lowe, Alice A. *Nauset on Cape Cod: A History of Eastham.* Falmouth, Mass., 1968.

McGiffert, Michael. "American Puritan Studies in the 1960's." *WMQ.* 3d Ser., XXVII (1970), 36-67.

McIntyre, Ruth A. *Debts Hopeful and Desperate: Financing the Plymouth Colony.* Plymouth, Mass., 1963.

McKinley, Albert E. *The Suffrage Franchise in the Thirteen English Colonies in America.* Philadelphia, 1905.

McLaughlin, Andrew C. *The Foundations of American Constitutionalism.* New York, 1932.

Mayo, Lawrence, ed. *The History of the Colony and Province of Massachusetts-Bay* (1765-68) by Thomas Hutchinson. 2 vols. Cambridge, 1936.

Miller, Perry. *Errand into the Wilderness.* Cambridge, 1956.

———— *The New England Mind: The Seventeenth Century.* Boston, reprint 1961.

———— *The New England Mind: From Colony to Province.* Boston, reprint, 1966.

———— *Roger Williams: His Contribution to the American Tradition.* Indianapolis, 1953.

Mitchell, Nahum. *History of the Early Settlement of Bridgewater in Plymouth County, Massachusetts.* Boston, 1840.

Morgan, Edmund S. *The Puritan Dilemma: The Story of John Winthrop.* Boston, 1958.

———— *The Puritan Family: Essays on Religion and Domestic Relations in Seventeenth-Century New England.* Boston, 1944.

———— *Roger Williams: The Church and the State.* New York, 1967.

Morison, Samuel E. "New Light Wanted on the Old Colony." *WMQ.* 3d Ser., XV (1958), 359-64.

Morris, Richard B. *Government and Labor in Early America.* New York, 1946.

———— *Studies in the History of American Law with Special Reference to the Seventeenth and Eighteenth Centuries. Columbia University Studies in Hist., Econ. and Public Law.* #316. New York, 1930.

Murdock, Kenneth. *Increase Mather, The Foremost Puritan.* Cambridge, 1925.

Neal, Daniel. *The History of the Puritans, or Protestant Noncon-formists from the Reformation in 1517 to the Revolution in 1688* (1733 and 1736). London, 1837.

"Notes on Plymouth, Massachusetts." *MHSC.* 2d Ser., III (1815).

Oberholzer, Emil, Jr. *Delinquent Saints: Disciplinary Action in the Early Congregational Churches of Massachusetts.* New York, 1956.

———— "The Church in New England Society." *Seventeenth-Century America: Essays in Colonial History.* Ed. Smith, James M. Chapel Hill, 1959, 143-65.

Osgood, Herbert L. *The American Colonies in the Seventeenth Century.* 3 vols. Gloucester, Mass., reprint 1957.

Palfrey, John G. *History of New England.* 5 vols. I-III. Boston, 1890.

Park, Charles E. "Friendship as a Factor in the Settlement of Massachusetts." *AASP.* XXVIII (1918), 51-62.

Parker, Joel. "The Origin, Organization and Influence of the Towns of New England." *MHSP.* IX (1867), 14-65.

Patten, Edwin B. *Isaac Allerton: First Assistant of Plymouth Colony.* Minneapolis, 1908.

Perry, Ralph B. *Puritanism and Democracy.* New York, reprint 1964.

Perry, Thomas W. "New Plymouth and Old England: A Suggestion." *WMQ.* 3d Ser., XVIII (1961), 251-65.

Plooj, Daniel. *The Pilgrim Fathers From a Dutch Point of View.* New York, 1932.

Porteus, Thomas C. *Captain Miles Standish: His Lost Lands and Lancashire Connections.* New York, 1920.

Potter, Elisha R. *The Early History of Narragansett* (with appendix and documents). Providence, 1835.

Pound, Roscoe. *The Spirit of the Common Law.* Francestown, N. H., 1921.

Powers, Edwin. *Crime and Punishment in Early Massachusetts, 1620-92.* Boston, 1966.

Pratt, Harvey H. *The Early Planters of Scituate.* Scituate, 1929.

Quinn, David B. "The First Pilgrims." *WMQ.* XXIII (1966), 359-90.

Reed, Susan M. *Church and State in Massachusetts, 1691-1740.* Urbana, Ill., 1914.

Reinsch, Paul S. *English Common Law in the Early American Colonies. Bulletin of the University of Wisconsin.* #31. Madison, 1899.

Richards, Lysander S. *History of Marshfield.* 2 vols. I. Plymouth, 1901.

Rothman, David. "A Note on the Study of the Colonial Family." *WMQ.* XXIII (1966), 627-34.

Rutman, Darrett B. *Husbandmen of Plymouth: Farms and Villages in the Old Colony, 1620-92*. Boston, 1968.

Schneider, Herbert W. *The Puritan Mind*. Ann Arbor, reprint 1966.

Scisco, L. D. "The Plantation Type of Colony." *AHR*. VIII (1903), 260-70.

Scott, William R. *The Constitution and Finances of English, Scottish and Irish Joint-Stock Companies to 1720*. 3 vols. Cambridge, Eng., 1910-12.

Shipton, Clifford K. "Puritanism and Modern Democracy." *NEHGR*. CI (1947), 181-98.

Simpson, Alan. *Puritanism in Old and New England*. Chicago, 1964 ed.

Smith, Bradford. *Bradford of Plymouth*. Philadelphia, 1951.

Smith, Joseph H. *Appeals to the Privy Council from the American Plantations*. New York, 1950.

Smith, Page. "Anxiety and Despair in American History." *WMQ*. 3d Ser., XXVI (1969), 414-23.

Smith, Timothy. "Congregation, State and Denomination: The Forming of the American Religious Structure. *WMQ*. XXV (1968), 155-76.

Steele, Ashbel. *Chief of the Pilgrims: The Life and Time of William Brewster*. Philadelphia, 1857.

Stoddard, Francis R. *The Truth About the Pilgrims*. New York, 1952.

Stokes, Anson P. *Church and State in the United States*. 3 vols. I. New York, 1950.

Swift, Charles F. *Cape Cod: The Right Arm of Massachusetts*. Yarmouth, 1897.

——— *History of Old Yarmouth*. Yarmouthport, 1884.

Terry, Roderick. "The Early Relations between the Colonies of New Plymouth and Rhode Island." *Bulletin of Newport Historical Society*. #34 (1920), 1-28.

Thacher, James. *History of the Town of Plymouth, 1620-1832*. Boston, 1832.

Towner, Lawrence W. "A Fondness for Freedom: Servant Protest in Puritan Society." *WMQ*. 3d ser. XIX (1962), 201-19.

Trayser, Donald G. *Barnstable: Three Centuries of a Cape Cod Town*. Hyannis, Mass., 1939.

Usher, Roland G. *The Pilgrims and Their History*. New York, 1918.

Vaughan, Alden T. *New England Frontier, 1620-75*. Boston, 1965.

——— "Pequots and Puritans: The Causes of the War of 1637." *WMQ*. 3d Ser., XXI (1964), 256-69.

Walker, Williston. *A History of the Congregational Church in the United States*. New York, 1897.

Ward, Harry M. *United Colonies of New England, 1643-90.* New York, 1961.

Ware, Horace E. "Was the Government of the Massachusetts Bay Colony a Theocracy?" *PCSM.* X (1907), 151-80.

Warren, Winslow. "Governor Edward Winslow." *MHSP.* LII (1919), 323-34.

Weeden, William B. *Economic and Social History of New England, 1620-1789.* 2 vols. I. Boston, 1891.

Willison, George F. *Saints and Strangers.* New York, 1945.

Winsor, Justin. *History of the Town of Duxbury, Massachusetts.* Boston, 1849.

Wolkins, George G. "Edward Winslow (O. V. 1606-11): King's Scholar and Printer." *AASP.* LX (1951), 237-57.

Wright, Otis O. *History of Swansea, Massachusetts, 1667-1917.* Swansea, 1917.

Zanger, Jules. "Crime and Punishment in Early Massachusetts." *WMQ.* 3d Ser., XXII (1965), 471-77.

Ziff, Larzar. *The Career of John Cotton: Puritanism and the American Experience.* Princeton, 1962.

Zuckerman, Michael. "The Social Context of Democracy in Massachusetts." *WMQ.* 3d Ser., XXV (1968), 523-44.

INDEX

188